STEAM ON THE
SIRHOWY TRAMROAD
AND ITS NEIGHBOURS

Thomas Ellis (right) and Isaac Thomas on the footplate of *St David*, c.1852.
(*TNA, COPY 1/449/268*)

STEAM ON THE
SIRHOWY TRAMROAD
AND ITS NEIGHBOURS

Michael Lewis

RAILWAY & CANAL HISTORICAL SOCIETY
2020

Seals of the Sirhowy Tram Road Company 1802, Rumney Railway Company 1825, and
Monmouthshire Railway & Canal Company 1848. (*NRM, 1975-7198, 1986-7697, 1986-7511*)

First published 2020
by the Railway & Canal Historical Society

www.rchs.org.uk

The Railway & Canal Historical Society
was founded in 1954 and incorporated in 1967.
It is a company (No. 922300) limited by guarantee
and registered in England as a charity (No. 256047)
Registered office: 34 Waterside Drive, Market Drayton TF9 1HU.

ISBN 978-0-901461-67-4

Design, cover and typesetting by
Stephen Phillips
Printed and bound in Great Britain by
Short Run Press, Exeter

Dedicated to Andy Guy
with gratitude

Contents

Foreword

THIS book began life as a modest study of the plateway locomotives that graced the Sirhowy Tramroad in South Wales. As is the way of such projects, however, it inexorably expanded to embrace not only adjoining lines but also aspects other than their motive power. In the process it became a much wider portrait of a tramroad system of major significance. Nonetheless, it is a selective portrait, for while it attempts to paint something of the formal background, it is not really about the topics that underlie so much of railway history. It is not about the politics of railway companies or of the iron and coal trades; nor is it an economic history; nor yet does it attempt to record such detail as the precise date of deviations or the exact route of branches. What it boils down to, rather, is a human story: the story of a happy-go-lucky workforce that was learning by trial and error – often much error, and in considerable danger – how to run a railway on which new-fangled steam power was awkwardly intermingled with old-fangled horse traction. At the same time it is the story of ordinary members of the public coming to terms with a new element in their lives, whether suffering innocently from its presence or deliberately exploiting it at the risk of life and limb.

This book, therefore, aims to make a contribution to social history, while it still remains a study of the early locomotives, many of them highly idiosyncratic, of a region that is all too often perceived as sitting – Trevithick apart – on the very fringe of the evolution of steam haulage. It covers all the known engines in the western parts of Monmouthshire that ran on plate rails or (during the painful conversion to standard gauge) those that were capable of running on plate rails. We know of a truly astonishing number of them – no fewer than eighty or thereabouts – and doubtless there were more that were never recorded.

The geographical focus is the busy main line owned by the Sirhowy Tramroad Company and its continuation owned by the Monmouthshire Canal Company (MCC) – or, after its change of name in 1848, the Monmouthshire Railway & Canal Company (MRCC) – which between 1804 and 1860 carried iron and coal from Tredegar to Newport. It was a plateway: that is, the vehicles were guided by flanges on the rails, not on the wheels. Physically joined to it were several other lines, most notably the Rumney Railway on the west, and on the east the Penllwyn and Hall's Tramroads and the Beaufort and Blaina branches of the MCC's Western Valleys lines. All of these were on the 4ft 4in gauge and, taken as a whole, they made up the longest connected system of plateways that ever existed. Pride of place is unashamedly given to the Sirhowy, the first long-distance railway to be built anywhere in the world and in a sense the premier line of the region. To complete the overall picture, the study also includes the narrow-gauge internal tramroads within the relevant ironworks and those that fed them with limestone. It makes no attempt, however, to deal with the railways of the Eastern Valleys and their feeders, which were of different gauge and were never connected to the Western Valleys system.

My thanks are due to many people. Above all, to Stephen Rowson for painstakingly combing the Rhymney Iron Company records which disability prevented me from seeing for myself; to Andy Guy for endless and ever-fruitful discussion and encouragement; to Jennifer Protheroe-Jones of the National Waterfront Museum in Swansea (part of the National Museums of Wales) for much help with pictures and other matters; to Jim Rees, Paul Reynolds and David Gwyn for information, insights and illustrations; to my son Hywel for help with maps; to David Joy and Stephen Phillips for seeing the book through the press; and not least to my students at Hull and Lincoln who, on the occasion of my final retirement, contributed a most generous sum towards the cost of illustrations in this book.

I am also grateful to all those who have allowed their images to be used. In a few cases it has proved impossible to trace the current owner of copyright, for which I apologise; notification to the publisher will ensure proper credit is given in any future edition.

Note on sources

DISTRESSINGLY, and with the few exceptions mentioned below, nothing beyond the odd legal document has survived of the archives of any of the relevant iron and railway companies of the area and period. As a measure of the wealth that has been lost, the papers of the comparable Dowlais Iron Company at Merthyr, preserved at Glamorgan Archives, include 563,000 letters. The first and main exception is the minute books and other papers of the Monmouthshire Canal Co and its successor the Monmouthshire Railway & Canal Co (TNA, RAIL 500); and through Stephen Rowson's good offices I have also had access to Gordon Rattenbury's work on the Sirhowy (Rattenbury 1987), which is a 'traditional' study of a kind very different from mine. It is still unpublished; much the best published outline of the MCC's formal history, based largely on the minute books, is Hadfield 1967, 127-59. The only other significant exception to this tale of loss is some of the Rhymney Iron Company's working papers: GlamA, DRH/12-21 (journals 1836-64), DRH/52-59 (ledgers 1838-64), and DRH/85 (1848 inventory).

This dearth of official records explains why much of the existing published literature is unsatisfactory. Although Barrie and Lee 1940, Byles 1982, Tasker 1992 and Hodge 2016 purport to cover the history of our tramroads, none of them is adequate, and hitherto not even a basic history of the Rumney, let alone of its locomotives, has ever been attempted. Frowen 1997, however, deals with Hall's Tramroad, and van Laun 2001 and Rattenbury's published articles, while not concerned with our main-line tramroads as such, are scholarly and reliable sources for many of the neighbouring lines.

Nonetheless a great deal of fresh material is available on issues great and small. By far the largest contribution is a huge range of day-to-day reports culled from that newly-accessible and vital resource for historians, the contemporary newspaper files which are now being digitised and made searchable online. These are Welsh Newspapers Online (free: http://newspapers.library.wales) and British Newspaper Archive (subscription: http://www.britishnewspaperarchive.co.uk.) Only those reports are cited – a fraction of the relevant total – which have something useful to say; and when they do, extracts are often quoted verbatim because nineteenth-century voices have more immediacy than modern paraphrases. To put it another way, they supply the brush-strokes that build up an unusually intimate portrait of a major tramroad.

At first, when there were no newspapers published in Wales, these reports are non-existent except for occasional notices in the press of neighbouring English cities – Gloucester, Bristol and Hereford. Then from 1804 they grow rather more numerous with the appearance of the *Cambrian* published in far-off Swansea. From 1829 they proliferate with the launching of the *Monmouthshire Merlin* (based initially at Monmouth, from 1836 at Newport) which was followed by more and more titles published in Cardiff and Merthyr Tydfil. Their predominant themes are twofold. One is the endless and acrimonious debates surrounding the modernisation of the MRCC's lines in the dozen years up to 1860. The other, throughout, is the deplorable number of accidents, recounted with a macabre relish for mangled bodies and amputated limbs which is typical of the period, but quite incidentally sheds much welcome light on the tramroads' working practices.

PART ONE

The Background

BEGINNINGS

THE South Wales Valleys, as they are generally called these days, were once more commonly known as the Hills. Both terms are appropriate, for the terrain verges on the mountainous, with the rivers and the natural transport routes funnelled south towards the Severn estuary by a succession of narrow and steep-sided valleys: the landscape at Crumlin on the Ebbw (Fig. 1.01) is entirely typical. We are concerned with the Western Valleys of Monmouthshire, a few miles east of Merthyr Tydfil and Taff Vale. They start at the watershed in limestone country, which after a few miles gives way to the coal measures that also contain ironstone (Fig. 1.02). The principal rivers are the Rhymney, formerly the western boundary of the county, whose mouth is a little east of Cardiff, and the Ebbw which, having been joined at Aberbeeg by the Ebbw Fach and at Risca by the Sirhowy, debouches just below Newport. Our area lies almost wholly within the historic county of Monmouthshire which, ludicrously but officially, used to be part of England but in 1974 became Gwent and part of Wales. The quarries

that supplied the iron industry with limestone, however, spilled over westwards into Glamorgan and northwards into Brecknockshire.

The ironworks that were the *raison d'être* of the tramroads discussed in this book were strung out in an irregular east-west alignment along the Heads of the Valleys, close to the northern boundary of the coalfield. All of them lay at approximately 1,000ft above the sea, while the ridges separating valley from valley rise to 1,600ft and more. The upland is agriculturally poor, and settlement before the nineteenth century was sparse. The Western Valleys proper, an area extending roughly twelve miles from the watershed down to the southern boundary of the coalfield at Risca and six miles wide from the Rhymney to the Ebbw Fach, was made up of four parishes – Llanhilleth, Aberystruth, Bedwellty and Mynyddislwyn, of which the last three were very large. At the end of the eighteenth century they were still utterly Welsh in culture and language, and in 1801 had a combined population of no more than 3,684, mostly in scattered farms. Yet, remote and impoverished though the region might be, it was rich in minerals, and industrialisation was already

Fig. 1.01
The Ebbw valley looking north to Crumlin viaduct, 1857. Foreground left, MRCC and [inaccurate] train; to right of river, Monmouthshire Canal. (*NLW, Mons. Top. D10 D002*)

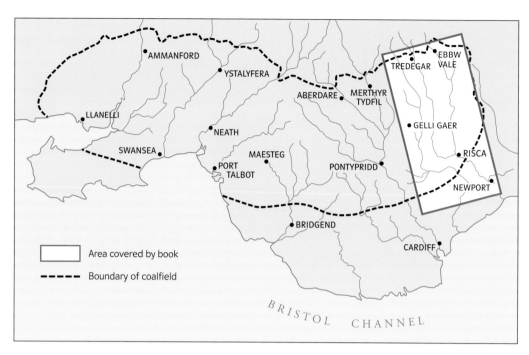

Fig. 1.02
The South Wales coalfield.

creeping in. Coal and ironstone were being dug albeit on a small scale, limestone was quarried, and there had been short-lived blast furnaces at Pont Gwaith yr Haearn in the Sirhowy valley and at Abercarn on the Ebbw.[1] The first big step came in 1778 when a partnership – composed, as was usual in South Wales, of Englishmen – built Sirhowy furnace beside the river a few miles below the watershed. Next year came the Kendalls' Beaufort Ironworks a couple of miles to the east, and there followed a succession of new furnaces at Ebbw Vale (1789), Nantyglo (1794), Clydach (1795), Tredegar (1800), Rhymney (also 1800), Coalbrookvale (c.1821), Blaina (1823), Bute (near Rhymney, 1825), Victoria (1836), and Cwm Celyn (1839) (Fig. 1.03).

Development in the Eastern Valleys, with furnaces around Pontypool from Tudor times and new ones at Blaenavon, Abersychan and Varteg from 1789, was rather different, and these works, although they used Newport as an outlet, hardly concern us. But the pattern that emerged around Merthyr Tydfil to the west, where the four ironworks of Dowlais, Plymouth, Cyfarthfa and Penydarren originated between 1757 and 1784, and rather later in the tributary Cynon Valley with Hirwaun, Aberdare, Abernant and ultimately Gadlys, was much the same as at the heads of the Western Valleys. Most of these eight works exported (via the north-south Merthyr Tramroad or the west-east Tappendens' Tramroad) from Cardiff, never from Newport, but as next-door neighbours their histories and their practices often overlapped with those of the Monmouthshire

works, and from time to time will call for mention by way of parallel (Fig. 1.04).

This great surge of industrial development meant that packhorses, the traditional mode of transport in the area, became wholly inadequate and that vastly improved methods were essential. 'On account of the wild state of the country, and no road or way to take the produce of the property to market,'[2] the ironworks were not easily accessible. Local roads were virtually non-existent. Archdeacon William Coxe, who personally experienced this deficiency during his travels in 1798-9, recites a telling anecdote. A local gentleman supporting a turnpike Bill was asked by a Commons committee, 'What roads are there in Monmouthshire?' 'None,' he replied. 'How then do you travel?' 'In ditches.'[3] Improvements were slow to take effect. The road from Merthyr to Abergavenny, bypassing most of the ironworks to the north and formerly little more than a horse track, was turnpiked under an Act of 1795, yet it was a good sixteen years before it achieved a reasonable state.[4] Much later, a folk-memory was recorded that when Tredegar was new,

it cost the company as much to transport one blast-engine from Neath Abbey to Tredegar as the value of such an engine today. Because there were no turnpikes at that time from Abergavenny or Merthyr to Tredegar, they were forced to transport the horse-head, the machine's main activator, from Neath Abbey to Newport, and from Newport to Abergavenny, and from Abergavenny over the mountain to Tredegar.[5]

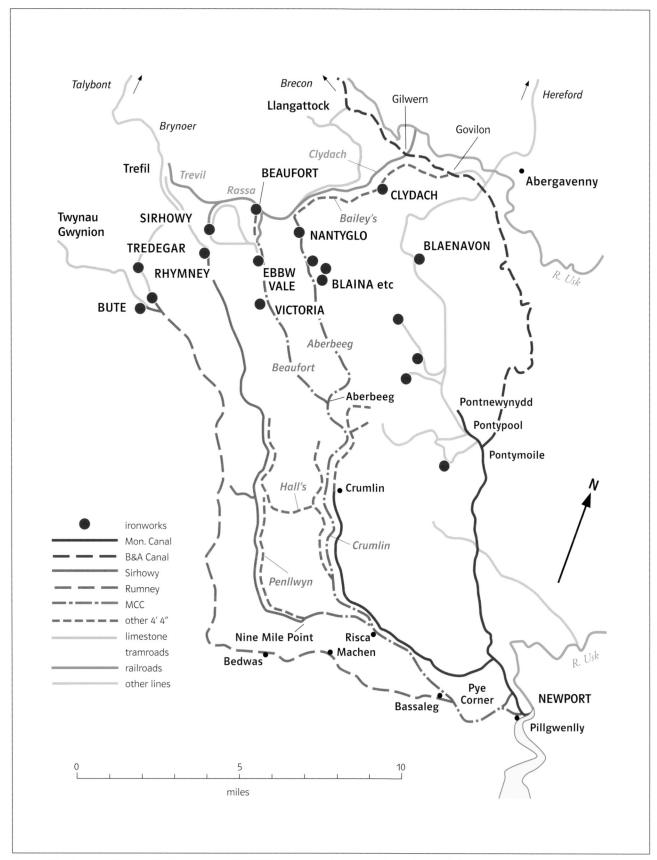

Fig. 1.03 The Western Valleys and their tramroads, c.1830-1850. Minor branches are not shown. For small places such as collieries, see Fig. 1.10

Legend:
- ● ironworks
- Mon. Canal
- B&A Canal
- Sirhowy
- Rumney
- MCC
- other 4′ 4″
- limestone tramroads
- railroads
- other lines

Labels on map:

Talybont, Brynoer, Trefil, *Trevil*, Twynau Gwynion, **SIRHOWY**, *Rassa*, **BEAUFORT**, *Clydach*, **TREDEGAR**, **RHYMNEY**, **EBBW VALE**, *Bailey's*, **NANTYGLO**, **CLYDACH**, Brecon, Llangattock, Gilwern, Govilon, Hereford, **Abergavenny**, **BLAENAVON**, *R. Usk*, **BLAINA etc**, **BUTE**, **VICTORIA**, *Aberbeeg*, *Beaufort*, Aberbeeg, Pontnewynydd, Pontypool, Pontymoile, *Hall's*, Crumlin, *Crumlin*, *Penllwyn*, Nine Mile Point, Risca, Machen, Bedwas, Pye Corner, Bassaleg, **NEWPORT**, Pillgwenlly, *R. Usk*

N

0 5 10
miles

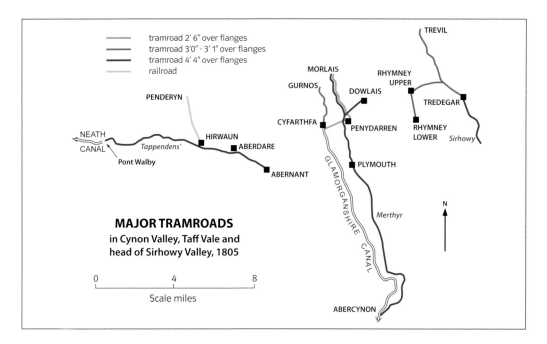

tramroad 2' 6" over flanges
tramroad 3'0" - 3' 1" over flanges
tramroad 4' 4" over flanges
railroad

MAJOR TRAMROADS
in Cynon Valley, Taff Vale and
head of Sirhowy Valley, 1805

Scale miles

Fig. 1.04
Map of major tramroads, 1805.

This tale, while one has one's suspicions about it, highlights the undoubted fact that Tredegar – and the other furnaces too – were hard to get at.

If at first the ironworks were small and remote, Newport, at the mouth of the Usk and the only possible point of export, already had a modest trade in coal which was sent largely up and down the Bristol Channel. Nonetheless it was an unprepossessing place. Coxe, visiting in 1798, remarks that

> the streets are dirty and ill paved; the houses in general wear a gloomy appearance. Not-withstanding its trade and situation, the population is very considerable. It contains only 221 houses and tenements, and 1087 souls.[6]

Another visitor in 1802 says of its harbour,

> Newport will appear contemptible from the slovenly mode of loading and unloading upon stages which totter under the work; and the vessels are lying on the bank at once steep and filthy.[7]

The solution to the difficulties of transport lay, as was already well known in the English Midlands, in canals leading to the ports and in railways feeding traffic to the the canals. An Act had been passed in 1790 for the Glamorganshire Canal to link the great ironworks of Merthyr Tydfil to the sea at Cardiff, and another in 1791 for the Neath Canal. In 1792 the Monmouthshire industrialists followed suit by obtaining an Act incorporating the Monmouthshire Canal Company.[8] As engineer

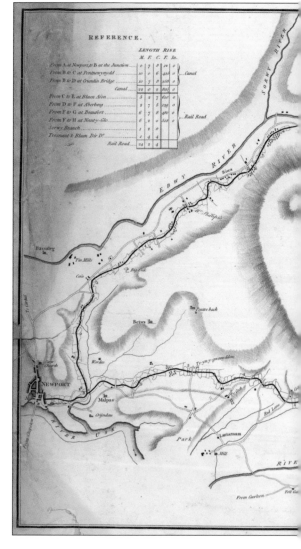

they chose Thomas Dadford junior who, with his father Thomas senior, was currently building the Glamorganshire. The Act authorised two branches that met near Newport and led inland. That up the Eastern Valley to Pontnewynydd near Pontypool, opened in 1796, falls outside our scope. What does concern us is the Western Valleys line to Crumlin, opened in stages between 1796 and 1799. The terrain being far from ideal for canal building, the navigation was heavily locked and often short of water. From the beginning, therefore, the company resorted to railways, not only to bring traffic down to its canal terminus but increasingly to parallel the waterway all the way to Newport. From Crumlin the original plan (Fig. 1.05) envisaged railways running northwards to Ebbw Vale and Beaufort (9¾ miles) and indirectly to Sirhowy (another 1½ miles), from Aberbeeg to Nantyglo (6¼ miles) and, from Pontnewynydd, to Blaenavon and other ironworks in the Eastern Valley. As was common

practice, the Act also authorised the building of such lines, whether by the company or (with its approval) by individuals, anywhere within eight miles of the canal.

A year later, in 1793, the Act was passed for the Brecknock & Abergavenny Canal (B&A) to the east, which, skirting the high ground by following the valley of the Usk, would connect those two towns to the Monmouthshire Canal at Pontymoile above Pontypool. Except at its southernmost point, its traffic was intended to be primarily agricultural, its only close approach to significant industry being in the neighbourhood of Abergavenny where the valley of the Clydach comes down to the Usk from the west. But the B&A was slow in the building, not being completed for almost twenty years.

With the canals, and even just before, came railways. A wooden one proposed for Plymouth Ironworks at Merthyr Tydfil in 1766-7 had come to nothing.[9] It was twenty years before Samuel

Fig. 1.05

Thomas Dadford's survey for MCC, 1792. Note north to right. Newport at lower left, Crumlin Bridge and Ponty Pool just left of central fold. Ironworks near right edge, Sorwy (Sirhowy), Ebbw Vale, Beaufort, Nantyglo, Blaen-Afon. (*GwentA, D38.41*)

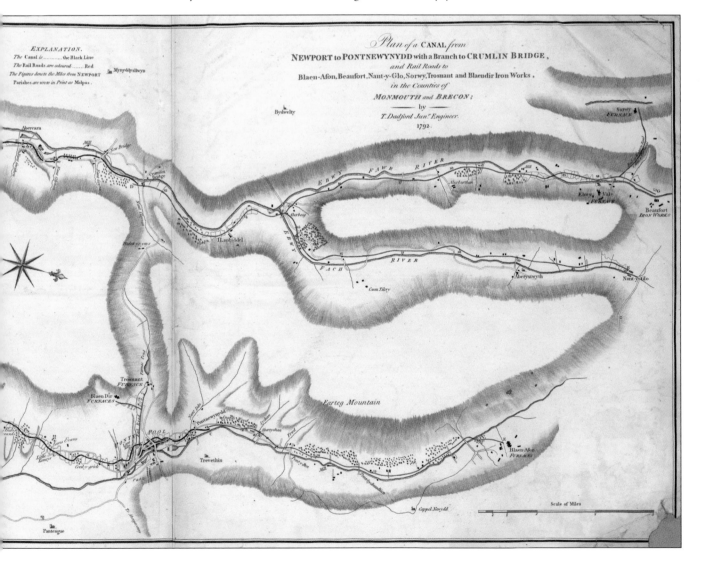

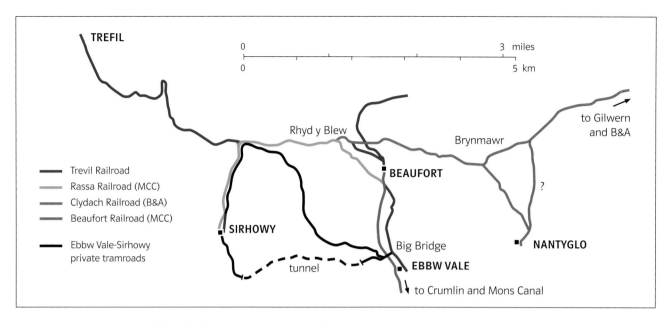

Fig. 1.06

Edge railroads at the Heads of the Valleys.

Glover laid a two-mile wooden line from Penderyn limestone quarries to Hirwaun furnaces in about 1786.[10] From that point the ironmasters of Merthyr got busy. Inspired by John Curr's introduction of iron plate rails at Sheffield, they pioneered their local use underground in mines from 1788 and on the surface from 1792. These rapidly spread, but at this early date their gauge was small, being always less than 3ft. In the standard terminology of the region, such plateways were known as tramroads (often written as *tram-roads* or *tram roads*), as opposed to edge railways which were called railroads. These too had already, in 1787-8, been pioneered locally at Merthyr, both underground and on the surface, in imitation of Shropshire practice.[11]

All this, then, added up to rapid industrial development along the Heads of the Valleys. To the east of Merthyr, there soon arose a sizeable connected system of railroads whose entanglements can only be understood from a map (Fig. 1.06). In 1794 the B&A, employing as engineer Thomas Dadford junior's brother John, built the Clydach Railroad that ran west-east from near Beaufort to its canal at Gilwern.[12] In 1796 the independent Trevil Railroad was joined to it to carry limestone to Sirhowy, Beaufort and Ebbw Vale furnaces,[13] and the MCC built the Rassa Railroad, which not only gave Sirhowy an outlet but looped circuitously back to Ebbw Vale. The MCC also built the Beaufort Railroad from Beaufort and Ebbw Vale south to the head of the Monmouthshire at Crumlin. The last three of these lines were engineered by Thomas Dadford junior, and all four were laid with edge rails to the

common gauge of 3ft 8in.[14] The line from Aberbeeg to Nantyglo, though authorised by the 1792 Act, was not however built at this time because of doubts about Nantyglo's viability as a concern.

A muddled tale survived in folk memory which seems to refer to the opening of the Clydach.

A tram, or carriage, was constructed for the purpose of travelling upon this railway; the tram consisted of four wheels, with a powerful brake, and was capable of conveying six tons of iron. Intelligence of this wonderful vehicle had spread over all the neighbourhood, and on the day of opening the railroad hundreds had assembled to witness the grand sight, waving handkerchiefs of various colours as a Sign of their approval. The wagon was drawn on its 'trial trip' by six horses, the most beautiful and powerful the company possessed, and the team was driven by John Moss.[15]

But although Ebbw Vale, Beaufort, and to some extent Sirhowy had an exit route to Crumlin and hence to Newport, the snag was that the B&A committee made the building of these west-east railroads its first priority. Only when they were in place did it begin to construct the canal itself, at first north-westwards from Gilwern to Brecon which it reached in 1800. Not until 1812 was Gilwern linked southwards to the Monmouthshire Canal near Pontypool.

Before that date, therefore, as far as the serious export of iron was concerned, the Clydach was a dead-end with no proper outlet to Newport, which was the only conceivable seaport. The small Clydach Ironworks, which it served along the way, had to send its iron out southwards, painfully hauling it 800ft up to the ridge and thence down via Blaenavon and the Eastern Valley. The Clydach Railroad, moreover, was a difficult line to work. In its last four sinuous miles, clinging as it were by its fingernails to the sides of the Clydach Gorge, it lost 727ft of height at the vicious average gradient of 1 in 30 (Figs. 1.07-08), and its 3-ton waggons had therefore to have double brakes.[16] For these reasons the Clydach saw relatively little traffic. Its staple trade was coal from Sirhowy, Beaufort and Clydach for local domestic markets and especially for Brecon. It also took limited amounts of pig iron from Sirhowy and Beaufort for refining at Glangrwyne Forge across the River Usk from Gilwern.[17]

Fig. 1.07
'A view of the iron mines and waterfall on the pitt road near Abergavenny,' a highly dramatised painting of the Clydach Railroad by Peter van Lerberghe, between 1794 and 1802. (© *British Library Board, Maps K.Top.31.5.b*)

Fig. 1.08
Detail from last.

TREDEGAR AND THE SIRHOWY TRAMROAD

In 1799 and 1800 two very important events took place. A second furnace had been added at Sirhowy in 1797 by the partners Richard Fothergill and Matthew Monkhouse, who began to think of expanding their activities yet further. They already leased a tract of land on the opposite bank of the river, little more than half a mile to the south, from Sir Charles Morgan of Tredegar near Newport, but the terms of the lease prevented them from developing it industrially. Having few strings to pull, they looked for help to Samuel Homfray of Penydarren Ironworks at Merthyr Tydfil (1762-1822, Fig. 1.09), an established ironmaster of wealth and ambition, who enjoyed the additional advantage of being Morgan's son-in-law and thus of having his ear.

Homfray leapt at the opportunity. On 20 March 1800 Morgan granted a lease of the land for a new ironworks, with full mineral rights and on very advantageous terms, to Homfray, Fothergill and Monkhouse. They were shortly joined by William Thompson and William Forman, Homfray's partners in Penydarren and wealthy London merchants; Forman was known as 'Billy Ready Money' from his willingness to give loans, and Thompson became an MP and Alderman of the City and later its Lord Mayor. As a nod to the landlord, the new works were named Tredegar after his stately home sixteen miles away. For a while thereafter, working almost in tandem, Fothergill managed Tredegar and Monkhouse Sirhowy; but there was never any doubt that the real boss was the domineering Homfray, a figure ever larger than life. An anecdote encapsulates his character: in 1816 William Wilberforce had the misfortune to be cornered by Homfray in a stage coach. 'Mr H– immediately recognised me, and with stentorian voice left me no peace till his whole tale was told … Inventor of Tram roads, founder of all great ironworks in Monmouthshire, &c.'[18]

As we have seen, the top of the Sirhowy valley already had some sort of rail transport eastwards, and the Tredegar partners must at least have considered the possibility of sending their produce out via the Rassa, the Beaufort and the Monmouthshire Canal. But this involved first a climb of 200-odd feet up to the ridge and then transshipment at Crumlin. They preferred a more direct route to Newport, downhill all the

Fig. 1.09

Samuel Homfray senior aged about 28, with Cyfarthfa Ironworks and Merthyr Tydfil in the background, c.1790. (*private collection*)

way and less dependent on the MCC. Thus arose the Sirhowy Tramroad and its continuation, the MCC's original main line. From the beginning the MCC had used railways to bring traffic down to its termini; now, and increasingly hereafter, it resorted to railways that paralleled the waterway all the way to Newport. The harbour of Newport, safe and reasonably deep but with the huge tidal range of 52ft at springs, was at Pillgwenlly on the estuary of the River Usk just below the town, and in 1804-5 the MCC opened its main tramroad from Court y Bella nearby to Risca on the Ebbw River. The mile of this line which ran through Sir Charles Morgan's Tredegar Park was built, maintained and owned by him, and was known as the Park Mile or (from its profitability) the Golden Mile. From Risca the route bore west up the Sirhowy valley to Nine Mile Point: nine miles, that is, from Newport. Here it made an end-on junction with the fifteen-mile Sirhowy Tramroad which continued northwards up to Sirhowy and Tredegar. Both lines were opened at the same time; and the whole length, although in three separate ownerships, was intended from the start 'to be one line of road, and all [the owners] subject to each other as though [it] belonged to one person only.'[19] Thus was begun the great network of tramroads which is our subject (Fig 1.10).

That is the bare outline of the story. The details were much more complicated. Of the local lines built before 1800, almost all of any length were railroads, and none of them, apart perhaps from the Clydach, could be called ambitious. The catalyst for change came when the B&A asked Benjamin Outram for advice on its canal and railroads, and six months later the MCC followed suit. These moves formed the second of the important events of 1799-1800. Outram (1764-1805),[20] a partner in Butterley Ironworks in Derbyshire, was currently the national protagonist of plateways, with strong views on their supposed advantages over railroads and on how they should be constructed. The two gauges he preferred – indeed insisted on – were 3ft 6in and, for heavy traffic, 4ft 4in.

At this point a word is needed on the tricky matter of how tramroad gauges are measured. A useful rule of thumb is that the gauge between the flanges, that over the flanges, and that between the wheels increased in two-inch steps. Thus on the MCC lines, as too on the Merthyr Tramroad, the figures were 4ft 2in, 4ft 4in, and 4ft 6in respectively. This is only a rule of thumb. Because there was a fair amount of play, half an inch or even an inch either way might not matter,

but a bigger difference could be crucial. It was discovered in 1849, for example, when new and better-built trams were tried, that one stretch of Hall's Tramroad, a private line feeding the MCC, was 'one inch and a quarter wider in the gauge than it ought to be; it was, therefore, found difficult to pass the new trams over this point,' whereas the crude old trams had evidently taken it in their stride.[21] Henceforth, unless stated otherwise, the gauges given here are those over the flanges, which operationally is the measurement that matters.

Outram's two reports, dated 1 July 1799 and 13 January 1800 respectively,[22] were couched in very general terms, preaching the supposed advantages of tramroads over railroads, rather than making specific recommendations about routes. But their effect was profound, and reached far beyond the MCC and the B&A. A great deal happened in a very short time. Owners hurried to build new lines according to his specifications, and sometimes to convert existing railroads. Thus the MCC converted the Beaufort in 1803-5, although the Trevil, Rassa and Clydach remained railroads to the end of their days. Over to the west was the Merthyr Tramroad, paralleling the Glamorganshire Canal down to Abercynon and engineered by George Overton who was an early admirer of Outram. Its construction began in 1800, and its first rails, described as of 'Outram pattern,' were cast in June of that year when the intended gauge was 3ft 6in. But very soon minds changed, and it was increased to 4ft 4in.[23] The Merthyr, when it opened at an unknown date in 1802, was the first significant Welsh line on this gauge; unless it was Tappendens' Tramroad at Aberdare, part of which was in operation by December 1802 (Fig. 1.10).[24]

Thus, when Tredegar began in 1800, the revolutionary Outram-style tramroad was a concept very new to the area, and it is no surprise that here as at Merthyr there were changes of mind about the gauge. The lease of 1800 permitted the Tredegar partnership not only to establish the furnaces and to mine raw materials but 'to make a Tram or other Road down Sirhowy Valley, to join the Canal' at Risca.[25] Although the legality of this lease was questioned, the resulting litigation need not detain us.[26] What is relevant is the *pas-de-deux* now performed by Homfray and the MCC. Hardly was the ink dry on the lease before the partners looked to their future transport needs. Tramroads were immediately built to the new Tredegar site from Sirhowy Ironworks

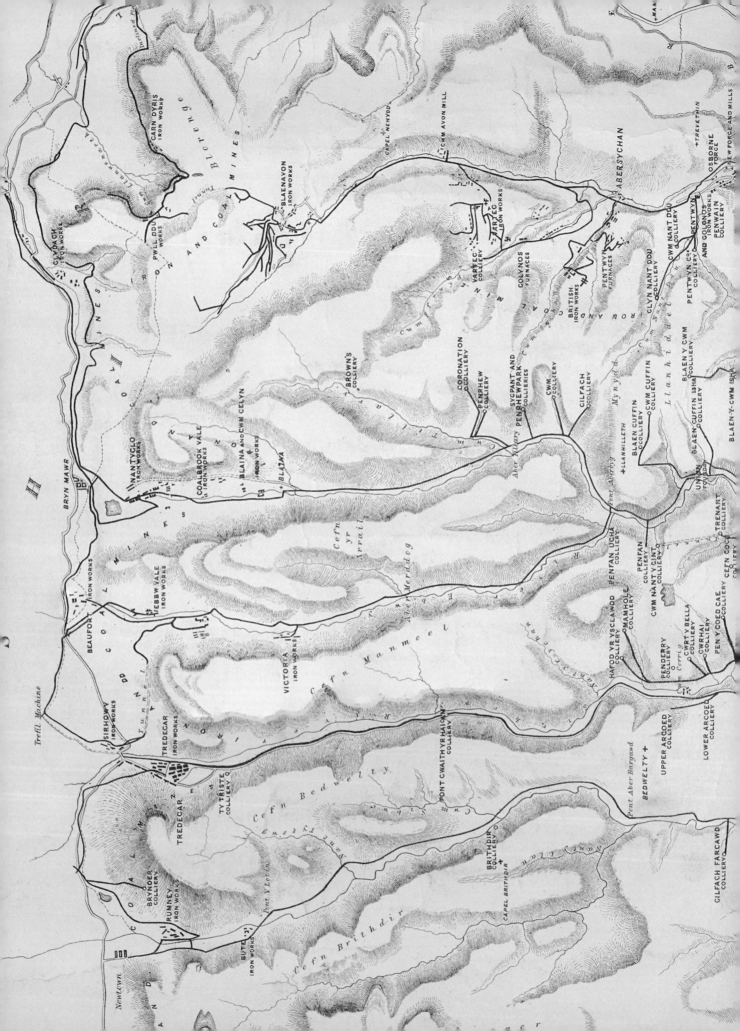

Fig. 1.10

Prujean's map of Monmouthshire tramroads, 1843. The limestone tramroads are not shown.

(NLW, Tredegar 458)

and from local coal and ironstone levels. More momentous still, within nine months of the signing, 'Homfray & Co had begun to make a tramroad to convey their iron, etc, from their works to a place called Pill, at Newport:'[27] not, be it noted, to the canal at Risca. The MCC, which would have been wholly bypassed by such a line, was horrified, and it hastened to lay claim to this potentially profitable traffic. On 18 December 1800 an agreement was reached whereby the MCC would within a year build the whole line from Tredegar to Risca 'according to the plans of Benjamin Outram,' and would even reimburse Homfray and his partners for the costs incurred so far on their uncompleted tramroad. This scheme, highly advantageous to Homfray, lasted only a day before the MCC shareholders turned it down in favour of a more equitable one, which embodied two major steps forward. It accepted Newport – or more precisely Pillgwenlly – as the terminus, which avoided transshipment to the canal at Risca. And it made Homfray responsible for the upper part of the line, the MCC for the lower. While the canal would still be bypassed, the company would nonetheless earn substantial revenue.

The full length, including the section Homfray had already begun, was surveyed in September 1801 by Outram's faithful assistant John Hodgkinson (1773-1861),[28] with the help of David Davies on the Sirhowy and of Walter Kenear on the MCC portion. The preparation of a Bill to put before Parliament generated much frantic and last-minute wheeling and dealing between the interested parties, as was spelt out by Homfray in an account written twenty years later.[29] In its final form the Bill incorporated the existing Tredegar partnership as the Sirhowy Tram Road Company, which was empowered to build a further line northwards from Tredegar to Trefil limestone quarries and with a branch to Rhymney Ironworks (Fig. 1.11).[30] The same Bill also authorised the MCC to build its main line from Nine Mile Point to Pillgwenlly (except for the Park Mile which Morgan was to make), and a branch from Risca to Crumlin (which in the event was long postponed) to join the Beaufort Railroad. The rough-and-ready estimate for the Sirhowy Tramroad was £25,000 with branches, the more precise one for the MCC lines £35,166. The Act was passed on 26 June 1802, and in October and November the MCC advertised for contractors for its portion and for 600 tons of rails.[31] The Act also laid down that the Tramroad Company and the MCC were to complete their portions by 29 September 1803, and Morgan to complete his Park Mile by 29 Nov 1803.

For the MCC this proved too optimistic. But Homfray was already hard at work, having jumped the gun and started building the tramroad under the terms of the Tredegar lease rather than of the Act. While his longer-term aim was unquestionably to create the first stage of the route to Newport, his immediate purpose was to bring coal to his furnaces. Limited supplies were already available from Bryn Oer Patch north-west of Tredegar, which was worked by primitive opencasting, and from a few small levels at Tredegar itself that were driven very soon after 1800. But the first shallow pit there (Duke's) was not sunk until 1806 and the first sizeable ones (Ty Trist) not until 1834.[32] Homfray therefore began by looking further afield, to levels and pits in the shallow Mynyddislwyn seam ten miles down the valley. One of these was Gellihaf Colliery, just on the Rhymney valley side of the ridge, which by 1804 was not only at work but already connected to the future main line by a branch tramroad 1½ miles long from a point on the main line between Gelligroes and Pontllanfraith (Fig. 1.12),[33] and

Fig. 1.11

Tramroads from Tredegar to Trefil and Rhymney, 1813. (*OS draft survey, © British Library Board, OSD 191*)

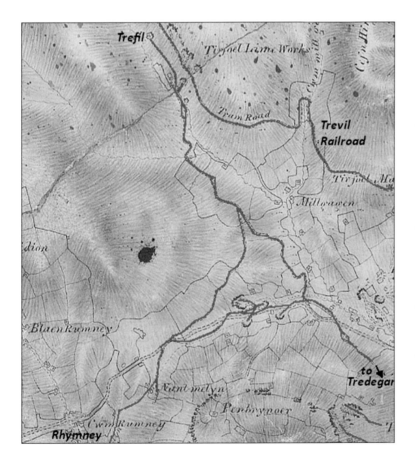

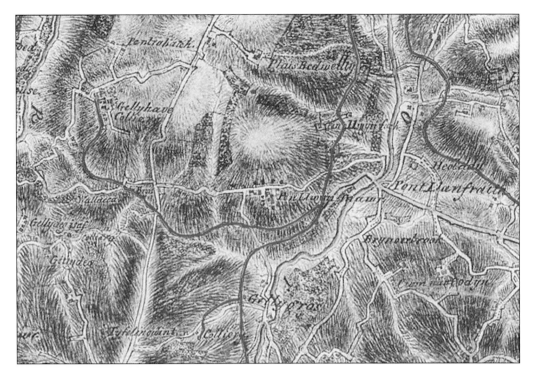

Fig. 1.12
Pontllanfraith-Gellihaf
branch, 1813. Sirhowy
Tramroad north-south
down centre, Rhymney
valley at top left, part
of Hall's Tramroad at
top right.
(*OS draft survey, ©British
Library Board, OSD 193*)

in 1805 its shaft was given a Tredegar-built Trevithick winding engine.[34] The drawback was that all this coal had to be hauled uphill to the furnaces, and although it was still being sold to Tredegar in 1822,[35] its place was gradually taken by supplies from collieries higher up the valley – Rock and Argoed and finally Ty Trist. When the Rumney Railway opened in 1826, Gellihaf was connected to it and the branch off the Sirhowy was truncated.

Behind Homfray was the Sirhowy Tramroad Company. Although none of its papers survive, and although it was legally a separate entity from the Tredegar Iron Company, there is little doubt that both were run in tandem. As far as we know – which is not very far – it was only towards the end that directors of the Tramroad Company were not necessarily current partners in the Iron Company.

The chronology of this proto-Sirhowy Tramroad can be traced only approximately, for until 1804 when the *Cambrian* began publication, the Hereford, Gloucester and Bristol newspapers carried few relevant reports. Already in June 1800 a tramroad was 'in contemplation' from Sirhowy to the canal at Risca,'[36] and by December Homfray had begun to build it.[37] In October 1801 an anonymous letter-writer said of the brand-new town called 'Tredegar Ironworks,' with which he was clearly familiar, 'from hence a rail or tram-road is making to Newport, a distance of 24 miles, of so regular a descent, that one horse

will draw ten tons down, and bring the empty waggons back.'[38] By October 1802 the MCC's portion had been marked out.[39] In February 1803 the line of tramroad from Sirhowy to Newport was 'now making, and in forwardness,'[40] and in April 1803 Eric Svedenstjerna, a Swedish visitor, reported that 'a tramroad fourteen miles long was laid, and is now united with another, belonging to the Canal Company of Monmouthshire, which is eleven miles long down to Newport.'[41] While 'to Newport' was premature – Svedenstjerna did not personally venture south of Tredegar – the implication is that a substantial amount of work had already been done.

In August 1803 two farms were advertised to let: Plas Bedwellty (a mile north of Gelligroes) and Buttry Hatch (named as Pentrabatch on Fig. 1.12 immediately north of Gellyhave). The notice states, not as a distant prospect but as a fact, that

the Sirhowy Tram-road, towards Newport [note: *towards*, not *to* Newport], passes through part of the Estate, by which lime and other manure, and also the produce of the Farms, may be conveyed at an easy expence; there is great plenty of Coal in the neighbourhood.[42]

By August 1803, therefore, the top two-thirds of the Sirhowy Tramroad proper, as far as Gelligroes and including the Gellihaf branch, were already at work if not yet fully completed.

The terminus of this first section, and the change of gauge, are both made plain by a new agreement between the Sirhowy and the MCC of 22 September 1803. This extended the time limit. The Tramroad Company would complete its section in two stages: part within twelve months 'on the plan of a Narrow Tram Road as now making from Sirhowy ffurnaces aforesaid down to and across the Gellygrose [Gelligroes] valley,' the rest within eight months 'on the plan of a wide Rail Way or Tram road as that now making by the said Canal Co;' and on twelve months' notice from the MCC it was to convert its line from Gelligrose to Pontgwaith yr haearn (the southern boundary of Tredegar's leasehold) from the narrow to the wide. The MCC was to complete its portion from Nine Mile Point downwards as a wide road within six months, except for the viaduct at Risca that was to be ready by 25 March 1805.[43] This new timetable was more or less adhered to. In October 1804 the colliery at Plas Bedwellty was advertised as adjoining 'the Sirhowy Tram Road, which runs through the property, and is now open for trade to Newport.'[44] As we shall see, however, the viaduct, the final link in the chain, was not completed until later. Exactly when the Trefil Tramroad and its Rhymney branch were opened is not known, but it was about 1804,[45] and maybe earlier because some feeder lines were already reported at work in April 1803.[46]

It has been suggested that the terms 'narrow' and 'wide tram road' do not mean what they seem to mean but, because the agreement was drawn up by lawyers rather than engineers, in fact mean 'single' and 'double track.'[47] This does not convince. It conflicts both with reality and with what later became reality. The 'wide Rail Way or Tram road . . . now making by the said Canal Co' was not, at the time, double track. Nor was there any move or suggestion to double the Sirhowy until 1860. Above all, 'narrow' and 'wide road' were terms already current in their obvious sense. Both are found, again in 1803 (July), apropos Penydarren's dual-gauge limestone tramroad (2ft 6in and 4ft 4in); 'narrow road' was applied in 1815 to the 2ft 6in line from Penydarren to the Glamorganshire Canal head in contrast to the 4ft 4in of the Merthyr Tramroad; and 'narrow tram-road' was used of Benjamin Hall's Tramroad before it was regauged in 1829.[48]

As for the precise gauge of the original Sirhowy line, Homfray, in common with the promoters of the Merthyr Tramroad of whom he was one, had begun by thinking small. His initial choice of 1800 for the Sirhowy was not the 3ft 6in initially intended for the Merthyr but even less – 3ft over the flanges – which long survived in the branches north of Tredegar.[49] But by the time of the Act in June 1802, and certainly by September 1803, it must have been agreed that the gauge the whole way from Sirhowy to Newport was to be the wide one of 4ft 4in. Everyone was now thinking big. The MCC had been convinced by Outram's recommendations, and Homfray was deeply involved in both the Merthyr and Tappendens' Tramroads which at this point were either complete or about to be completed. If a narrow gauge had hitherto sufficed for feeder tramroads, the more capacious 4ft 4in was now established as the 'main line' gauge in South Wales.

From Nine Mile Point to the entrance to Sirhowy Ironworks, the length of the Sirhowy Tramroad proper was (at least as measured in 1860) 14 miles 2 furlongs 2½ chains. At about 24 miles – including an extension of 1806 from Court y Bella to Pillgwenlly – the conjoint Sirhowy and MCC line was, by a very considerable margin, the longest railway yet built anywhere. John Hodgkinson was put in overall charge of the construction, to Outram's requirements, of the whole length from Sirhowy to Pillgwenlly including, presumably, the change of gauge in the course of 1804 of Homfray's line from Tredegar to Gelligroes. The resident engineer seems to have been Walter Kenear. The three owning parties – Tredegar, Morgan and the MCC – paid in proportion to the length of their sections. Contracts for construction were let in November 1802, but the names of only two contractors are known: Henry Lewis for the portion from Court y Bella to Tredegar Park (3,000 yards for £1,257; he already held the contract to maintain the Blaenavon Railroad), and Walter Walters from the Park to Risca (6,380 yards for £3,600; he had built Brynich aqueduct on the B&A).[50] Blaenavon Ironworks won the tender for rails for the MCC line (with assistance from Alexander Raby of Llanelli), while Tredegar no doubt cast those for the Sirhowy. The final cost of the whole tramroad is said to have been about £74,000, or £14,000 more than the estimates;[51] but it was apparently the MCC's section that was responsible for this over-run, because according to Homfray the Sirhowy cost £1,000 less than estimated.[52]

From the beginning, relations between the MCC and Homfray, both father and later son, were frosty. Both, and especially the Homfrays, were past masters at delaying tactics, so that disputes were liable to rumble on for years. So it continued to the end.

In 1818 Sirhowy came to a crisis point. Sixteen years previously the land on which the furnaces stood had been bought by the Harfords of Ebbw Vale, and now Fothergill and Monkhouse's lease expired. They fondly expected a renewal, but the Harfords stood by their rights and took possession. Sirhowy became, and remained, part of the Ebbw Vale empire. Fothergill, in a fit of pique, immediately removed all links to Tredegar, including the connecting tramroad. Sirhowy having no puddling furnaces, it had hitherto sent its pig at first to Glangrwyne and then to Tredegar for turning into wrought iron.[53] Now it had to carry it to Ebbw Vale by way of either the circuitous Rassa Railroad or an equally circuitous private railway, and then to send its iron for export down the Beaufort Tramroad rather than the Sirhowy; until 1832, that is, when a connecting tunnel was driven through the ridge to Ebbw Vale. Another upshot was that for many years not only the ironworks but the two communities of Tredegar and Sirhowy were at loggerheads, glowering at each other across the river.

For the first eighteen years of the Tredegar partnership the dominant member, though not the day-to-day manager, was Samuel Homfray senior, who continued to live at Penydarren House. But in 1818 he transferred his superabundant energies from iron to politics, and left Penydarren to his two partners William Forman and William Thompson. At the same time, with the change in Sirhowy's ownership, Richard Fothergill stood down as manager of Tredegar, to be replaced by Homfray's young son Samuel junior (1795-1882, Fig. 1.13), who henceforth ruled from Bedwellty House and in his turn became a power in the land. He was a crusty and eccentric character but, as ironmasters went, not unpopular. If he lacked his father's outspoken drive, he was a bold innovator, and under him the works expanded mightily, advancing from strength to strength.

The population of the new town expanded even more mightily, from virtually nothing in 1801 to 28,598 in 1861, many of whom, lured by employment, had moved in from England and Ireland.[54] Much the same could be said of all the other towns generated by the ironworks, and indeed of Newport itself (just over a thousand in 1801, about 19,000 in 1851). This did not, however,

Fig. 1.13
Samuel Homfray junior in old age.
(*Newport Museum and Art Gallery, TEMP_2006_1556*)

mean a rapid anglicisation, because even more moved in from rural parts of Wales. The Western Valleys did not become predominantly bilingual until quite late in the nineteenth century, much later than the more cosmopolitan Merthyr.[55]

OTHER IRONWORKS

Such, then, was the basic artery of the Western Valleys system. Feeding it, as well as the canal itself, were many branches both short and long. Some of course served the ironworks, which grew in number and in size. In 1823 there were 23 blast furnaces in our area; in 1830, 33. Their product was pig iron, of which more and more came to be processed by puddling and rolling into bar iron. Cyfarthfa's rolling mills, for example, began in 1788, Tredegar's in 1807, Nantyglo's in 1811, Ebbw Vale's in 1818-20, while Sirhowy and Beaufort never had them. The works' relative standing may be seen in the annual tonnages of iron sent down the Monmouthshire Canal and its tramroads:[56]

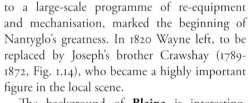

	1805	1810	1815	1820	1825	1830	1835	1840
Tredegar	956	7,696	9,225	8,211	11,012	12,303	13,909	15,288
Nantyglo			4,684	8,826	16,536	17,115	24,957	26,662
Coalbrookvale					3,596	1,905	3,211	7,824
Blaina					1,588	4,195	9,233	8,937
Beaufort	4,605	3,948	3,767	3,132	7,091	5,065	12,976	10,049
Ebbw Vale/Sirhowy	1,012	2,758	4,953	3,605	10,325	18,133	25,392	24,199
Victoria								6,436
Rhymney/Bute						5,728	4,198	18,581

Fig. 1.14

Crawshay Bailey
(1789-1872).

(author's collection)

Nantyglo's childhood was spasmodic and unhappy. In its first phase under Harford and Hill it was in production only from 1794 to 1796. A new partnership of Hill, Harrison and Griffiths lasted only from 1802 to 1808. But on 25 March 1811 the works were leased to Joseph Bailey, nephew of Richard Crawshay of Cyfarthfa, and to Matthew Wayne of Cyfarthfa who supplied the technical know-how. This step, which led to a large-scale programme of re-equipment and mechanisation, marked the beginning of Nantyglo's greatness. In 1820 Wayne left, to be replaced by Joseph's brother Crawshay (1789-1872, Fig. 1.14), who became a highly important figure in the local scene.

The background of **Blaina** is interesting. William (1770-1853) and Richard Brown (1773-1851) were brothers whose family migrated in the 1780s from Broseley in Shropshire to Penydarren, where they made a name as mechanics and smiths.[57] They knew Trevithick and helped build his 1804 engine, and we will return to them more than once. In 1811 they moved to Nantyglo to assist in setting up the new rolling mills there, and later they bought shares in Blaina Ironworks a little further down the valley, which had started in 1823, and by 1827 the firm was known as R. Brown & Son. In the early 1830s the brothers pulled out of active management, leaving Richard's son Thomas as manager in partnership with John Russell. They, in 1839, bought the new **Cwm Celyn** furnaces nearby and operated as the Cwm Celyn and Blaina Iron Co, selling out in 1844 to a new partnership whose manager was Frederick Levick. Under him was brought in the small **Coalbrookvale** Ironworks, also nearby, which had originated in about 1821.

Ebbw Vale remained under the Quaker Harford family, in partnership with various others, until it went bankrupt in 1842. In 1844 it was sold to a consortium known as the Ebbw Vale Iron Co., headed by Abraham Darby IV of Coalbrookdale fame. Its manager was Thomas Brown (1804-84),[58] formerly of Blaina, who thus became one of the grand figures of the industrial scene (Fig. 1.15). Its coal selling agent was his mercurial brother James (1809-89),[59] well known as three times mayor of Newport and a fierce critic of the current transport system who had 'undertaken to thrash the Monmouthshire Railway Co.'[60] In their hands Ebbw Vale prospered mightily.

In 1836 the new Monmouthshire Iron & Coal Co's Victoria Ironworks sprang up immediately south of Ebbw Vale, but its finances were not sound and in 1840 it went bankrupt, to be sold in 1844 to Ebbw Vale, into whose works it was absorbed although the finances of the sale were not sorted out until 1849.[61]

The next (and last) location to be noticed demands a rather fuller introduction because in a sense it was out on limb, and the history of its tramroad has never yet been explored. At **Rhymney**, two miles to the west of Tredegar, another new works was created in 1800 by a consortium of Bristol men who built the Upper Furnace and, a few years later and a mile to the south, Rhymney Lower Furnace. Together these were known as the Union Ironworks. Very soon – in 1803 – it came into the hands of Richard Crawshay of Cyfarthfa, and in 1810, on Crawshay's death, into the sole control of his son-in-law Benjamin Hall. When Hall died in 1817 it passed to his son of the same name (1802-67, later Sir Benjamin, later again Lord Llanover) who was still a minor. In 1824, once he was of age, the whole Rhymney estate was put up for auction and, after a bidding contest between the Marquess of Bute and Crawshay Bailey of Nantyglo, knocked down to Bailey.[62] The legitimacy of the sale, under the terms of Crawshay's and Hall's wills, was questioned, and the resulting litigation rumbled on for decades; but for the time being the proprietors were Joseph and Crawshay Bailey and William Thompson (1793-1854, co-partner in Penydarren).[63] On the principle, presumably, that possession is nine-tenths of the law, they acted fast, in two directions.

A new ironworks was built, called **Bute**, on the Marquess of Bute's land on the west (Glamorganshire) side of the river opposite Rhymney lower furnace. Its foundation stone was laid in April 1825 and it was well on the way to production by June 1826. It was nominally in different hands from Rhymney, the managing partner being William Forman (1767-1829), the other co-partner in Penydarren. The firm was thus known as Forman & Co.[64] It acted in close cooperation with Rhymney, where Thompson and the Bailey brothers stayed on.

Secondly, something was done about Rhymney's transport, for it had suffered for want of an exit route to Newport. In the early days much of its pig iron had been carted to Merthyr for processing, and some was carried to Tredegar by the narrow-gauge branch of the

Tredegar-Trefil tramroad for sending down the Sirhowy to Newport. In 1815 a brand-new line on the 3ft 6in gauge, the Brynoer and Hall's Trefil Tramroads which joined end-to-end, were opened to the north to connect Rhymney to the B&A at Talybont. These were fine for bringing limestone in from Trefil and surplus coal out to Brecon, but did nothing for the export of iron. But a decade later Rhymney promoted a 22-mile tramroad down the Rhymney valley to join the MCC's Western Valleys line at Pye Corner near Bassaleg, which it used for the final three miles to Newport. The gauge, of course, was 4ft 4in. It was plain from the outset who the leading Spirit was: thirty-odd years later it was still 'commonly known as Crawshay Bailey's line.'[65]

By January 1825 the route had already been marked out by George Overton, one of the leading South Wales engineers of the day who had built, among others, the Merthyr and

Fig. 1.15
Thomas Brown (1804-84). In the background Ebbw Vale ironworks with a Neilson 'box' 0-4-0ST, one of the first standard-gauge engines here. Mezzotint by George Raphael Ward, 1854. (*author's collection*)

Brynoer Tramroads,[66] and in February the necessary Bill was introduced to Parliament by Sir Charles Morgan of Tredegar, son of the original Sir Charles who had died in 1816. He became the company's first chairman.[67] The Rumney Railway Act was passed on 20 May 1825,[68] and the line opened in March 1828. It had been built with remarkable speed and remarkable economy, the estimate being £47,850, the actual cost £51,000. The sole shareholders were Crawshay and Joseph Bailey, Sir Charles Morgan and William Thompson.[69] Crawshay Bailey, it was remarked in 1843, 'made the Rhymney Tramroad when iron was more than double its present price, at a cost so small that it would absolutely cause to every Railway Engineer of the present day "each particular hair to stand on end."'[70] Its low cost, and the speed with which it was constructed, were largely because it hugged the landscape with few earthworks, very sharp curves, and frequently-changing gradients. It terminated a mile short of the ironworks, the rest of the distance being on Iron Company metals.

Pre-modern Welsh orthography was not standardised. In nearly all cases this book uses the modern or reasonably modern form,[71] reserving older spellings for quotations. Thus the river and the ironworks are spelt as Rhymney. In the case of the railway, however, to avoid confusion with the latterday Rhymney Railway to Cardiff authorised in 1854, the form 'Rumney Railway' or 'Old Rumney' has to be retained, which was then the usual anglicised spelling. Confusion, nonetheless, has long reigned. From the 1840s it was increasingly if inaccurately known as the Rhymney Railway; and the wonderful (if perhaps apocryphal) tale is told that somewhere in the 1860s, when railway take-overs were in the air, a party of Midland Railway officials surreptitiously inspected the ramshackle Old Rumney under the misapprehension that it was the spanking new Rhymney.[72] Despite being a tramroad, from the start the Old Rumney was officially called a railway, or even just the 'Rumney Road' (Fig. 1.16).

In 1835, as one result of the litigation mentioned, the Rhymney estate was again put up for auction. It was bought by the new Rhymney Iron Co, led once more by William Thompson, Forman having died in 1829; and in 1837 Rhymney and Bute were formally amalgamated and run as a single concern.[73] The Bailey brothers were no longer involved in the works, but remained as directors of the railway company, along with

Fig. 1.16
Rumney Railway milepost.
(*Oxford House Industrial History Society, Risca*)

various Morgans of Tredegar (who held a third of the shares) and Alderman William Thompson (or after his death in 1854 his trustees).[74] But it was reported in 1859 that there had been no meeting of the company for 26 years, the other directors kowtowing to Crawshay Bailey's decisions.[75]

The Rumney acquired an evil reputation for inefficiency, summed up by such comments as these of 1853:

Hitherto the natural riches of the Valley have depended for their conveyance to a shipping port upon the antiquated contrivance of a Tram road, which is traversed in common by locomotive engines, and by the public on foot, in gigs, carriages and carts. Moreover, the curves and gradients of this Tramroad are so severe that a locomotive engine has difficulty in transporting from the Bristol Channel to the Rhymney Iron Works, a distance of only 25 miles, thirty tons of iron ore during a whole day.[76]

And,

The distance from the Rhymney Iron Works to the Port of Newport is only 25 miles, yet it is considered an excellent day's work to go there and back over that Tramroad in a day; and often the return train does not arrive at the Rhymney Works till after midnight, although it may have started long before the break of day.[77]

Thus, unlike the situation in the neighbouring valley where the Sirhowy Tramroad Co and the Tredegar Iron Co were in effect the same, the Rumney Railway Co did not see eye to eye with the Rhymney Iron Co which was its principal customer. When in 1853 the trustees of the Marquess of Bute, who controlled vast mineral rights and were responsible for massive dock developments at Cardiff, promoted a new Rhymney Railway to take the valley's traffic to Cardiff rather than to Newport, the Iron Company, in the hope of more efficient transport and no doubt afraid of offending the Marquess who was their landlord, wholeheartedly supported the scheme. The Rumney Railway Co, led by Crawshay Bailey, a diehard conservative, opposed it; yet, despite anguished pleas from the Newport interests who saw their port losing out to Cardiff, they were reluctant to improve their own line. 'The new Rhymney line would never have been started,' it was said in 1856, 'if the old line had been properly managed.'[78]

BRANCHES

To return to the MCC. Between 1827 and July 1828 its original main line from Nine Mile Point to Newport and its isolated **Beaufort Tramroad** were connected by a new line from Crumlin to Risca (sometimes called the **Crumlin Tramroad**), thus allowing through transport by rail all the way to Newport from the head of the Ebbw Fawr. Rather over six miles long, this was surveyed by the MCC's engineer William Wells, opened on 28 September 1828, and cost £12,193.[79] At the same time it also added the 5½-mile branch (often called the **Aberbeeg Tramroad**) down the Ebbw Fach from Blaina and Coalbrookvale, with Wells again as engineer and Edmund Hodgkinson, son of John, as contractor. The cost was £8,473.[80] The final mile from Coalbrookvale to Nantyglo was completed privately by Joseph and Crawshay Bailey, and at long last all the tramroads authorised by the MCC Act of 1792 were a reality.

Branches off the Sirhowy, the Western Valleys lines and the Rumney were many. Some served foundries and similar concerns which were ever growing in number and size. Such were the Union Copper Co's works, later converted to an iron foundry, at the end of Risca Long Bridge; the Pontymister Iron Works nearby; the Union Foundry at Llanhilleth; Benjamin Hall's Abercarn works; and a thick cluster of foundries and forges at Pillgwenlly – Uskside, Tombs',

Cambrian, Newport and Pillgwenlly, and so forth. But the great majority of the branches served coal pits. Most of them were quite short, and some necessitated inclines. Thus Archdeacon William Coxe recorded on his travels in 1799 that the Crumlin branch of the Monmouthshire Canal was fed at Newbridge with coal 'brought down a rail road, from the mines of Mynydd Islwyn, and conveyed by the canal to Newport.'[81] And again,

> In my way to Risca, I crossed a bridge over a rail road, lately formed by Mr Edward Jones … The expedition and security with which the cars are conveyed up and down the steep side of the precipice, appear singular to a spectator on the bridge. Two parallel rail roads are carried from the canal to [a coal mine on] the opposite side of the Ebwy, along which two cars are drawn up and let down at the same time, by means of an engine; they appear to pass each other alternately, like buckets in well; a boy descends with the empty car, nearly midway, and after adjusting the machinery is again drawn up with the loaded car, which empties the coals into the boats on the canal.[82]

This line, short and short-lived, was unusual in that it climbed up to the canal, whereas most dropped down to it. Opened in 1799, it was probably an edge railway and lasted until the Sirhowy Tramroad was completed; although by 1806, when Jones was using the new line, it was a tramroad, and Jones was reprimanded by the MCC for employing trams which damaged their track.[83]

Other early examples of branches lay further north, like that from the Sirhowy to **Gellihaf Colliery**, already noted and sometimes called the Bryn branch. One, later known as **Phillips' Tramroad**, joined Trinant Colliery by an incline down to the Beaufort at Crumlin. Another, with an incline from **Llanhilleth Colliery** on the east of the Ebbw valley near Aberbeeg, was built in 1798 but dismantled in 1819.[84] Yet another, some 600 yards long, from **Penyfan** pit on the opposite side of the valley may well have been of a similar date, and was certainly at work by 1808.[85] A drawing of its incline in 1845 (Fig. 1.17) is self-explanatory: the endless iron chain, supported on iron rollers, passed round horizontal sheaves mounted in pits at the head and foot, and beneath the upper sheave was the brake wheel.[86]

Two further lengthy but private branches were

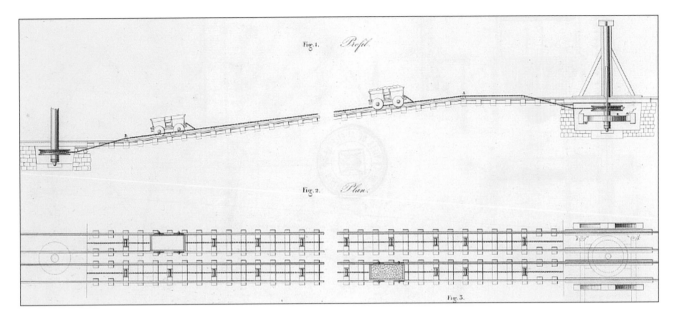

Fig. 1.17

Penyfan incline, 1845
(*Combes 1845, Atlas,*
pl. xxxiii)

the 8½-mile Benjamin Hall's Tramroad with a complex network, ever changing as pits opened and closed, running from collieries to the canal at Abercarn. Beginning as several short railroads laid in 1798 by Samuel Glover, it was rationalised by Hall when he took over the Abercarn Estate in 1808 and became a tramroad of a narrow but unknown gauge. One might guess that it was 3ft as at Rhymney in which Hall was a partner, his agent at Abercarn being John Llewellin who had also come from Rhymney. With the opening of the Crumlin Tramroad, Hall's had to be enlarged to the standard MCC gauge of 4ft 4in,[87] and in 1852 it was bought by Ebbw Vale.[88] The other long branch was the 5½-mile **Penllwyn** or **Jones's Tramroad** built in 1824 from pits on the floor of the Sirhowy valley to Nine Mile Point, the bottom two miles being vested in the Sirhowy.[89] Both contributed sizeable amounts of coal to the main line's traffic: in 1848 50,201 tons from the Penllwyn, 96,230 from Hall's. Neither line was ever locomotive-worked during plateway days.

Yet another branch, of a rather different sort, was **Crawshay Bailey's tramroad** of 1821 from Nantyglo to Govilon, a little east of Gilwern on the B&A. Steeply-graded – too steeply for locomotives of the day – and 5½ miles long, its purpose was to free Nantyglo from bondage to the Clydach Railroad, especially before 1828 when the ironworks were linked by the Aberbeeg branch to the MCC system. The gauge was again 4ft 4in, so that at least in theory – though in practice there would be little call for it – a tram could travel all the way from Govilon

to Rhymney, a distance of some 46 miles. At Govilon Bailey's Tramroad made an end-on junction across the canal with the 3ft 6in-gauge Llanvihangel Railway which carried on to Abergavenny and, ultimately, to Hereford.

Captain Simmons' report on the MRCC of 1849,[90] a valuable source and frequently referred to hereafter, gives lengths for the track inside those ironworks served directly by the MRCC: Ebbw Vale (probably including Sirhowy) 10¾ miles, Victoria ¾ mile, Blaina 4 miles, Nantyglo (probably including Beaufort) 1½ miles. Even these figures sound like underestimates because Rhymney Ironworks, according to an inventory of 1848, had over 33 miles of cast-iron tramroad and perhaps 2 miles of wrought-iron on the surface, as well as more than 48 miles underground.[91] The weight of the surface plates – 150 lb/yd – shows that these are lengths not of rail but of track including iron sills. They do not include the Rumney Railway itself, which belonged to the Railway Company rather than the Iron Company, but surely do include Hall's Trefil Tramroad (about 3 miles), the Rhymney Limestone Railway (about 4 miles) and the top mile of the Rhymney that was ironworks property. Yet that still leaves around 25 miles for internal lines and sidings. By a similar token, the very much smaller Coalbrookvale, when sold in 1841, had 27,883 yards of tram plates in place.[92] If meant literally, this equates to nearly 8 miles of track.

For total mileages, various sources give conflicting figures.

	MRCC	public branches	private branches	total branches	total
Company version 1849	30¾			72½	103¼
Freighters' version 1849	46	54	35	89	135
MB 19 Sep 1846	51¾				
MM 22 Dec 1849	43				
MM 4 Apl 1851	54			123	177

The first two sets of figures were given to Captain Simmons. The route mileage of the Western Valleys lines, Park Mile included, is easily measured and indeed was, as the Company said, 30¾. The 46 miles given by the freighters was approximately the track mileage. The true length of the branches is harder to calculate – exactly what is included? – and here most of the figures given defy neat explanation. But even 123 miles does not seem excessive, if they are track miles including such internal works lines as discussed above. It seems best to accept the Company's figures as minimum ones. At all events, a total of 103¼ miles made by far the largest connected system of plateways that ever existed anywhere; much more so if the total was 177 miles or more.

The MCC was not a common carrier: it provided the track but did not operate the traffic. This was done with a minimum of regulation by the freighters – the coalowners, ironmasters and other parties – who owned the vehicles, organised their own motive power and paid tolls to the Company. Such an arrangement was standard on early public railways; but while it worked very well on small and simple lines, it became an operational nightmare as mileage and traffic expanded and as some freighters adopted steam traction instead of horses. These awkwardnesses lay at the root of the anguish when the system, now extensive but antiquated, had to be dragged screaming into the Railway Age. Nor was the MCC (or, after its change of name in 1848, the MRCC) much loved, for it lived in a constant state of financial stringency, its rates were high, its tramroads ill-maintained, and its inefficiencies notorious.

TRAFFIC

For the overall volume of traffic carried, reliable and consistent figures are hard to come by. Some idea of the general growth of trade may be gained from comparative figures of coal shipments from South Wales ports (in thousands of tons).[93]

	1840	*1851*	*1874*
Newport	490	603	1,066
Cardiff	166	750	3,780
Swansea and Neath	493	394	1,043
Llanelli	212	229	222
Milford	77	49	34

This shows very clearly how – once the main line railways arrived with the Taff Vale in 1840-1, and once the east-west lines offered a choice of route – Newport lost out to Cardiff, where the rates were always lower. Another, more local, idea may be gained from the five-yearly average tonnages set out below of iron and coal delivered to Newport.[94] These embrace everything from Eastern and Western Valleys alike, although the great majority, especially in later years, arrived by tramroad rather than by canal. Apart from Newport's own needs, all of it was for export. For comparative purposes, the figures for Tredegar iron are included.

	Iron	*Coal*	*Tredegar iron*[95]
1807-11	26,368	185,820[96]	6,622
1812-16	41,666		8,263
1817-21	45,176		8,776
1822-26	68,780		10,284
1827-31			13,434
1832-36	121,468	480,074	12,909
1837-41	153, 268	523,293	14,479
1842-46	187,594	629,311	18,380[97]
1847	240,637[98]		

Tredegar, of course, was only one player among many. Early on, it accounted for a quarter of the total iron shipped, but by around 1830 this had slipped to a tenth. About 1825 it was overtaken by Ebbw Vale, which from then on produced considerably more. With coal, in 1839 Tredegar contributed only about 9 per cent of the total. These figures may not sound particularly large. But there was plenty of non-Tredegar traffic in the Western Valleys, by far the biggest player being the Newport Coal Co, a cartel headed by Thomas Prothero and Thomas Powell. Only for 1842 is a complete breakdown available of tonnages on the Sirhowy. Alongside Tredegar's own contribution of 18,380 tons of iron and 31,455 of coal, Ebbw Vale sent out 13,120 tons of iron (in addition to what it sent down the Western Valleys line), and there was 14,000 tons of back carriage to Tredegar. Of pits further south, Argoed sent out 28,347 tons of coal and Gelligroes and Gellideg 22,914. Thus the total on the Sirhowy main line in 1842 was 128,216 tons. But there were also 59,219 tons of coal on the Penllwyn Tramroad, the lowest two miles of which belonged to the Sirhowy; include this, and the grand total sent on from Nine Mile Point in 1842 amounted to 187,435 tons.[99] This probably does not incorporate coal from Sirhowy pits; certainly by 1859 they were sending out some 78,000 tons.[100]

The feeder tramroads had a big financial advantage over the waterways of the high-charging MCC. In 1818 Samuel Homfray senior wrote,

> The Sirhowy Tram-road is 23 miles long, and the hauliers[101] find their own oil, and every expence [sic] (except trams,) and take our iron for 21d per ton, long weight (120 lbs to the hundred); this is less than 1d per ton per mile. If, therefore, we add tram dues [i.e. tolls] 1½d per ton per mile, we have 2½d per ton per mile, which, on 28 miles, is 5s 10d.

The comparable cost by canal, by which he seems to mean at MCC rates, would be 10s 6d per ton, or nearly twice as much.[102] The Sirhowy Tramroad therefore did well financially. Its capital of £30,000 was in 300 shares of £100, and until 1832 it paid an average dividend of 14 per cent (18 per cent in 1818 as against the MCC's 8 per cent, and 30 per cent in the early 1820s), but in 1833-5 it fell to 10-12 per cent because of the cost of new rails.[103] Even in the 1850s it was still a regular 10 per cent, and shares changed hands

at £200.[104] For many years the Rumney Railway paid a dividend of 8 to 12 per cent,[105] despite charging only 1d per ton per mile as opposed to the MCC's 1½d.[106] These are impressive figures. The Stockton & Darlington is often held up as an outstandingly profitable concern, with dividends of 10 per cent or more from 1836 to 1848 and peaking at 15 per cent in 1840-41;[107] but those figures were equalled or handsomely exceeded by the Sirhowy and the Rumney.

It was because of its high rates that the MCC lost out to rivals. The B&A rates were lower, which meant that for lengthy periods, once that canal had opened throughout in 1812, Ebbw Vale found it cheaper to export via the Clydach Railroad to Gilwern wharf, until the through tramroad to Newport was complete. Nantyglo did likewise, and for even longer because of the steep gradients on the Aberbeeg. The creation in 1832 of the tunnel between Ebbw Vale and Sirhowy led, as we shall see, to the claim that Ebbw Vale was thus evading tolls that rightfully belonged to the MCC. On a smaller scale, in 1835 Thomas Prothero's Rock Colliery on the Penllwyn was extended westwards underground to emerge in the Rhymney valley, and much of its coal was covertly sent out by the Rumney so that the MCC lost six miles-worth of tolls.[108]

Despite the MCC being, by origin, a canal company, its canals carried an ever-diminishing proportion of the valleys' traffic. The bypassing in 1828 of the Crumlin branch by the Crumlin Tramroad exacerbated the trend, and by the 1870s water-borne trade had dwindled to virtually nothing.

ENGINEERING

Although the Sirhowy, Rumney and the MCC's Western Valleys tramroads were separately-owned entities, as connected lines they necessarily had a great deal in common. In general terms, and until at least 1850, much of what can be said of the track and rolling stock and operation of one holds true for the others. The whole of the Sirhowy and the MCC main line was originally laid as single track with passing places. The MCC's doubling of its portion from Nine Mile Point downwards was probably not completed until 1813, and of the Beaufort and Crumlin Tramroads not until about 1839.[109]

The valley sides along which the tramroads ran on a shelf are less precipitous than in the Clydach Gorge, but as far down as Risca the track was rarely more than two hundred yards from the

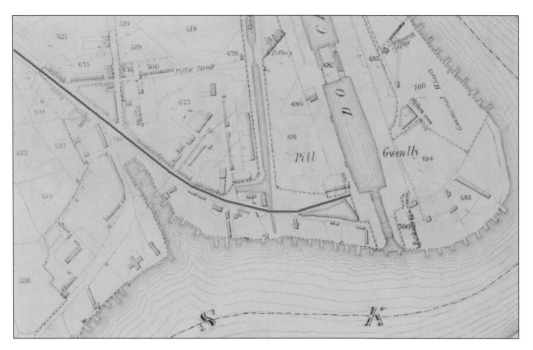

Fig. 1.18
Pillgwenlly in 1841. Only
the main route of the
tramroad is shown; there
were many branches
to individual wharves,
constantly changing with
time. (*Tithe Map*)

rivers, which dictated the ruling gradient. On the Sirhowy it was 1 in 98 (maximum 1 in 72, at Tredegar) reducing to 1 in 130, and reducing again to 1 in 176 on the MCC section. The Crumlin was 1 in 106, the Beaufort 1 in 75, the Aberbeeg 1 in 50 but increasing to an evil 1 in 30 or thereabouts on the final mile built by Bailey to Nantyglo. Hall's was 1 in 54, the Penllwyn gentler at 1 in 156.[110] The Rumney, overall, was equally gentle, although the top eight miles averaged 1 in 105.[111]

Curves were sometimes vicious: one at Tredegar was of 34ft radius,[112] and even sharper ones of 15ft 2in and 14ft 4in radius were to be found, before they were ironed out, on the MCC lines at Risca, Crumlin and Blaina.[113] There were weighing machines and toll houses at Nine Mile Point and at Court y Bella just outside Newport. At Pillgwenlly, to which the track had been extended from Court y Bella in 1806,[114] the tracks fanned out to the various wharves and jetties (Fig. 1.18), the detail of the layout constantly changing over the years. This was the territory of the Tredegar Wharf Company, a partnership of Sir Charles Morgan, Samuel Homfray, Rowley Lascelles and Richard Fothergill set up in 1807, which made huge profits in developing the port area.[115] In 1842 the first dock was opened at Newport and the tramroad extended to it, and in 1854 a second dock was authorised.

Because the routes largely followed the contours rather than crossing the grain of the country, the engineering feature that stood out as the most impressive was the Long Bridge over the Ebbw at Risca. The contract was let in November 1802 for £3,600 to Richard Thomas, William Homfray (no relation, it seems, of Samuel) and Walter Walters. Completion was delayed, and to enable traffic to flow the MCC allowed the Sirhowy any extra costs incurred as well as 'a Man and Horse to assist in conveying their waggons across the said Valley'[116] on a temporary bridge. By October 1804 the man and horse had not yet materialised,[117] and yet further delays meant the bridge was not complete in May 1805.[118] But it was passable, and this, it seems, was the date when through traffic began. In the very same month Benjamin Outram died at the early age of 41; but John Hodgkinson stayed on in Monmouthshire and set up there in practice as surveyor, engineering many more tramroads. In 1806 the MCC committee was prodding him to build the bridge's parapets,[119] and the final touches were made only in mid-1811; hence the date of 11 August 1811 occasionally given for the full opening.[120]

The Long Bridge (Fig. 1.19), at first intended as single arches over the river and road with embankment in between, was in fact built as a continuous structure. A proposal of 1803 to create dwellings under the arches was not realised.[121] The thirty-two arches were of 24ft span and an average height of 28ft 6in, the deck was 16ft wide between parapets, and the overall length was 930ft which at the time made it the longest railway viaduct in existence.[122] Hodgkinson

Fig. 1.19 Long Bridge, Risca, *c.*1900. (*author's collection*)

Fig. 1.20 'View of a Stone Bridge,' aquatint by Thomas Cartwright after Edward Pugh, 1810. Pugh's original drawing was done after 1807 when the copper works in the background were built. The tramroad is shown continuing up the valley beyond the right-hand end of the bridge, but in fact this was not built until 1828. (*Sir Arthur Elton Collection, Ironbridge Gorge Museum*)

Fig. 1.21
Long Bridge under
demolition, 1904.
(*author's collection*)

was justly proud of his creation, and in 1810 he published a splendid aquatint of the bridge (Fig. 1.20).

The Long Bridge suffered subsidence in two of its spans in 1855,[123] and was superseded in 1858-9 when the tramroad was revamped as a full-blown railway with easier curves.[124] It was demolished in 1903-4 (Fig. 1.21).[125] The only original bridge that now survives on the Sirhowy is the stone arch across the river at the northern terminus which probably belongs to 1800 and the first rail link to Tredegar, thus preceding the Sirhowy Tramroad proper. Its side arches and splayed deck are perhaps a later addition to allow the tracks to fan out into the Sirhowy works yard (Fig. 1.22).

In contrast to the Long Bridge is the much-altered Big Bridge or Newtown Bridge at Ebbw Vale (SO 170099), a causeway carrying at first only a high-level tramroad to the furnace tops, but later the private line from Sirhowy and later still the line from the 1832 tunnel. It originally had two stone arches (with a date-stone of 1813), of which one crossed the river, the other the Beaufort Tramroad and alongside it the road; and it was later heightened with a mini-viaduct of small arches built on top, visible from only one side, which reached a final height of 75ft above the river (Fig. 1.23).[126] In 1859, when the line to Beaufort was being improved, a new arch was created for the road by cutting through the

Fig. 1.22
Tramroad bridge over
Sirhowy river at Sirhowy.
(*Robin Drayton,
cc-by-sa/2.0*)

embankment and erecting a temporary timber bridge 35ft long to span the gap. It collapsed without warning, sending a train of four iron ore trams, two horses and the haulier plunging to the valley floor. The cause, the contractor thought, was either heavy rain washing out the supports or the trams derailing, the consequent jerk bringing the timbers down.[127]

The Rumney crossed the Ebbw at Bassaleg by George Overton's fine viaduct with semicircular

Fig. 1.23

Big Bridge, Ebbw Vale, arch with 1813 date stone for Beaufort Tramroad and road. Tall arch on left added in 1859 for new road.

(*Colin Cheesman, Wikimedia cc-sa/2.0*)

arches each of 26ft span (ST 278872) (Fig. 1.24). Dated 1826 and widened for the standard gauge, it claims to be the oldest railway viaduct in the world still to carry traffic, albeit nowadays only stone from Machen Quarry. The Penllwyn, almost at its junction with the Sirhowy, crossed the Sirhowy river by a fine masonry bridge of 44ft span which is still extant (ST 203911, Fig. 1.25). Hall's boasted a respectable tunnel at Pennar (ST 195963) which was originally about 540 yards long but was later enlarged in bore and reduced in length. It also had another fine eight-arched viaduct of 1828 over the Ebbw at Pontywaun, which was built for Hall by an illiterate Pontypool mason named Jones, the agreed price being £1,910. But it turned out that the tramroad either side was 13ft higher than the contract specified, and Jones had to rebuild the bridge taller. Having been paid £3,995, he was still £1,000 out of pocket. The Assizes jury awarded him another £674.[128] Phillips' Tramroad that fed down to Crumlin had a three-quarter mile tunnel connecting Trinant and Cwm Nant y Gint Collieries.[129]

The first rails on the MCC lines and the Sirhowy were of Outram's standard design, cast-iron, 3ft long, and spiked directly to the stone blocks. One of the men involved in laying the Sirhowy's original track was William Lewis ap Meredith of Argoed (1760-1836), who in 1811-36 also held the contract for maintaining it. Two further generations of his family followed in his footsteps:[130] his son William (1809-86) became its permanent way inspector;[131] and his grandson William Lewis Meredith (1843-1924) also worked on it until the Sirhowy Railway was completed, when he left for the Midland Railway and in 1884 founded the Permanent Way Institution. They, and their counterparts who maintained the trams, seem to have done their work well, for contemporary writers speak approvingly of the line's quality. It was said in 1819,

> From the Tredegar iron-works a railway, for a length of nearly twenty-four miles, is laid down through the valley … This railway, which is travelled by waggons carrying weights of two tons and a half, is, perhaps, in dimensions, both as to breadth and length, the first thing of the sort in existence. It has several lateral lines of road connected with it.[132]

Another report of 1826-7 says, 'One horse will draw downwards 10 tons, 200 cwt, and bring up the empty waggons, a performance which far surpasses that usual on the tramroads of South Wales.'[133]

Maybe. But this underlines the inherent defects

of plateways. They suffered heavy friction from the wheels rubbing on the flanges, the flat of the rails was often encumbered by accumulated dirt, and in general their trams were crudely built and maintained. On any decently-kept edge railway, traffic could run down Sirhowy-like gradients by gravity alone. Thus experiments in 1834 on the Liverpool & Manchester, on long wrought-iron rails, showed that trains of loaded waggons would freewheel down a gradient as shallow as 1 in 276.[134] On the Hetton Colliery railway in 1824,

with cast-iron edge rails 4ft long, the gradient 'such as would cause the carriages to descend with an accelerated velocity' was 1 in 104.24.[135] On tramroads, by contrast, the friction was such that the trams had to be hauled downhill even on quite steep slopes. According to George Overton, the shallowest gradient that allowed gravity running on a well-kept cast-iron plateway was 1 in 53.[136] It was only wrought-iron plates and better trams that improved the situation, a topic that will be pursued in Part 3.

Fig. 1.24
Rumney Railway, George Overton's viaduct over the Ebbw river at Bassaleg, 1826. (*Jaggery, Wikimedia cc-by-sa/2.0*)

Fig. 1.25
Nine Mile Point, Penllwyn Tramroad bridge over Sirhowy river, 1824. (*Oxford House Industrial History Society, Risca*)

Fig. 1.26
Tredegar Ironworks, 1809,
by Richard Fothergill junior.
Sirhowy Tramroad across
foot, feeder lines coming
down from above.
(*GwentA, D.1147.13*)

Fig. 1.27
Tredegar Ironworks, 1864.
(*NMW, P76.419*)

EARLY DAYS

Of the day when the Sirhowy Tramroad first began proper business, at some unrecorded point in the summer of 1805, Tredegar's historian wrote,

> Iron was conveyed to Newport at the first opportunity. A splendid team of horses, driven by Morgan Humphrey Richard, conveying from ten to twelve tons of iron on carriages, completed a successful journey to Newport in one day, and returning the following day with provisions, &c., to supply the Company's Shop.[137]

On 7 August 1809 Richard Fothergill junior drew a pencil sketch, microscopic but carefully done, of Tredegar works and a line-up of trains on the Sirhowy Tramroad, with further trams coming down from the pits above (Fig. 1.26).[138] An engraving of 1864 from the same viewpoint shows how the works and the town had grown (Fig. 1.27). The place might be perpetually filthy, the housing inadequate, the sanitation shameful, the wages miserly and the people downtrodden, but these were exciting times.

One such excitement came on 27 November 1821. John Jones, the owner of Penllwyn Colliery near Gelligroes which lay on the valley floor below the Sirhowy tramroad, was faced with the cost of lifting the coal a substantial height up to rail level. He therefore invoked the eight-mile clause of the MCC Act of 1792 and set about building his own low-level tramroad, surveyed by George Overton, alongside the river to Nine Mile Point. The Sirhowy Tramroad Company did not like such competition; nor did John Llewellin, agent of Benjamin Hall's rival collieries to the east. Between them they bought a field on the intended route and obtained injunctions to prevent Jones crossing it. Before Overton was even aware of the problem, a horde of five hundred Tredegar men, allegedly led by Samuel Homfray in person, descended on the site 'on foot, on horseback, in tram-waggons, and by other modes of conveyance,' and tried with 'pick axes shovels and other instruments forcibly to prevent the men in the employ of George Overton proceeding with that part of the road.' They ripped up the plates already laid, destroyed the earthworks, and were stopped only by the magistrates reading the Riot Act. Jones appealed in Chancery, and eventually a peaceable settlement was hammered out.[139] As a result, Jones's line was built in 1824, with a continuation northwards as far as Rock Colliery

where for some distance the Sirhowy River and three tramroads – Hall's, Jones's and the Sirhowy – were bottlenecked side-by-side into a strip little more than 300 yards wide.

In the early days traffic could hardly be called heavy: in December 1810, for example, the Park Mile carried only a weekly average of 215½ tons of coal on 93 trams from various collieries – that is, roughly 2,500 tons a year – and 12 trams of iron from Tredegar.[140] The coming of branches, most notably the Penllwyn and Hall's Tramroads, raised these figures substantially. In 1838, out of a particular 68,000 tons on the Park Mile, the principal contributors were:[141]

	Coal	Iron
Hall's	32,320	
Sirhowy	9,620	3,440
Penllwyn	8,050	
Rumney	4,600	2,720

In the year 1832/3, the Park Mile brought Sir Charles Morgan an annual income of £3,335.[142] Because his only outgoings would be the maintenance of a mile of track, he was veritably sitting on a gold mine. The same year saw roughly 450,000 tons of coal pass down the tramroad. From this may be drawn a salutary antidote to the common belief that plateways were but poor relations of 'proper' railways. Lumbering, antiquated and inefficient they may be been; but in that year the Western Valleys lines still carried more coal than even that success story of the day, the Stockton & Darlington with its 424,274 tons.[143] It was probably not until 1836 that the S&D, with a sudden surge past the half-million mark, finally overtook the Western Valleys. Certainly by 1838/9, when we have a rare figure for coal carried to Newport by tramroad – 442,882 tons[144] – the S&D was carrying 669,729 tons.

The Sirhowy's primary *raison d'être*, of course, was to take iron out, increasingly in rolled form rather than as pig, and to bring provisions in. But as a public railway it might carry almost anything. An unusual and interesting consignment in 1810 was the prefabricated iron roof for a building 40 by 21ft in plan, made at Aberdare and carried in pieces by road waggon to Tredegar and thence by tram to Newport, all in twenty-four hours. It weighed 2¼ tons.[145] From the beginning, moreover, all the ironworks along the heads of the valleys were supplied with their raw materials from relatively nearby sources, until in the early

1830s, as local supplies were outgrown, increasing quantities of ironstone had to be imported and carried uphill. The time also came – earlier than is often thought – when significantly more coal was raised than the ironworks needed, and it was carried in quantity down to Newport for shipping coastwise.

On 18 December 1821 the neighbourhood enjoyed another excitement. In celebration of Tredegar's early entry into this trade, Homfray junior laid on a grand demonstration train which was timed to coincide with Sir Charles Morgan's popular annual Cattle Show held beside the tramroad at Court y Bella just outside Newport. The scene was memorably depicted by John Thomas in an extraordinary painting, measuring 12ft by 2ft 10in, inscribed

> A Plain Representation of the Teams & Trams of Coal, brought down to Pillgwenlly, by Samuel Homfray Esqr on Tuesday 18th December 1821. Weight of Coal 79 Tons 10 Cwt. To Samuel Homfray Esqr The Independent Iron Master & Coal Merchant, Whose Exertions Have Benefited the town & Neighbourhood of Newport by reducing the Price of Coals. This Piece is Humbly Inscribed by his Humble Servant Ino Thomas (Fig. 1.28).[146]

Featuring prominently in it are the huge and novel bogie coal trams, of which more later. There are also two written accounts of the occasion.

> A contract was made to deliver the 'best coal' at Pillgwenlly, Newport, and to convey the first coal carriages were specially constructed, and taken into the shop level to be loaded; twelve carriages were loaded and brought to the surface; some of the lumps of coal weighed several tons. On the

appointed day two teams of splendid grey horses, each team consisting of four beautiful animals, fully equipped and decorated, started with six carriages for each team; the huge masses of coal were decorated with flags of various colours, and arrived safely at their destination, to the satisfaction of the proprietors, and to the astonishment of the large and interested crowd collected together to witness the curiosity. S. Homfray, Esq., junior, who at that time was a young man about 19 years of age [actually 26], accompanied the first train of coal conveyed to Newport, and was enraptured with joy at its safe arrival. The collier who dug the coal was George Williams, and the hauliers, who drove the teams were John Davies (Jack y Bugail) and David Williams.[147]

The *Cambrian* too pulled out all its journalistic stops.

> A long train of waggons, called trams, gaily surmounted by waving banners, drawn by a team of superb grey horses, in their best gear, escorted by detachments of horse and foot recruited on the way, all enlivened by a good band, playing patriotic and martial airs, were hailed on their arrival at the Pill-wharves by repeated salvos of artillery, and by the cheers and acclamations of a large multitude collected on the occasion. Some dozens of immense pieces or knobs of coal, weighing from 5 cwt to 3 tons each, intended as specimens for some distant ports, attracted particular notice and curiosity. About 30 tons or more of large coal, of the finest quality, were distributed among the poor. The jolly tars and hardy operatives, with their numerous friends, after being well drenched with rain, were counter-drenched with copious libations of *cwrw da* [beer], supplied by their liberal and public-

Fig. 1.28
'A Plain Representation', by John Thomas, 1821. (*NMW, A2834*)

spirited employers, and as the well-drained casks were in succession rolled away, to make room for new guests and fresh taps, the air was rent by the reverberating shouts of *Success! Success!–work and wages for the winter! our Masters, our Masters, our noble, kind, and bounteous Masters, Homfray and Co for ever!* [148]

Tredegar, now twenty-one years old, had so to speak come of age. Yet industrial and social unrest, however much the broadly conservative local press might play it down, was never far below the surface. Only four or five months after helping Homfray to vandalise the Penllwyn Tramroad and shouting their loyal huzzahs at the Cattle Show, his and other iron and coal workers were not only on strike for higher wages but quite literally on the warpath. The military had to be called in

A large party of colliers assembled at Gellyhaw colliery [Gellihaf, already discussed], stopping by force and chaining together nineteen waggons, laden with coal for the Tredegar works…The Riot Act was read…In less than twenty minutes, however, an attack was made on the waggons in the rear, and the coals were thrown out…The cavalry were then ordered to clear the ground… The waggons were then forwarded under guard of the cavalry, and, together with 55 others, making in the whole 74 waggons, were conveyed, notwithstanding repeated attempts to break up the roads in advance, to within three miles of the Tredegar works, where they were met by a detachment of the Scotch Greys. [149]

A few days later, in the narrows of the Western Valleys line above Crumlin, came the orchestrated ambush of a coal train that was heading north under armed escort for Ebbw Vale. It was decided that a detachment of the Chepstow Cavalry

should form a kind of advanced guard, and should precede the main body about a mile, to prevent the breaking up the road. The road in those parts winds along a narrow valley, with an immense mountain almost perpendicular on the right hand, at the foot of which runs the river on the left. The detachment had hardly proceeded three-quarters of a mile when a most furious attack was made upon it from the sides of the hill on the right, down which immense stones and fragments of rock were hurled with great violence. The bugle was at once sounded for assistance, and the party halted; but not having any proper means of defence at hand against this species of assault, a retreat was sounded: having retired about 150 yards, it took up a less exposed station, till it was joined by the whole corps.

The Riot Act was again read, in vain, and although growing numbers of men hid in the thickets on the hillside, it was stalemate for three hours until the Scots Greys worked their way round along the ridge and cleared the ground from above. [150]

At the same time, despite the defeat of this ambush, other strikers

during the night destroyed or disabled about twenty wagons which (deserted by the halliers in the course of the day) had been left near the Monmouthshire Canal Company's reservoir at Lanhilleth: four of them, with their contents, were rolled over the precipice, and dashed into the river below; others were sunk in the reservoir, and

the wheels of about fourteen more were broken to pieces on the road. Not content, however, with these depredations, the coals (more than two tons in each wagon) were set on fire, and with everything combustible about the wagons, totally consumed, some of the great masses of fire continuing to burn till Monday morning. While this was effecting in the valley above Crwmlin, another body of rioters … attacked and destroyed, in several places above the 18 milestone,[151] nearly half a mile of the Sirhowy tramroad … Not only were the iron plates ripped up and carried away, but the stone blocks raised and rolled down into the river; and in order to prevent a further supply being sent up, this fine public work, from which the country (and no portion of it more than the workmen themselves) have derived such great advantages, was thus feloniously destroyed. Great numbers of the work-people have, however, since been employed upon the road, and we are happy to learn that it is, by great exertion, already restored to its former state of usefulness and repair.[152]

The strike, as usual, fizzled out, but unrest continued. In the 1820s and 30s the iron towns were terrorised by the anti-immigration faction that called itself the Scotch Cattle. In 1830, when the Luddite-like anti-mechanisation movement known as Swing was under way, 'Mr Homfray, of Tredegar, and Mr Bailey, of Nantyglo, have received "Swing" letters, imperatively calling upon them to destroy their respective locomotive engines;'[153] which they ignored. There followed two popular uprisings which, in terms of casualties, were the worst in mainland Britain for many centuries, worse even than the Peterloo massacre of 1819. In 1831 the ironworkers contributed to the Merthyr riots that ended with

twenty-odd fatalities. And in the great Chartist rising of 1839 hordes of thousands of them converged on Newport along the tramroads on foot or by rail. After the bloody debacle at the Westgate Hotel that left more than twenty dead and fifty injured, they made their escape by the same route; some, tragi-comically, in steam-hauled trains travelling at walking pace.[154]

There had already been a few experiments with steam haulage in South Wales, but the real revolution dated from 1829 when locomotives began to be adopted ever more widely. For the period between 1829 and 1860 much of the detailed story of the tramroads will emerge in the following pages. But to complete the outline of the formal background, let it be said here that as early as 1842 the MCC began to think of modernising its lines in the interests of efficiency, in the face of opposition from the freighters who were frightened of the cost. The committee sent a deputation to the North of England 'for the purpose of ascertaining and reporting upon the system there pursued, more especially in regard to the transit of coal.'[155] The only immediate result was the substitution of wrought-iron plates for the old cast ones, and it was not until 1849 that the MRCC finally embarked on the much more painful process, no less than eleven years in duration, of replacing its plate rails with standard-gauge edge ones, partly by laying temporary 'combined rails' which could take both flanged and unflanged wheels, partly by using 'combined wheels' which could run on either kind of rail. The Rumney followed a similar path. The Sirhowy Tramroad was likewise converted between 1857 and 1860, but rather by omitting the combined rails and employing only standard-gauge edge rails and combined wheels.

Notes to Part One

1   King 1994; Burland Frowen and Milsom 1977.
2   NLW, Tredegar MS 611 011 11 6.
3   Coxe 1801, vol. 1, 14. For further contemporary accounts see Baber 1973, 9-10.
4   *Cambrian*, 23 Sep 1809; *GJ*, 28 Oct 1811.
5   Morris 1868, 12.
6   Coxe 1801, vol. 1, 46.
7   Manby 1802, 96.
8   32 Geo III cap.102.
9   Lewis and van Laun 2001.
10   Lloyd 1906, 113-4.
11   Van Laun 2001, 205-6, 215.
12   For the Clydach, Rattenbury 1980, 59-81.
13   Rattenbury 1989.
14   Van Laun 2001, 204-5.
15   Powell 1902, 31-2, who rather implies that it refers to the opening of the Sirhowy Tramroad, which he later describes in quite different terms.
16   Hadfield 1967, 132; Rattenbury 1980, 64. The scene was painted by Peter van Lerberghe between 1794 when the Clydach Railroad opened and 1802 when his artworks were sold (Myrone 2015)
17   Rattenbury 1980, 65-6; van Laun 2001, 86.
18   Wilberforce 1838, vol. 4, 302.
19   NLW Tredegar MS 611 011 11 6.
20   For his career see Schofield 2000.
21   *MM*, 7 Apl 1849.
22   NLW, Maybery 383 (B&A); TNA, RAIL 1005/54 (MCC).
23   Van Laun 2001, 172-3.
24   NLW, Maybery 10-11.
25   NLW, Maybery 226, printed in Lloyd 1906, 139-40.
26   Dowden 1993.
27   NLW, Maybery 229; Lloyd 1906, 143.
28   Copy of survey in NLW, BRECS Q/RP/49.
29   NLW, Tredegar MS 611 011 11 6.
30   42 Geo. III cap. 115, 26 Jun 1802.
31   *GJ*, 8 Nov, 6 Dec 1802. These notices refer, inaccurately but understandably, to the whole length to Newport as the Sirhowy Tramroad, as was not uncommon in later days too.
32   Powell 1902, 25, 27, 44.
33   Lovering 1998, 5; *Cambrian*, 18 Apl 1807; Hassall 1815, 15-18.
34   The cylinder was 8in by 3ft: *Monmouthshire Evening Post*, 22 Feb 1912, an entry drawn by Charles Ellis from Thomas Ellis senior's notebooks, of which more in Part 2. This entry, however, is not in any of the six volumes currently at the NLW.
35   *Cambrian*, 4 May 1822.
36   *GJ*, 16 Jun 1800.
37   NLW, Maybery 229; Lloyd 1906, 143.
38   *GJ*, 26 Oct 1801.
39   *GJ*, 8 Oct 1802.
40   *GJ*, 14 Feb 1803.
41   Svedenstjerna 1804, 107; translation, 61 (wrongly giving twelve miles).
42   *GJ*, 8 Aug 1803.
43   NLW, Maybery 240. Much the best, though not perfect, account of the tramroad's early history is Schofield 2000, 263-74, from which some of the following details are drawn.
44   *GJ*, 8 Oct 1804.
45   Van Laun 2001, 136.
46   Svedenstjierna 1804, 104; translation, 59.
47   Rattenbury 1987.
48   Van Laun 2001, 174; Elsas 1960, 152; *MM*, 7 Nov 1829.
49   Schofield 2000, 268 is certainly wrong in assuming it was edge-railed.
50   TNA, RAIL 500/5, 4 Nov 1802.
51   Cumming 1824, 26.
52   NLW, Tredegar MS 611 011 11 6.
53   Svedenstjerna 1804, 105; translation, 60.
54   For the history of Tredegar and Sirhowy, both as ironworks and as communities, the major source, to be used with much caution, is Powell 1902 (written in 1884). Jones 1969 leans heavily on Powell. See also Hilling 2003.
55   Thomas 2000.
56   Scrivenor 1854, 127, 258
57   Wilkins 1867, 160, 171-2. His account is muddled.
58   Obituary, *MM*, 12 Dec 1884.
59   Obituary, *South Wales Daily News*, 19 Aug 1889.
60   *MM*, 23 Jun 1854.
61   *MM*, 21 Feb 1846, 7 Apl 1849.
62   *Cambrian*, 10 Jul 1824; *HJ*, 2 Mar 1825; *Cambrian*, 12 Mar, 23 Apl, 7 May 1825.
63   *Cambrian*, 22 Jan 1825.
64   *Cambrian*, 16 Apl 1825, *Birmingham Journal*, 2 Jul 1826; *Morning Advertiser*, 7 Jul 1830.
65   *CT*, 1 May 1863.
66   *Cambrian*, 22 Jan 1825.
67   *Cambrian*, 12 Feb 1825.
68   6 Geo IV cap. lxii.
69   Gerstner 1831, Bd. 1, 638-9.
70   *MM*, 28 Jan 1843.
71   Or that still in normal circulation; thus Blaenavon rather than Blaenafon, Abertillery rather than Abertileri, Trefil rather than Trevil (except for the Trevil Railroad which was the official title).
72   Barrie 1957, 111.
73   *MM*, 2 May 1835; *London Courier*, 1 Mar 1836; *MM*, 26 Mar 1836.
74   *MM*, 29 Jun 1843, 16 Jun 1854
75   *MB*, 16 Apl 1859.
76   *BM*, 17 Dec 1853.

77 *CMG*, 17 Dec 1853.

78 *MB*, 16 Apl 1859; *CMG*, 22 Nov 1856.

79 Gerstner 1831, Bd. 1, 637.

80 Rattenbury 1980, 50-1; Gerstner 1831, Bd. 1, 637.

81 Coxe 1801, vol. 2, 257.

82 Coxe 1801, vol. 2, 258.

83 Meredith 1913, 221; Rattenbury 1983b; Morgan 2017.

84 Hadfield 1967, 131.

85 *Cambrian*, 5 Nov 1808.

86 Combes 1845, vol. 3, 53-5 and atlas, pl. xxxiii; Lewis 2017b.

87 Rattenbury 1988; Frowen 2007a and 2007b.

88 *CMG*, 27 Nov 1852.

89 Rattenbury 1983a.

90 Report of the Commissioners for Railways for 1849, Appendix 74, 157-178 = *PP* 1850, vol. xxxi, 179-200. Discussed in Lewis 1996.

91 GlamA, DRH/85 f. 101.

92 *MB*, 30 Jan 1841.

93 Morris and Williams 1958, 32, 91.

94 Hadfield 1967, 139.

95 Scrivenor 1854, 127, 258.

96 1809 only (Hassall 1815, 116).

97 1842 only (*MM*, 29 Apl 1843).

98 Byles 1982, 111.

99 *MM*, 29 Apl 1843.

100 *MM*, 30 Jul 1859.

101 *Haulier* was the regular term in Wales for horse tram drivers, and often later for locomotive crew.

102 Anon 1818, 7.

103 *BM*, 5 Dec 1835; Tomlinson 1914, 51; Cumming 1824, 29.

104 *CMG*, 4 Sep 1852; *MM*, 17 Sep 1852.

105 *MM*, 5 May 1854.

106 *MM*, 12 Feb 1831.

107 Kirby 1993, Appendix 1.

108 Rattenbury 1983a, 194.

109 Hadfield 1960, 137, 145.

110 Figures mostly from Simmons' report, but other sources vary, though not wildly.

111 Meredith 1913, 238-9; Barrie 1980, 117.

112 NLW, MS 5157 f.8v, of 1842.

113 *MM*, 29 Apl 1843.

114 GwentA, D.749/111.

115 Its papers are in NLW, AN.

116 NLW, Maybery 240.

117 TNA, RAIL 500/5, 4 Oct 1804.

118 Schofield 2000, 269-70.

119 TNA RAIL 500/5, 7 May 1806.

120 Meredith 1906, 254; 1913, 228.

121 TNA, RAIL 500/5, May 1803.

122 Its nearest rival was a 494ft timber viaduct of the 1790s at Wallsend near Newcastle (Lewis 1970, 152).

123 TNA, RAIL 500/9, 25 Jan 1855.

124 *CMG*, 20 Nov 1858.

125 By Alfred Sidney Morgan, a Newport contractor. A man was killed during the work, and a few months later eleven arches collapsed of their own accord. The last arch standing was blown up on 31 Oct 1904 (*CT*, 2 May, 17 Oct 1903, 5 Nov 1904).

126 Gray-Jones 1970, 76; Hughes 1990, 318; Hill and Green 1999, 86; van Laun 2001, 127-8.

127 *CMG*, 11 Jun 1859; *CT*, 11 Jun 1859; *HT*, 11 Jun 1859.

128 *MM*, 31 Mar 1832; illustrations Frowen 2007b, 36; 2010, 4-7.

129 Prujean 1843.

130 Meredith 1906; Moore 2017.

131 *MM*, 28 Aug 1858; *MT*, 27 May 1863.

132 *BM*, 12 Apl 1819.

133 Oeynhausen and Dechen 1971, 65.

134 De Pambour 1836, 102-6 and especially 105.

135 Wood 1825, 189-90 ('one yard in 104.24') and 198 ('1 yard in 200 yards, or 134 inches in 13968 inches'). This '1 yard in 200 yards' is a mistake or a misprint: the inches give the gradient as the same 1 in 104.24.

136 Overton 1825, 43, 47: on the Twynau Gwynion-Dowlais tramroad of this gradient a loaded tram would run without accelerating or slowing down. Comparable figures are given by Palmer 1823, 29, 31.

137 Powell 1902, 32. Morris 1868, 15, however, followed by Jones 1969, 43, names this first haulier as Morgan Saunders.

138 GwentA, D.1147.13.

139 *BM*, 8 Dec 1821; Rattenbury 1983, 191-2.

140 NLW, Tredegar 45/204.

141 NLW, Tredegar 57/101.

142 GwentA, D.43/4661.

143 Kirby 1993, 185.

144 Totalled from the monthly figures published in the *MM*.

145 *HJ*, 6 Jun 1810.

146 NMW, A2834. Discussed in Gwyn 2003.

147 Powell 1902, 35.

148 *Cambrian*, 22 Dec 1821.

149 *Cambrian*, 4 May 1822.

150 *Cambrian*, 11 May 1822.

151 Under the 1802 Act mileposts were set up every quarter of a mile.

152 *HJ*, 15 May 1822.

153 *MM*, 18 Dec 1830. These locomotives will be discussed shortly.

154 Gwyn 2003, 46.

155 *MM*, 6 Jan 1849.

PART TWO
The Locomotives

THE core of our subject is the locomotives which operated on the three tramroads of 4ft 4in gauge (the Sirhowy, the MCC/MRCC Western Valleys lines, and the Rumney Railway) that led from the various ironworks and collieries down to Newport, as well as those on the narrow-gauge internal and feeder lines of four of the ironworks concerned. The number of these engines is truly astonishing: no fewer, first and last, than eighty, belonging to fifteen different owners. Such an assemblage of plateway locomotives was wholly unparalleled. The Merthyr area could claim a dozen, other parts of South Wales perhaps five, and the whole of England and Scotland only a further dozen.

As everyone knows, in 1804 Richard Trevithick had built an engine at Penydarren for Samuel Homfray, winning for him the 500-guinea wager with his sceptical fellow-ironmaster Richard Crawshay of Cyfarthfa. Yet for twenty-five years after that pioneering venture, South Wales remained almost fallow ground for locomotives. The only exceptions were a rack engine of about 1814 at Nantyglo, William Stewart's locomotive probably tried on or near the Sirhowy in 1816 (of both of which more below), and one by George Stephenson at Llansamlet near Swansea from 1819.[1] To these must be added the bare possibility that another Trevithick engine ran on one of Tredegar's 3ft-gauge tramroads in or soon after 1804. All these early efforts are of very great interest.

Then suddenly in the late 1820s South Wales began to take a more persistent interest in steam traction. This was in line with the quickening pace of development in the North East, which had begun in 1812-15 with Blenkinsop and Murray, Hedley, Chapman and Stephenson. In South Wales it was no doubt stimulated by news from Killingworth and the Stockton & Darlington, even before the nation's attention was seized by the Rainhill trials; but why South Wales lagged fifteen years or so behind the North East is a more complex question. It would be facile to suggest that after Trevithick (who was a Cornishman anyway), there was no engineer or ironmaster there of sufficient calibre and

imagination. The incentive, rather, when it did come, arose from industrial growth. The North East had been carrying coal by rail in huge quantities for two centuries. Monmouthshire had not. But between 1822 and 1828 its output of iron more than doubled, and its output of coal grew in parallel; good reason to look for ways to expedite the traffic and reduce costs of haulage. In 1827-8 the completion of the Crumlin and Aberbeeg Tramroads, which funnelled much traffic from canal to rail, must have been a further stimulus.

It is also open to debate who was responsible for setting the Welsh ball rolling. On the face of it, it was William Forman with his order for a narrow-gauge engine for Bute in early December 1828, which was closely followed by Homfray's order for *Britannia* later in the same month. But Bailey's Llangattock Tramroad, seemingly designed as a locomotive line, was already being surveyed in August 1828. In the light, therefore, of the part Crawshay Bailey had played in introducing the Nantyglo rack engine, it may very well be he who led the way. Other collieries and ironworks followed – in 1830 Blaina Ironworks and Thomas Prothero the freighter, in 1831 Ebbw Vale, in 1832 Martin Morrison the freighter, and so on. Further west at Merthyr, too, Cyfarthfa was showing an interest in locomotives in 1829 and experimenting with them in 1830, followed in 1832 by Dowlais and Penydarren.[2]

For a number of locomotives we have a fair amount of information, for many virtually nothing. Technical details of some of the many engines built by Neath Abbey are to be found in the incomparable collection of works drawings preserved at Swansea;[3] although, because many are untitled or undated (or both), allocating such drawings to the right engine can be problematic or even impossible. It is like doing a jigsaw puzzle without a picture to follow; but one guide to assembling it is the table of rolling stock belonging to each ironworks and freighter in April 1849, published in Captain Simmons' report of which more later.[4] This gives Tredegar nine engines, Rhymney and Ebbw Vale six each, and Blaina two. While this provides a useful check on the tally of locomotives described in these pages, it cannot tell us how many engines had already been sold or scrapped before that date. The impression remains that there must have been a number which have escaped all record.

The firm that built more of our eighty engines than any other – over a quarter of the total – was the Neath Abbey Ironworks. To look at it another way, a good half of Neath Abbey's locomotive output before 1860 went to the Western Valleys system, and about two-thirds of it if one includes the Merthyr ironworks too. The Neath Abbey Iron Co was a Quaker concern founded in 1792 and specialising at first in stationary engines, but later adding marine engines and from 1829/30 locomotives to its repertoire. Dominated by the Price family who hailed from Shropshire,[5] its designs were innovative and imaginative, brazenly using its customers as guinea pigs for experiments which, if they did not work well, were promptly dropped. In earlier days, before its ideas became more conventional, it tried, apart occasionally from direct drive from inclined cylinders, both rocker-beam and bell-crank drives. It tried various boiler arrangements, from the single-flue and return flue to the straightforward multi-tubular with horizontal fire tubes or even with vertical water tubes. One feature common, it seems, to all its locomotives before the mid-1840s was a feed water heater wrapped around the exhaust pipe.

Neath Abbey's products were distinctive: sturdy workhorses, for the most part, that did not pretend to emulate the latest advances of main-line technology. Rather, like Timothy Hackworth's engines in the North East, they were adopted because they were cheap to build, easy to maintain, and designed specifically to haul heavy loads at low speeds on gradients that were often steep. As such, they must be counted a success. Above all, Neath Abbey was that great rarity of early days, a firm which specialised in industrial locomotives where almost all of its contemporaries concentrated on supplying public railways.

What is remarkable about the Welsh engines of this generation is that, until the late 1840s when more orthodox designs came to be adopted, they were little influenced by English practice. True, there were the original two Stephensons of 1829, of which *Britannia* provided the model for Tredegar engines through the next three decades. True again, a few technical features were picked up by Welsh engineers at the Rainhill trials. There were also two collieries near Swansea – Llansamlet and Hendreforgan – whose English owners mistrusted Welsh engineers and insisted on managers and machinery from the North East,[6] and in 1850 the Llanelly Railway contracted its locomotive and operation departments out to a consortium from the North East.[7] A number of ex-main line locomotives, too, were bought second-hand from England. But, all that having been said, until the mid-1840s the bulk of the design and construction was of local origin, and in the Western Valleys English engineering exerted little influence.

2A THE EXPERIMENTAL PERIOD

2A i. Possible Trevithick locomotive, 1803/4

We begin (to adopt a phrase from a rather different context) with a riddle, wrapped in a mystery, inside an enigma. It seems that a Trevithick engine was at least contemplated for the 3ft-gauge tramroads at Tredegar or Rhymney. Everything hinges on the famous but controversial drawing of the 'Tram Engine,' the oldest illustration of a railway locomotive that exists (Fig. 2.01).[8] Its provenance and background are discussed at length elsewhere,[9] and here a summary must suffice. Dated December 1803 and blatantly depicting an engine on Trevithick's principles, it shows the single cylinder as 4¾in by 3ft and the wheel gauge as 3ft 1¼in, which demands a rail gauge over the flanges of 3ft 0in or something very close to it. The boiler clearly held a return flue, but under the crankshaft at the non-firebox end is a rectangular feature which suggests that the flue, rather than returning in a U-bend – difficult to fabricate on this small scale – went in and out of a box fixed to the boiler end. One notable feature is that the design keeps the overall width to an absolute minimum – 4ft 5in – to the tune of paring off the sides of the boiler flanges and endplates and bringing the wheels, gears and flywheel as close inboard as possible. There was clearly a strict limit on width, although the available height allowed a large flywheel and a chimney 8ft 5in above the rails. In this it differed from the Penydarren engine, whose height as well as width was restricted by Plymouth tunnel. It differed markedly too in its overall size and power. Whereas the Penydarren's weight when full was about 5½ tons, the Tram Engine's would be very roughly 1½; and whereas the Penydarren's brake horse power can be calculated as about 10.5, the Tram Engine's, assuming the same steam pressure, turns out to be a feeble 2.3 hp.[10] The full-size replica at Ironbridge reminds us just how small the engine would have been: not so very much larger than a horse (Fig. 2.02).

The drawing was made by John Llewellin

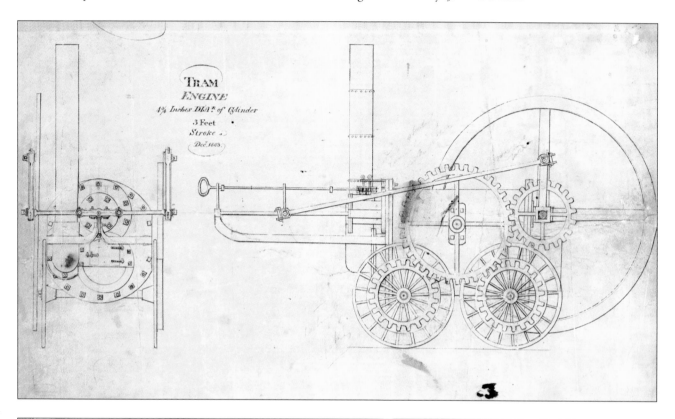

Fig. 2.01
The Tram Engine drawing.
(*NRM, 1903-102*)

Fig. 2.02
Reconstruction of the Tram Engine at Ironbridge Gorge Museum. (*Andy Guy*)

(1779-1845), a mining agent who before 1805 was working at Cyfarthfa Ironworks at Merthyr but by 1807 had moved to Rhymney Ironworks. He became agent to Benjamin Hall (both father and son) at Rhymney and then at Abercarn. Later sources describe him as 'a personal friend of Trevithick'[11] and 'engaged with him at Merthyr.'[12] Another mentions that 'one of his pupils, John Roe … supplied a correspondent to our pages with many particulars of the old engine,'[13] namely the Penydarren. Evidently, then, Llewellin was well acquainted with Trevithick and had ready access to him while he was at Merthyr. From John Llewellin the drawing descended to his nephew William, who in 1855 gave it to William Menelaus the manager of Dowlais Ironworks, who in turn presented it in 1862 to the Patent Office (later Science) Museum, describing it as 'found at Penydarren Iron Works.'[14] The details of the Tram Engine are somewhat amateurishly drawn, and it is no doubt a copy rather than an original; but at the time it greatly excited such people as Francis Trevithick and Thomas Ellis, who assumed it was of the Penydarren engine itself. This was naive, because the dimensions are utterly incompatible.

In 1952, however, E. A. Forward suggested that it was was the locomotive which Trevithick had begun to build at Coalbrookdale in 1802 before his patron William Reynolds died and the other ironmasters there lost interest.[15] Forward's theory has been almost universally accepted ever since. He claimed, on the authority of the German engineers von Oeynhausen and von Dechen who visited in 1826-7, that there was a tramroad at the Dale of 3ft gauge.[16] But this is very much in doubt. Oeynhausen and Dechen's practice was to measure plateway gauges not only in Prussian units (3ft Prussian equalled 3ft 1in English) but also between the flanges (therefore about 3ft 3in English over them). In hard fact there is no known evidence for any line in the Coalbrookdale area which the engine could have fitted.[17] Nor is there much likelihood of it. The drawing was done by a South Wales man and resurfaced in South Wales; and the very title 'Tram Engine' is wholly out of place in a Shropshire context, where the word 'tram' was not in the local vocabulary; but it admirably suits a South Wales one. Much more probably, then, the engine was designed both in and for South Wales.

There were few tramroads there of 3ft gauge, and none at Merthyr of exactly the right figure. That commonly said to have existed at Penydarren

seems (as is explained later) to be illusory: the internal gauge there, as on its tramroads from the limestone quarries and to the canal, was 2ft 6in.[18] The line from Gurnos quarries to Richard Crawshay's Cyfarthfa works was 3ft 1in over the flanges,[19] which in theory could take an engine 3ft 1¼in between the wheels but in practice would be too tight a fit. There is an even more telling consideration: would Crawshay commission Trevithick, the engineer employed by his arch-rival Samuel Homfray, to design a locomotive for his own use at precisely the time when he was pooh-poohing Trevithick's application of steam at Penydarren? It seems beyond belief.

But the right gauge of 3ft 0in did exist at Tredegar and Rhymney.[20] In December 1803, when the Tram Engine drawing was made, both of these ironworks were almost new, feeders to them already existed,[21] and there were still about ten miles of narrow-gauge track on the Sirhowy Tramroad. While Rhymney must remain as a possible destination for the Tram Engine, it had just – in September of the same year – come into the hands of Richard Crawshay, who seems no more likely to have countenanced steam traction here than at Cyfarthfa. But in December 1803 Trevithick was constructing his Penydarren locomotive for Homfray, who was lord not only of Penydarren but of Tredegar too; and who was also, for that matter, a partner at Aberdare where, as we shall find, another Trevithick engine is said to have run.

The finger thus points at Homfray's Tredegar as the customer. If so, where on the Tredegar lines was the Tram Engine meant to run? Hardly hauling coal up from the Mynyddislwyn seam in the Gelligroes area, because with its paltry 2.3 hp it could not handle any worthwhile load against the stiffish gradient; and what would have been the sense in designing it for a 3ft gauge line which, as Homfray had agreed in September 1803, only three months before the drawing was done, was at any moment to be converted to 4ft 4in? The engine might well have difficulty too in hauling a worthwhile number of empty limestone trams up the even stiffer gradient to Trefil quarries. Conceivably it was meant to bring coal or iron ore from a nearby opencast or level. On none of those lines, however, was there any known structure or cutting that would limit the width of a locomotive.

This leaves Tredegar Ironworks themselves. There would be no shortage of work in the furnace yard. In 1805 the recorded output of iron from the furnaces there generated roughly 13,500 tons of cinders or slag which would need to be moved off-site. Was the Tram Engine's width dictated by the arched doorways to the cast-houses which, if about 4ft 8in wide and 7ft high to the springing, would accommodate not only the original horses but a narrow replacement locomotive? The track would be near enough level and the individual loads modest. The Penydarren engine itself, Homfray said in 1804, was 'as tractable as a Horse, will back its load, and move it forward as little (& slow) at a time as you please,' all of which are qualities highly desirable for shunting; and it is said by a late source to have spent some years after its trials as a works shunter.[22] In the next generation – in 1832, very shortly after the reintroduction of steam to South Wales tramroads – Penydarren, Dowlais and Sirhowy all acquired such yard engines, and in 1837, as we shall find, so too did Tredegar itself.

The suggestion is therefore that Trevithick designed the Tram Engine, no doubt at Homfray's instigation, as an experimental and small-scale shunter for Tredegar works

It is unlikely that it ever left the drawing board. Yet it might, just conceivably, have become a reality. In 1849 Joshua Field (1786-1863), the renowned mechanical engineer and partner in Maudslay, Sons & Field, gave his presidential address to the Institution of Civil Engineers. In an overview of locomotive development to date, he described the famous London locomotive of 1808 (which he misdated to 1804) as designed and constructed by Trevithick, who also made an engine about the same year, of different construction, which was employed on the Tredegar tram-road, for conveying minerals and iron, between Tredegar iron-works, and Newport.[23]

Tredegar may of course be a simple mistake for Penydarren, which is not mentioned, and certainly no 3ft gauge locomotive ever reached Newport. Yet in 1803-5, at the very date in question, Field had been working as a pupil of Simon Goodrich the Admiralty mechanist,[24] who knew Trevithick personally and took a keen interest in his work. In his memorandum book he described and illustrated the London steam carriage of 1803. He was kept informed by Samuel Homfray about Trevithick's trials at Merthyr, and would have witnessed them in person had not an accident to Homfray postponed his visit indefinitely. Later, in 1807, he inspected Trevithick's model locomotive and in 1808 corresponded with him about the Thames Tunnel.[25] At the same time he held Field

in high regard as a promising young man, and helped to forward his career by seconding him to Maudslay's works. It cannot therefore be ruled out that Goodrich had heard news of a Trevithick locomotive at Tredegar, and had passed it on to Field, who somewhat garbled it.

What is more, local historians – admittedly late sources and far from the horse's mouth – have further tantalising snippets. The originator of this thread was a certain William Turner who wrote under the pseudonym of 'Cheviot.' In an article of 1886 on Newport's history he said, 'In 1802 an act was obtained to construct a railway – called the Sirhowy Tramroad Company – upon which Trevethick's [sic] famous locomotive was the first in this district.'[26] Turner was superintendent of the Mercantile Marine Office in Cardiff. Would such a man be likely to have read Field's address in an engineering journal nearly forty years old? More probably he came across this information in South Wales, where 'Trevethick' was a widespread mis-spelling. Next year an anonymous article – possibly also by Turner – states,

> As early as 1802 an Act of Parliament was obtained for making a railway from Newport to Nine Mile Point, from which place a tramway had already been constructed to the iron furnaces at Sirhowy. This was the line upon which Trevethick's first essay on steam locomotion was attempted.[27]

A year later again, Charles Wilkins of Merthyr Tydfil picked up the same information. On the Sirhowy, he said, 'Trevethick experimented with his locomotive, a similar one to that used on the Penydarren tramway;' and after a highly romanticised account of the Merthyr trials of 1804, he added a new teaser: 'the efforts of Trevethick, who ran a locomotive also from Mill Street [Aberdare] to Hirwain, and those who followed him, led gradually to changes.'[28] These statements he repeated in later publications: 'Trevethick, as is well known to those versed in local history, had tramways at Hirwain, Tredegar and Merthyr' – an odd remark, but meaning tramway locomotives?[29] And again, 'Trevethick assisted after this in forming an engine for Tredegar, and another for the tramroad between Hirwain and Aberdare, and then disappeared from Wales.'[30] Finally, as late as 1927, the first Lord Aberconway, members of whose family had been directors of the Tredegar Iron & Coal Co since 1873, wrote that 'Trevethick built a high-pressure steam locomotive in 1801, which was

Fig. 2.03

Pencil notes on the Tram Engine drawing under infrared light.

(*NRM 1903-102*)

worked over the Tredegar tramway for more than half a century.'[31] Although muddled – and perhaps confusing a locomotive with the Tredegar puddling mill engine of which more in a moment – this statement may represent the same tradition.

A hitherto unknown Trevithick locomotive actually running at Hirwain, while not wholly implausible, cannot concern us here. Another actually running at Tredegar is not wholly implausible either, and deserves serious consideration.

When Francis Trevithick, who had trained under Tredegar's chief engineer Thomas Ellis junior, was researching his father's life he renewed contact with his former teacher.

In 1854 the writer revisited the Welsh works to inquire more particularly about the blast pipe. Mr Ellis's relative, while standing in one of Mr Homfray's Tredegar workshops, remarked that pieces of Trevithick's early engines had remained for many years in the old scrap-heap, in the corner of the shop; on turning over the surface pieces, and directing Mr Ellis's attention to one in particular, he replied, 'That is Trevithick's first blast-pipe, or a copy of it.'[32]

Ellis's relative was perhaps his brother-in-law Charles Hunter. The pipe may of course have been from a stationary engine, and, being where it was, presumably from a Tredegar one. But which? The only recorded Trevithick engine

there was the 'puddling engine' of perhaps 1805 that drove the rolling mill[33] and was built by William Aubrey and Ellis' father, Thomas Ellis senior.[34] But because it was not taken down, Ellis junior said, until 1856,[35] it could not have been the source of the pipe on the scrap heap in 1854. Ellis was well aware of Francis's interests, and his own professional memory must have reached back to at least 1820. Yet he never mentioned any other Trevithick engine at Tredegar. Had he done so, Francis, an avid if indiscriminate collector of whatever information he could lay hands on, would assuredly have published it. Thus the possibility remains that the pipe was from the Tredegar locomotive; and that, because it was very ancient history and perhaps because it was not a success, Ellis (who was only born in 1804) had never heard of it.

Yet more frustrating but of yet greater potential interest, there are on the Tram Engine drawing three faint pencil notes in a nineteenth-century hand. One by the valve gear perhaps begins 'Detail ... ,' but the rest of it, and a second note inside the flywheel, defies all attempts at reading, even under ultraviolet and infrared light (Fig. 2.03). The third, beside a running wheel, says 'Casting of spokes', which implies that somebody at some point was at least considering the practicalities of building the engine. Alternatively, the scribbles may be no more than instructions to the lithographer when the drawing was published as a print in 1857; but unless they can be fully deciphered, no more can be said.

Drawing apart, nothing of all this is recorded in contemporary sources, of which we have very few. The silence of Trevithick's correspondence is no surprise, for a mere fraction of it survives: only once, for instance, does it mention the Gateshead locomotive. In any case it was rarely that Trevithick, once he had made the drawings and pocketed the royalties, played any part in building or testing his engines. The Penydarren locomotive was an exception, because it was a pioneer and sizeable machine for hauling significant loads on a 'main line' from a populous town. A Tredegar locomotive, by contrast, would be small, and it might do no more than potter unsung in what was then the back of beyond. Its very existence is far from proved, but it cannot be wholly dismissed. Nor should it be forgotten that, if it was a reality, it might have preceded, if only by a few months, the Penydarren engine itself.

2A ii. Nantyglo's Blenkinsop rack locomotive, *c.* 1814

As is well known, Trevithick built the last of his locomotives in 1808, and his mantle fell upon John Blenkinsop and Matthew Murray who were the first to demonstrate, at Middleton Colliery near Leeds, that steam traction by rail was a viable proposition. They ignored, however, the lesson taught by Trevithick that simple adhesion between wheels and rails was perfectly adequate, and instead they used only a rack drive as patented by Blenkinsop in 1811. The first of these engines, built by Fenton Murray & Wood in 1812, had two vertical cylinders, 8in by 24in, mounted on a cast-iron boiler. There was a single fire tube, incorporating the fireplace, of constant 14in diameter (Fig. 2.04). Three further engines followed at Middleton in 1812-15, and three on

Fig. 2.04

Blenkinsop rack locomotive, Middleton, 1815. (*Andrieux 1815*)

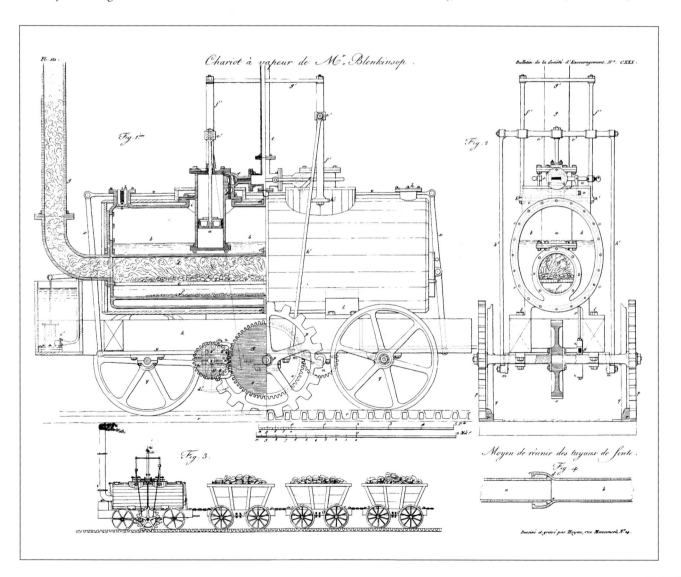

Chariot à vapeur de Mr. Blenkinsop.

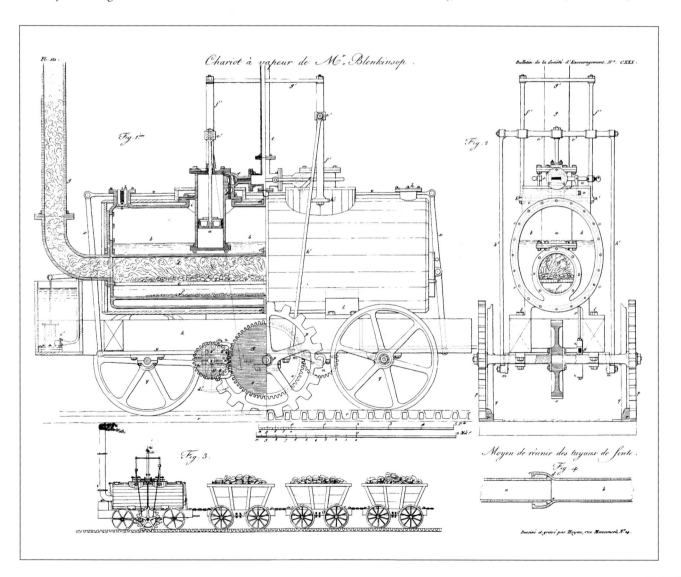

the Kenton & Coxlodge Railway near Newcastle in 1813, all built by Fenton Murray & Wood. Yet another three were made for Orrell Colliery near Wigan from 1813 by the nearby Haigh Foundry, under the oversight of Robert Daglish the viewer.[36]

These ten engines, though all for edge rail, were far from identical. At first the boilers were of cast iron, but from 1813 of wrought iron with 'a double Iron Tube' – a return flue?[37] Precise dimensions differ considerably, and evidently did not matter; so long as the cylinders and drive conformed, any suitable design would serve. No doubt Blenkinsop sent generalised specifications to prospective customers, but the only part under patent was his rack drive, for the use of which he demanded royalties. The Middleton and Orrell locomotives were long-lived, some of them lasting well into the 1830s.

Blenkinsop's rack drive also found use in Wales. In January-March 1813 he had been in correspondence with Lockwood & Co near Swansea and Alexander Raby at Llanelli, coal-owners who were potential customers,[38] but there is no hint whatever that anything came of the negotiations. On 10 October 1813, however, John Watson of Coxlodge wrote, 'I understand he [Blenkinsop] has agreed with some Gentlemen in Wales lately, that he should receive £50 p Annum for each Mile of Way they use his Invention.'[39] In other words, as at Orrell, they would use it under licence.

There, at the Blenkinsop end, the trail goes cold. But in March 1830 the *Monmouthshire Merlin* reported that 'in the mining districts of this county the steam carriage is not a novelty, one having been in use for a considerable time, on a railway (laid down with cogged nails [*sic*: read rails] purposely to suit the machinery,) leading to the extensive iron works at Nanty Glo'.[40]

Such a statement seems most unlikely to be a journalistic invention. True, it raises potential awkwardnesses, but they are not insuperable. In October 1814 Blenkinsop himself, listing railways which used his patent, included only Middleton, Coxlodge and Orrell;[41] but perhaps the Nantyglo engine was not yet at work or even, conceivably, it had been built without telling Blenkinsop or paying the royalties. Again, in 1818 Joseph Tregelles Price of Neath Abbey stated flatly that 'in Wales there are no Locomotive Engines employed at present;'[42] but perhaps the Nantyglo one was temporarily out of commission, or it had not come to the ears of Price who lived at the

opposite extremity of the coalfield. Whatever the reasons, the existence of the engine is beyond doubt.

Full proof, and the identity of the man responsible, comes from a much later source. In November 1858 a meeting was held in Abergavenny to promote the proposed Merthyr Tredegar & Abergavenny Railway, with Crawshay Bailey of Nantyglo in the chair. Given the terrain, the gradients of the intended line could not be other than steep, and in the event, when the line was opened from 1862, the steepest was 1 in 34.

> The Chairman said that about 22 years ago he went to the North of England to consult some engineers about a locomotive line, and he was told that locomotives could not travel with a less gradient than something like 1 in 200 (laughter). He then went to Leeds to see a railway worked by a rack and pinion, and he came home and adopted the rack and pinion, never thinking that the gradients in Monmouthshire and Breconshire could be worked by locomotives. That journey to the north cost him £10,000; and now some engineers would almost tell the public they could go up the side of a house (laughter).[43]

The date of 'about 22 years ago' – 1836 – must be wildly wrong. Even in his old age Bailey was good at remembering dates,[44] and perhaps this was a mistake by the reporter or typesetter for 'about 44 years ago,' namely about 1814. Although Crawshay did not become a partner in Nantyglo until 1820, he had worked there alongside his brother Joseph from the take-over in 1811.[45] Alternatively, were Bailey's words misreported, having really been 'when I was about 22 years of age'? That would give about 1811. The £10,000 – quite possibly an inflated figure – presumably represents the cost of the locomotive and the special track needed.

Historians have hitherto had difficulty in locating on which of Nantyglo's tramroads this engine ran. The limestone line to Llangattock was opened in 1830, the link south to the MCC's Aberbeeg Tramroad in 1828, Bailey's tramroad east to Govilon in 1821, and the limestone line north to Disgwylfa in 1816/18, all too late for the arrival of the Blenkinsop engine. But the works lay about a mile south of the east-west Clydach Railroad, which belonged to the B&A Canal and fed down to it at Gilwern. Short of sending its iron via Beaufort and Crumlin, which would involve two transshipments, this was at the time

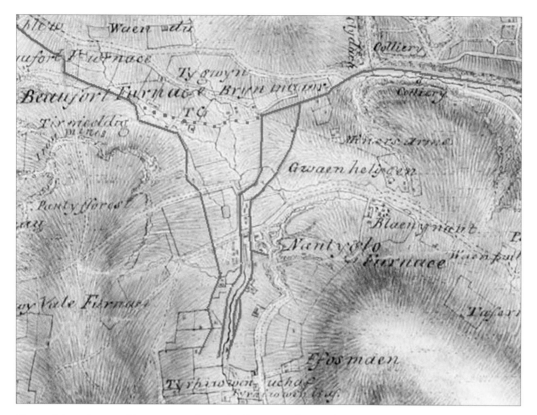

Fig. 2.05
Railways at Nantyglo, 1813. The Clydach Railroad, tinted a pale pink in the original and here strengthened in red, runs west-east across the top; but the stretch past the 'Upper Toll-Gate on the Mountain' (labelled TG) and here highlighted with red dots, though undoubtedly in place at the time, is unaccountably not coloured in on the original.
(*OS draft survey*, ©British Library Board, OSD 194)

Nantyglo's only possible way out by rail. The draft Ordnance Survey map of 1813 marks three branches of the Clydach running to Nantyglo (Fig. 2.05). Of two from the north-east, one perhaps brought in limestone (from its then quarry at Daren Ddu) to the furnaces. This was in existence by 1810 when coal workings on the farm of Ty Blaenant were advertised 'workable from the Level of the Tram Road leading from Waniyelligan [Waen yr helygen] to Nant y Glo.'[46] This being prior to Bailey's take-over, it must have been laid before 1808. The second line from the north-east features in July 1810 in an advertisement for coal workings close to the furnaces as 'a Tram Road is now making from these works to join the Railway communication with the Brecon and Abergavenny Canal.'[47] By November 1811 this line was complete,[48] though it may well have been extended later. Whether these were really plateways, as 'Tram Roads' would normally suggest, we cannot say.

The third branch ran, slightly east of south, from the Clydach Railroad's 'Upper Toll-Gate on the Mountain' (SO 1819 1132) to the works, with a length of about a mile and a gradient of roughly 1 in 50. This had been twice requested by the earlier partnerships but turned down by the B&A. Now, in December 1811, with the canal on the point of completion from Gilwern southwards,

Bailey and Wayne did obtain permission to lay rails on the B&A's pre-existing 'stone road' – that is, metalled but not railed – from the tollgate to Nantyglo. This line was completed by January 1814,[49] a date that fits perfectly with Blenkinsop's agreement with 'some Gentlemen in Wales' reported in October 1813. Because the Clydach was (and remained) an edge railway, it seems likely that this branch from it was also edge-railed. The Clydach's gauge is commonly given as 3ft 4in but, as John van Laun has shown, was really 3ft 8in.[50] Thereafter we know nothing definite until the *Merlin*'s report of 27 March 1830 that a rack engine had run at Nantyglo 'for a considerable time.'

As to who built the engine, we have no direct clue. Had it been Fenton Murray & Wood, we might expect to have heard of it from the Leeds end. Most probably, like the Orrell engines, it was a local product, and it may very well have been built in-house by Nantyglo itself. An interesting point to note is that at this date the ironworks had on its payroll the brothers Richard and William Brown, whose claim to fame deserves spelling out in full. They made their name at Penydarren as smiths of high skill, and there they had been responsible for fabricating the flue for Trevithick's engine of 1804, which is usually interpreted as a simple return flue. A typical

Fig. 2.06
Return flue from a Trevithick-type semi-portable engine built at Dudley about 1845. Boiler 5ft 6in by 3ft 6in. (*Science Museum, 1881-57*)

flue of this sort – with all the craftsmanship demanded of the boilermaker – is very well illustrated by Fig. 2.06.[51] By the 1830s, if not before, the Browns were great friends with the Baileys, the proprietors of Nantyglo.[52] Moreover, much earlier, they had befriended Trevithick himself who, while at Penydarren, lodged with Richard Brown's family.

The ingineous [sic] Trevethick was a lodger in his father's house in Pendarren [said Richard's son Thomas many years later], when he constructed the first locomotive engine ever made. His father made the first locomotive boiler with his own hands, and assisted Trevethick on the other parts of the engine.[53]

Richard Brown's widow Betty likewise stated that Trevithick 'had many meals at our house. He used to come in every day.'[54] Rees Jones, the Penydarren fitter who also assisted Trevithick, confirmed Richard's role: 'Richard Brown made the boiler and the smith-work … the boiler was made of wrought-iron, having a breeches tube also of wrought-iron, in which was the fire.'[55]

William Brown also played a part. While researching his biography of his father, Francis Trevithick, who had met him in 1837, claimed, 'I know the man who was my Father's right-hand man in making the engine, and who is now I believe a partner in an iron-works, a little below the Nanty-Glo works … who had to do with the first locomotive' of 1804.[56] And when Francis finally got in touch with him again, William

briefly replied, 'Concerning the late Captn Trevithick's Locomotive Engine. There was only one tube contained in the Boiler of it. A Breeches tube in the making of which I was concerned.'[57] Old men's memories may falter – the Penydarren boiler was actually of cast iron, not wrought – but there is no reason to doubt the essential truth of these statements, that the two brothers assisted at the birth of the first locomotive in Wales. It is only natural to wonder, since they were in the right place at the right time, if they also assisted ten years later at the birth of the second, the Nantyglo rack engine.

'Breeches tube' or 'breeches flue' denoted a pair of flues running from a single fireplace to the chimney, where they reunited, thus resembling a pair of trouser legs. This principle was certainly used by the Brown brothers in their locomotive for Blaina in 1830 (*see* 2C i). It seems likely, therefore, that the boiler of the Penydarren engine had not a simple return flue but a double one, and that the Nantyglo and Blaina engines imitated it.

We next hear of the Nantyglo engine in 1829-30, between the opening of the Aberbeeg line in July 1828 and of Bailey's Llangattock Tramroad in December 1830, when something was afoot with it. In the memorandum books of Thomas Ellis senior, the head patternmaker of Tredegar – whom we will meet many times more – there is an intriguing cluster of entries. An undated and more than usually mis-spelt note says,

'1802 Tevethig took is Patent want of Condensing water in Cornwall, made him persevere in high Pressure Steam & work Expancive, Encourag'd by Davice Giddey Member of Parlement. Blenkensop was the first wo introduced Steam Waggons at Leeds Yorkshire For Tram Roads at the Coal Works.'[58]

This proves no more than that Ellis was aware of Blenkinsop's place in locomotive history. But another entry is certainly relevant to us here:

'Nantyglo locomotive Engin Steam Valve 3 Inches Diameter July 1830.'

This is typical of a number of entries in Ellis' notebooks, each with a simple diagram of a weighted lever valve with its diameter (in this case 3in), the length of arm (24in plus 3in), and the weight required (60 lbs) for it to blow off at a given pressure (Fig. 2.07);[59] for another example

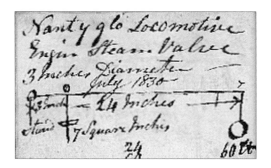

see under *St David* (2B i). Such valves being susceptible to the motion of the engine, sprung ones, pioneered by Hackworth, were already beginning to come into use in the North East.[60]

In similar cases, Ellis made such calculations as one of the last jobs before a new boiler was completed, and this entry surely ties in with two others. One runs:

Thos Myric boyler Maker Engages to Make the boyler – Tubes – Stack & water Tank for Locomotive Engine rivetes for Water tank Excepted for 10£ per Ton Leaving 2£ per ton in hand until the Above is aproved of, & all alterations to be considered in the 10£ per Ton. Decr 1829.[61]

Perhaps the tank, not being under pressure, did not need such careful riveting as the boiler. The last entry reads:

Jun 23 – 1830. Wm James Boyler Maker took to Myric's Job – –

Plates for a Locomotive Boyler & Tube

3 Plates 4ft 9½ In long 1ft 11in wide ⅜ thick outside tube

Inside 3 Plates 5-0 long 1-6 wide ¼ thick

Outside boy[l]er or Large End 3-3 long 1-11 wide ⅜ thick

fire place 3-6 long 1-9½ wide ⅜ thick --- Ends ½ Inch thick.[62]

These entries are enigmatic. They cannot refer to the boiler of Tredegar's first home-made engine *St David* which, as we shall see, had already been completed by May 1830. We can only conclude that Nantyglo had contracted this work out to Tredegar, possibly because it was itself then short of the necessary expertise, the Brown brothers having moved on to Blaina. The 1841 census finds both Thomas Mirrick and William

James at Tredegar still, as fitter and boilermaker respectively. Conceivably they were building a brand-new engine; but the coincidence of dates strongly suggests that they were giving a new lease of life to an existing boiler – whether a complete replacement or the patching of weak parts – for which the Blenkinsop-type engine is the only possible candidate. It would also need the rack drive removed, gears added on the wheel axles, and the edge-rail wheels, now with a geared drive for adhesion only, replaced with tramroad ones.

Any attempt to reconstruct the boiler from these meagre details is fraught with difficulty. The iron plates that James took are not nearly enough to make a complete boiler. Maybe Mirrick had already made most of it. Allowing 2in overlap, the three plates of the first item ('outside tubes') would make a tube 4ft 9½in long by 1ft 8in diameter, or 4ft 7½in by 1ft 5⅔in, depending on whether the plates were fitted longitudinally or circumferentially. The three plates of the second item ('inside') would make a tube 5ft by 1ft 3¼in or 4ft 8in by 1ft 4½in. These are difficult to interpret. Was the first tube a fire tube to be set in front of the fireplace (of nearly the same diameter), which would make the boiler 8ft 1½in long? But if so, what was the other tube for?

An alternative solution is that the 'outside' plates could make three smaller tubes 4ft 9½in by 6⅔in diameter, the 'inside' ones three smaller tubes 5ft by 5in diameter. But what does 'outside boyler or large end' mean? Can it be, as deduced for the Tram Engine, an external box or reservoir where the gases in a return flue changed direction? Or can it, more probably, be an external smokebox at the fireplace end, where the gases from a number of relatively small return tubes were united into the chimney? If so, its 3ft 3in dimension would represent the boiler diameter.

Sadly, the details remain mysterious, but the fact of a major replacement of the boiler's internal elements seems likely enough. Then about 15 years old, they would be due for replacement. Certainly Nantyglo had a locomotive at work 'for a considerable period' before March 1830, and certainly it had a locomotive actually at work in December 1830. Everything points to this being the Blenkinsop-type engine revamped. The gauge was now 3ft 6in over the flanges, which comes to almost exactly the same as the old 3ft 8in edge rail gauge. For Bailey's Llangattock Tramroad in which it ran, see 2F i.

Fig. 2.07
Thomas Ellis senior's diagram for safety valve for Nantyglo locomotive, July 1830.
(*NLW, MS 5157 f.42v*)

2A iii. Stewart's locomotive, 1816

William Stewart is an elusive character. Nothing certain can be found of his background before September 1815 when he and John Ramsdin, engineers and millwrights of Newport, were advertising for sale a thrashing machine, a mill and a steam engine; and next January their partnership was dissolved.[63]

In September 1844 Stewart wrote a letter from Drogheda in Ireland which at first sight seems irrelevant to us. In 1814 when he was at Newport, he says, he offered the Parkend Coal Co in the Forest of Dean, for use on the Severn & Wye Railway, a locomotive that he had built knowing 'nothing at that time of Mr Stevenson's more successful attempts.' Negotiations with Parkend broke down, and Stewart 'was obliged to abandon the engine to that Company in lieu of a small sum they had advanced to him.'[64] The Severn & Wye minutes are silent on this matter; but on 7 November 1815 they do record 'that the Company hereby approve of any person or trader hauling coal or other articles over the railway, by steam engine, provided the engine be within the weight allowed … and not interrupting the general trade.' The weight limit for trams on the Severn & Wye was one ton (plus tare) per axle,[65] the plate rails weighed 42 lbs, and the gauge was 3ft 6in.[66] It sounds as if someone was after all contemplating the use of Stewart's locomotive. But because it must have weighed at least 5 tons (as did Trevithick's 1804 engine), it was surely on four axles or eight wheels to meet the weight limit.

There this particular story would have petered out, had not Francis Pettit Smith, curator at the Patent Office Museum in South Kensington (later to become the Science Museum), made an expedition to South Wales in 1862 in search of relics of Trevithick's Penydarren locomotive. Apart from the Llewellin drawing, his only acquisition was a wrought-iron plate which, he recorded, 'was found at Treforest, S. Wales and presented to the Museum by Francis Crawshay

Esq.' With it went an explanatory label, which Smith transcribed:

> Piece of S. Homfray's engine that took the load of iron to navigation house for the £1000 bet. Trevithick builder, and with two cylinders. The history of our getting it. After taking the iron down it was made into a small planishing hammer engine at Penydarran, brought into the Forest by Mr Protheroe thirty years ago [i.e. c.1820] to sink pits at Castle rag colliery, from there to Protheroes lower pits and sank them, then to Links delight for our old company, and we pulled it down and cut a piece out for you. This is as I copied it from old Broad, our manager. Henry Crawshay March 14 1850.[67]

There follows a crude pencil sketch. Henry and Francis Crawshay, sons of William Crawshay II of Cyfarthfa, ran the Treforest tinplate works near Pontypridd. Castle Rag and Link's Delight pits were part of their coal empire in the Forest of Dean, and the Protheroes (not to be confused with the Newport Protheros) were also large coal-owners there.[68] But, while Trevithick's engine did indeed work a hammer at Penydarren, its removal to the Forest of Dean does not ring true. Crawshay's engine, having (as we shall see) two vertical cylinders and a wrought-iron boiler, cannot have been Trevithick's, which had a single horizontal cylinder and a cast-iron boiler. The Science Museum, most deplorably, surrendered the plate to the scrap drive in World War II, and all we have now is the sketch, in plan and section, of the curved top plate of a boiler about 4ft 3in in diameter with three circular holes in it (Fig. 2.08).

The two outer holes, 12in in diameter, were clearly for the cylinders, which would be about 9in in bore. The central hole was perhaps for the manhole cover (awkward to install in a domed boiler end) with the regulator mounted on it. The cylinders, however, being set at roughly 2ft 6in centres, are far too close together for a direct drive to the wheels. They can only have driven a pair of intermediate shafts from which gear trains went to the wheels; which was precisely the point where locomotive technology stood at the time when Stewart's machines were built. This, in 1814-16, was how engines were driven: Blenkinsop's, Hedley's at Wylam (both original and modified), Stephenson's at Killingworth, Buddle and Chapman's at Wallsend and Chapman and Crowther's at Whitehaven.[69] And if Stewart's engine had eight wheels to conform with the weight limit, it will have looked,

Fig. 2.08
Boiler plate from the Forest of Dean. (*after sketch by Francis Trevithick in NRM, T/1903-102, p 28*)

at least as far as the drive is concerned, very much like the Whitehaven engine (Fig. 2.09).[70] Both Wylam and Whitehaven eight-wheelers were on bogies, which were one of Chapman's specialities, and whose wheel arrangement is best described as 0-4-4-0. So too must Stewart's have been. The overall wheelbase of the Whitehaven engine was 10ft, surely too great, if fixed, for a plateway with sharp curves; on the MCC, many years later (as we shall find) 9ft 6in proved to be beyond the limit. If the Crawshay boiler plate was indeed from the Forest of Dean locomotive – which seems highly likely if beyond categorical proof – how did Stewart come by the design? Whether or not we believe that he was ignorant of Stephenson's work, he had surely heard of current work by others – and especially by Chapman – in the north.

The relevance of the last few paragraphs can now at last emerge. On 8 January 1816 Stewart wrote a letter to the chairman of the MCC.

> Being at present engaged in Making a Steam Engine intended for the purpose of hauling Carts, or Waggons, on Rail Roads or Turnpike Roads, which may ultimately prove beneficial to the Coal and Iron Trades by reduceing the expence of hauling … I now humbly Petition for Leave to try on the railroads belonging to the Monmouth Shire Canal Company, the effects of a Locomotive Engine … [71]

This sounds like a different engine from the Forest of Dean one. Here too the company minutes are silent on the matter, and one might assume that nothing resulted were it not for a reminiscence by William Lewis Meredith, whose family was long involved (as we saw) in the maintenance of the Sirhowy's permanent way. He quoted a recollection of his father, who was born in 1809, 'of first seeing a locomotive engine on the Sirhowy tramroad when he was barely 10 years of age … the first engine tried was set aside for some time near to the present Tredegar Junction' (that is, Pontllanfraith).[72] Nothing further is on record. Possibly, if the MCC turned his request down, Stewart asked the Sirhowy Tramroad Co instead because Homfray senior, as a protagonist in the 1804 trials, might be expected to lend a more sympathetic ear. Meredith's memory, while far from the horse's mouth, is not easily disdained. His dates fit. In 1816 he was indeed a small boy of seven. Nor was he prompted by leading questions from an interviewer, for Stewart's letter to the MCC was long forgotten

and its publication lay far in the future. While the jury must remain out, Meredith may very well be right.

One wonders, without expecting an answer, whether his mention of Pontllanfraith is relevant. This seems a curious place to put a dysfunctional locomotive out to grass. Was it because Stewart's engine had been working, or trying to work, the private branch to Gellihaf from Pontllanfraith, where it was stabled (Fig. 1.12)? Gellihaf Colliery belonged to Thomas Edwards of Newport, who sold up and left the district in August 1816.[73] Did the engine cease to run because of the departure of its patron?

Exactly the same technical considerations apply to this engine as to the Forest of Dean one. The requirements, whether for the MCC or the Sirhowy, were almost identical, except that the scale was presumably larger to suit the larger gauge. At 45 lb or more, the tramplates here were heavier, and at the time the maximum permitted weight for a tram was 56 cwt or 28 cwt per axle.[74] With eight wheels, i.e. four axles, the locomotive

Fig. 2.09

Chapman, Buddle and Crowther's Whitehaven locomotive, 1816. (*Rees 2001, 156*)

ought therefore to weigh no more than 5.6 tons. And one is prompted to ask further unanswerable questions: did Stewart's engine sow a small local seed? In 1831 Neath Abbey designed for Dowlais a gear-driven 0-4-4-0 rack engine to run on the Merthyr Tramroad (Fig. 2.45). Were its gears and bogies inspired by Stewart's locomotive, whether during its brief working life or while languishing at Pontllanfraith? And was its rack element inspired by the Nantyglo engine?[75]

More is known of Stewart's movements thereafter than of his earlier career. He was not the William Stewart who from 1818 to 1832 was manager of Hendreforgan Colliery in the Swansea valley and who had been recommended to the owner by Nicholas Wood of Killingworth.[76] Rather, he was in France c.1819-43, working on steamboats, bridges and optical lenses. After ten years in England and Ireland, he returned to France, and died some time after 1862.[77]

In the North East the years 1814-16 saw a burgeoning of interest in steam traction. This is palely reflected in South Wales too, both by Stewart's attempts of 1814 and 1816 to sell his own engines and by a letter of 7 March 1815 by Benjamin Hall to John Llewellin his agent: 'Chapman the Engineer called on me today. He says one of their Engines will cost about £400 & 30 G[uinea]s per [year?] for his Patent. He gave a bad account of the Collieries at Newcastle, that they do not clear 5 per cent.'[78] This must be William Chapman (1749-1832) of Newcastle.[79]

In view of Stewart's evident familiarity with his work, this sounds more than coincidental, but the details of the link elude us. Chapman had at the end of 1812 taken out a patent which covered not only pivoting bogies for locomotives but also traction by a chain laid between the rails along which it hauled itself by means of a roller (Fig. 2.10). A promotional pamphlet, issued in 1813 and republished next year,[80] invited enquiries to Chapman or to John Buddle, with whom he worked on later engines. It may have been this that led to Chapman's meeting with Hall, unless it was a description of the Lambton locomotive in the *Cambrian* in January 1815.[81] Chapman's six-wheeled chain locomotive underwent trials on the Heaton Waggonway in 1813-15, and an eight-wheeled one with both chain and adhesion drive was demonstrated on the Lambton Waggonway in 1814; neither, it seems, with any great success. Thereafter, from 1815, Chapman seems to have given up the chain principle, and the date of his meeting with Hall rather suggests, though it does not prove, that only the bogie element of the patent was under consideration here. If so, the engine proposed would have resembled the Whitehaven one (Fig. 2.09). Presumably the letter refers to Hall's Abercarn Tramroad, though the possibility remains that his line from Rhymney to Trefil is meant. Nothing, however, resulted from Chapman's overtures, for there is no hint that steam power was ever used on either of Hall's tramoads in their plateway days.

Fig. 2.10
Chapman's chain-haulage locomotive, 1813. The four-wheel bogie on the left is unpowered. Rollers on the right wind-in on a chain laid between the rails.
(*Engineer, 14 Sep 1936*)

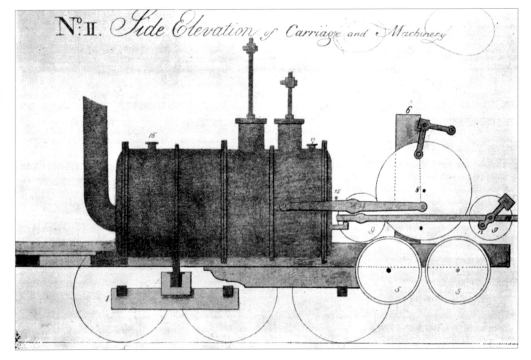

2B THE SIRHOWY TRAMROAD

2B i. Tredegar Ironworks

As far as Tredegar's locomotives are concerned, the major player was Thomas Ellis junior (1804-69). His father, Thomas senior (1781-1850), had been born at Wappenshall near Wellington in Shropshire and migrated to Wales in 1800. He spent a brief period (1801-2) at Penydarren under William Aubrey (1759-1827, the Homfrays' chief engineer at both Penydarren and Tredegar), and a shorter spell (1802) at Dowlais, before moving in 1803 to Tredegar where he spent the rest of his life as foreman patternmaker.[82]

His only son Thomas junior was baptised at Bedwellty (then the parish church for Tredegar) on 23 June 1804, and stayed for fifty years, living at relatively humble addresses. In 1829 he married Ann Hunter, one of a family that had migrated from Gosport in Hampshire, with whom he had twelve children. From boyhood he was employed at Tredegar works, at first, like his father, under William Aubrey.[83] He must have shown precocious talent, for in 1828 he was promoted to Aubrey's post at the tender age of 24. Samuel Homfray junior never regretted it. At the farewell dinner held in 1853 to mark his own retirement as manager, he paid tribute to his assistants.

> There was one agent who was absent, whose health would not allow him to be present, but he was obliged to mention his name, William Ellis, engineer [the reporter's obvious mistake for Thomas]. (Cheers.) He felt proud to do so … because he was one of his own rearing, and that he was rising in his profession.[84]

But for Ellis the writing was now on the wall. Homfray was replaced as manager by Richard Powell Davies, a new broom who made enemies and drove a number of senior staff to resign.[85] Ellis was evidently one. In 1854 he left and moved to Tymawr at Pontypridd. There we find him running a brickworks, starting a foundry, opening collieries, acting as a corn factor and serving as a director of the New Steam Packet Co.[86] Perhaps he had too many irons in the fire, for after four years he was bankrupt.[87] But he recovered, and in 1861 became manager of the new Great Western Railway rolling mills at Swindon. On retiring from there in 1865,[88] he spent his final years at Newport,[89] where he died on Christmas Day 1869 aged 65, to be buried at Bedwellty. Beyond a bare notice of his death, the press carried no obituary.[90]

Thomas Ellis junior was a self-effacing character rarely mentioned in the local press and, if his few surviving letters are any guide, a man of no great culture or polish. Unlike many contemporaries of his standing he played no significant role in local affairs.[91] Only once did he hit the headlines, so to speak, at the opening in 1849 of the new Tredegar rolling mills which he had himself designed and built. Homfray, at the ensuing dinner, proposed Thomas Ellis's health.

> We have a man in Tredegar who was born and educated here, and whose father worked here, who could produce such machinery as you have seen in motion today … I take delight in being the instrument to endeavour to bring a young man's name forward in society and in public, who should be esteemed by all, that he may be known as a person whom any one, let him be ever so high in his engineering qualifications, may be glad to consult as a careful, calculating, and steady engineer (Loud cheers.) I do not hesitate to say that I am proud of him (Cheers.) He was reared under my own eye, and I have given him all the advantages I could, and he has shown … what he can do. Mr Ellis briefly responded to the toast, and was loudly cheered.[92]

Next year, by way of thanks, Ellis was presented with a silver-plated tea service.[93] But, from all his time at Tredegar, it may be that he took greatest pride in having had under his wing the young Daniel Gooch and Francis Trevithick (of both of whom more later), who by now were the chief locomotive superintendents at Swindon and Crewe respectively. In 1854 Trevithick, then beginning work on his biography of his father, met up with his old mentor again, and they corresponded until Ellis's death.[94] Both were deeply interested in the Penydarren locomotive of 1804. When the famous Llewellin drawing surfaced in 1855, Ellis was the first to bring it into the public domain by publishing it as a lithograph in 1857 although, like his contemporaries, he mistakenly assumed it was of the Penydarren engine itself.[95]

With Ellis's departure, the link with Tredegar was not broken. His wife's family, the Hunters, had some interesting members. One of her brothers, George, whom we shall meet again, was something of a black sheep. But another, James, went in the late 1820s with Rhys Davies, a fellow Tredegar man, to work in the French iron industry; and then in 1833 they crossed the Atlantic to set up the important Tredegar Iron Works at Richmond, Virginia, where James died in 1867.[96] A third brother, Charles (1811-61), was the Welsh Tredegar's estate agent, and his son Charles Lafayette Hunter (1839-1902), who had joined the works as an apprentice in 1853, was appointed chief engineer and locomotive superintendent in 1860 at the astonishing age of 21.[97] In that year not only had R. P. Davies died, to be replaced as manager by the more congenial James Reed, but Ellis's successor as chief engineer, James Watson, had disgraced himself when his monstrous new blast engine failed to work and he was sacked.[98] Charles Hunter junior progressed further to become works manager in 1869, but resigned in 1874 when the works were sold,[99] having presided mechanically over the transformation of the Sirhowy Tramroad into the Sirhowy Railway.

For the Tredegar-built locomotives, the old sources are few because no working documents of the ironworks survive. The earliest significant source, newspapers apart, is Evan Powell's history of Tredegar, written for an eisteddfod competition in 1884. Powell (1840-91) spent his whole life at Tredegar, where he was born, starting off as an ironstone miner and becoming an inspector of weighing machines at the works. But his book being largely based, like most of its kind, on memory and on hearsay, it is full of inaccuracies and unreliable on dates, yet is a source that cannot be ignored. It gives a list of eight locomotives.[100]

Much more important is a miscellany that derives ultimately from Charles William Ellis (1841-1929), Thomas junior's fifth son, who became an iron merchant and colliery owner of no great distinction. But he kept his father's memory alive, and it is through his efforts that the Tredegar engines remain to this day much the best known of all the plateway locomotives that ran in western Monmouthshire. This miscellany preserved by Charles Ellis consists of four short published letters and articles which contain some bald information, vague in date and unreliable in detail, as well as a few illustrations and a small but illuminating handful of manuscripts:

- Memorandum books of Thomas Ellis senior which span almost the whole of his career at Tredegar.[101] They now comprise six postcard-size volumes of very miscellaneous notes ranging from biblical extracts and medicinal remedies to detailed dimensions of engine and machine parts, particularly for blast engines and rolling mills. The delightfully mis-spelt entries are far from arranged in date order, and some are not dated at all. Sadly, at least one volume, quoted in his grandson's letter of 1912, never reached the National Library as its fellows did. Yet they contain material of very great value.

- Letter of 1889 by Charles Ellis quoting his grandfather's notebooks on Daniel Gooch.[102]

- Anonymous article of 1901 derived indirectly, by way of a certain C. T. Johnson, from Charles Ellis (it quotes, or misquotes, from his grandfather's notebooks). The only locomotive it names is *St David*.[103]

- Letter of 1912 by Charles Ellis on a Trevithick winding engine built by Tredegar for Gellihaf Colliery in 1805.[104]

- Anonymous article of 1915 with acknowledged input by Charles Ellis, naming thirteen engines as well as mentioning two narrow-gauge ones. This, being the last and fullest of the lists, seems the most authoritative.[105]

- Original drawing by Thomas Ellis junior of *St David* in 1848,[106] and a redrawn copy of it.[107]

- At least three photographs of locomotives evidently taken for him by Charles Eastment of Ebbw Vale, including a copy of the very early one of *St David*.[108]

There is also an anonymous paragraph of 1905 which, although it includes (slightly altered) the redrawn version of the drawing of *St David*, seems to be independent of Charles Ellis. Derived from John Williams, son of the driver of *Laura*, it names only those two engines.[109]

These lists, skimpy though they are and evidently drawn from fading memories, are as follows:

Powell 1884	Railway Mag 1901	Loco Mag 1905	Loco Mag 1915
Dispatch	10 locos 1838-48	4 locos 1846-48	*Britannia*
Speedwell	(eight 0-6-0 including	including *St David*	*Hercules*
Lord Rodney	*St David*, and two	and *Laura*	*Speedwell*
St David	0-4-0 for 2ft 6in)		*Tredegar*
Lady Mary			*Jane*
Lady Charlotte			*Lord Rodney*
Bedwellty			*Lady Sale*
Tredegar			*Prince Albert*
			St David reb. 1848
			Fanny
			Charlotte
			All above 1832-38
			Dispatch 0-4-0 shunter
			1832-48
			2 for coal lines 1832-48
			Bedwellty 1853

For the past century, accounts of the Tredegar locomotives have derived exclusively from these lists.[110] Now, however, the newspapers and Ellis senior's notebooks between them go a fair way towards correcting, refining and expanding the old information, although plenty of questions remain. One further guide to the approximate dates of construction and withdrawal of engines is a series of statements of Tredegar's total stock of locomotives:[111]

1835	8
1843	9
1849	9
1862	7
1869	6

Another tentative guide is that Tredegar's home-built engines seem in almost every case to have been named after ships that were currently trading into Newport, which are easily checked through the weekly shipping news in the local press. True, some ship-names like *Britannia* and *Dispatch* were two-a-penny, but the correspondence of dates seems beyond coincidence. No pattern can be found in the ownership or trade of these vessels, which varied from sloops to steamers, none of them devoted to carrying Tredegar products and three – *St David*, *Lady Charlotte* and *Lady Rodney* – being steam packets on the Bristol run. It looks as if Homfray or Ellis (or whoever was responsible for naming the locomotives) chose whatever ship-name had caught his fancy on a recent visit to the wharves.

BRITANNIA, 0-6-0 Robert Stephenson 1829

Samuel Homfray junior had long been aware of steam locomotion. As a boy of eight, he was surely at his father's side to witness the Merthyr trials of 1804, and it would be surprising if he was not treated to a ride. Nor was South Wales totally isolated from the rest of the country. When, shortly before 1820, moves were afoot to build a railway from Stockton to Darlington, the committee not only appointed George Overton – one of the leading lights among Welsh engineers – to make a survey but also canvassed opinions from others. One reply came from Joseph Tregelles Price of Neath Abbey Ironworks,[112] another from Josiah John Guest of Dowlais,[113] and a third (of which more later) from Homfray senior with information about the Sirhowy Tramroad. Thereafter Homfray junior, no doubt already predisposed to steam haulage, kept his ear to the ground.

Whether Thomas Ellis junior was equally predisposed we do not know. Trevithick's Penydarren engine was built after his family had left for Tredegar and 'before I saw the light.'[114] But manager and engineer must have debated the possibilities of steam. In December 1828, hearing, it is said, of the 'wonderful travelling engines at Newcastle which were reducing the cost of haulage by 50 per cent,' Homfray sent Ellis and his mining agent Theophilus Jones to see for themselves and to enquire about a locomotive for the Sirhowy.[115] Their tedious six-day journey to Newcastle by coach had three outcomes. Having talked to Robert Stephenson and inspected the Killingworth engines, they went off again, armed with a letter of introduction to Thomas Gooch, George Stephenson's assistant at the western end of the Liverpool & Manchester. On their return home, Ellis senior copied this letter (with his own spelling mistakes) into his notebook:

Mr T. L. Gooch Raylway Office Liverpool

Dear Gooch,
the two Gentlm who hand you this are from Wales and have been examining the Engins in the North of England. Especialy the Locomotive Engins. You will be so good as shew them the Tunnel and any of the other works at your end of the line.
Your kind attention will oblige yours most truly
Robert Stephenson
New Castle Decr 11th 1828.[116]

Thomas and his younger brother Daniel were sons of John Gooch, a Northumbrian friend of the Stephensons and formerly cashier at Bedlington Ironworks, and it is hardly over-fanciful to suppose that this meeting played a part in John's appointment in 1831 as cashier at Tredegar. With him he took his wife and his younger children; and there, until John's death in 1833, the teenaged Daniel received his first mechanical training from Ellis senior and under the overall eye of Ellis junior.[117] He wrote of this period,

The foreman in the pattern shop was a Mr Ellis; his son was the engineer of the works – that is, had charge of all the mechanical department. Old Ellis, as we used to call him, was somewhat of a character; but he was always a kind friend to me, and gave me

any information he could. He had a book with a store of facts valuable at the time as the result of a life's experience, and this was always at my service … I look back upon the time spent at Tredegar as by far the most important years of my life.

In the 1850s Gooch gave an apprenticeship at Swindon to Thomas Ellis junior's third son George Falconer,[118] who by 1861 was sharing lodgings with a nephew of Daniel's. In this we may see the hand of friendship at work, and even more so in Thomas Ellis's final employment at Swindon.

The second outcome of the Newcastle expedition was that, in all probability, Ellis and Jones described to Stephenson their home-grown bogie trucks and waggons and that this information was disseminated directly or indirectly to America. This is a topic we shall pursue in Part 3.

The third outcome was the locomotive for Tredegar. Stephenson's 'No. 15 Travelling engine' or 'Humphrey's engine,' soon to be called *Britannia* (Fig. 2.11), was ordered in late December 1828, a few weeks before the 3ft-gauge 'No. 14' or 'Forman's engine' which, as we shall later see, was destined for Bute Ironworks.[119] Both left Newcastle on 18 July 1829 and were shipped together to Pillgwenlly at a joint freight of £30.[120] A fortnight later came the bill.

The Tredegar Iron Co Abergavenny
For one Locomotive Engine complete delivered at their wharf Pillgwenlly as p Agreement
£550.0.0
One strong Packing Box hooped with Iron
£1.18.0.[121]

Britannia's cylinders, 10½ by 20in, were steeply inclined, an arrangement recently inaugurated on Stephenson's *Lancashire Witch* for the Bolton & Leigh Railway. The wheels were 3ft 6in, the weight 8 to 9 tons full, the return-flue boiler 4ft 4in by 9ft.[122]

After being put together, *Britannia* was no doubt tested around the works. Then on 16 September Homfray wrote to the MCC 'recommending the introduction and patronage of Locomotive Engines on the Sirhowy Tram Road and stating that the only thing required is an alteration in the partings [i.e. points] and to make a few more communications between the two roads.'[123] He also recommended the lengthening of points to 'ten plates between the

Fig. 2.11

Tredegar's *Britannia*, 1829.
(*Warren 1923, 154*)

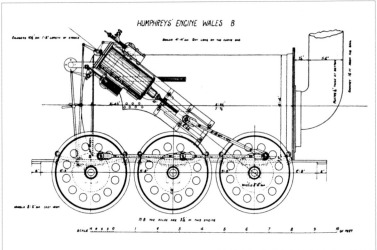

wing and the Cross' (compare the drawings of points in Figs. 3.20-21);[124] in other words that rails at points diverged at too great an angle for the engine, much longer in the wheelbase than a tram, to take easily. But it was not until 17 December that *Britannia* made its public debut, which was once again – and surely with another very deliberate eye to publicity – on the occasion of the Cattle Show at Court y Bella. Leaving little to chance, Homfray informed the MCC,

> It is my intention to make a trial of the locomotive engine to go down to Newport on Thursday next and shall feel obliged by your allowing your men to use their endeavour to keep the road as clear as possible so as to meet with no impediments. The partings of the Canal Company will be sent down as fast as you can have them put down.[125]

But the best-laid plans…

> It was confidently stated for some weeks past that the Tredegar Iron Co at Tredegar Iron-works were to start a locomotive engine the day of the Cattle Show on Thursday last, to bring the iron from this Works to this port, a distance of twenty-four miles. The persons assembled at the Cattle Show (which was close to the tram-road) were looking anxiously for the steam-engine, but it did not make its appearance. The engine did, however, start from the Works early in the morning, but, unfortunately, at one of the crossings in the tram-road, which was not long enough for the steam-carriage, the wheels got out of the tram-plates, which caused a detention of some hours; and on coming through Tredegar Park the chimney was carried away by the branch of a tree hanging over the tram-road. In consequence of these accidents, it did not arrive in Newport till the evening. The engine is very neat and compact – the carriage consists of six wheels, on which is the boiler and machinery, behind which the engineer stands to work it – there is also a carriage attached, carrying the coke for immediate use, and a reservoir of water to supply the boiler; besides which is another tram with coke to supply the above as required. The engine is about eight horse power, and brought down 53 tons of iron, besides its own weight, making altogether about 80 tons, at the rate of six miles an hour, with much ease, and without forcing the engine. The next day the chimney was repaired, and we saw the engine at work; she went at the rate of ten miles an hour, having nothing attached to her then but the carriage with the reservoir of water. It is generally believed the engine will answer the purpose intended, and that horses will soon be put out of request. The engine stops twice in the twenty-four miles for a supply of water, which takes about a quarter of an hour each time. We understand the Canal Company are disposed to encourage the working of steam-engines, and to alter the tram-roads as may be found necessary.[126]

Sadly John Thomas was not present, as he had been in 1821, to depict the scene. But the overall appearance of the locomotive with its double tenders must have been akin to Hackworth's inclined-cylinder design of 1838 for the Stockton & Darlington (Fig. 2.12).

For some months all went well with *Britannia*, which is said to have reduced the cost of haulage by 35 per cent.[127] In March 1830, when a Gurney locomotive passed through Newport on its way to Cyfarthfa works at Merthyr, the press reminded readers that

> Another steam-tug has been nearly twelve months [an exaggeration] successfully employed at the

Fig. 2.12

Hackworth locomotive and double tenders, Stockton & Darlington, 1838. (*Engineer, 31 Oct 1879*)

works of Messrs Homfray, at Tredegar, of sufficient power to drag seventy tons, exclusive of its own weight, which is about eight tons, at the rate of six miles an hour. The boiler with the propelling machinery of this engine is on six wheels, and is connected with and preceded by another carriage holding the water tank to feed the boiler, and the coke with which the fire is kept up.[128]

But on 30 June 1830, when *Britannia* had been at work for only six months,

the boiler of one of the steam engines on the railroad between the Tredegar Works and Newport unfortunately bursted on Wednesday last, about nine miles from the latter place, by which accident, we lament to say, one man was killed.

The ensuing inquest on 'a boy, unknown' recorded a verdict of accidental death.[129] While *St David*, the next engine, may just have entered service, the likelihood is that the accident was to *Britannia*. Three months later, after due time for repairing or replacing the boiler, Ellis senior noted the calculations for 'Tredegar Locomotive Engin by Stevinson New Castle Steam Valve Octer 21st 1830.'[130]

Within a month of the boiler blowing up, the local press published some tactful words on the occasion of the first run of Thomas Prothero's *Speedwell* built by Price & Co of Neath Abbey, of which more later:

Mr Homfray, of Tredegar Iron Works, who is always amongst the first to promote every object of utility, having during the last six months used Loco-motive Engines, constructed on Stephenson's plan, for conveying his Iron along the Sirhowy Tram-road, it was perceived that the great defect in those engines was the want of a regular supply of steam to keep them going; and to remedy that defect was the matter of the greatest care and consideration with Messrs Price and Co in the plan and construction of their engine. Another great object of their attention was to prevent the possibility of explosion by improperly charging the boiler, and thereby remove the chance of any accident fatal to life from that cause.[131]

It is clear enough that, here as elsewhere, this shortage of steam led to drivers holding down the safety valves, with sometimes fatal results. It may also have led to the replacement of the return-flue boilers with multi-tubular ones. Boiler pressures recorded at Tredegar by Ellis senior at various

dates from 1830 to 1840 were all in the range of 50 to 58 psi, which was typical of the early 1830s, except for *Speedwell* at 71 and *Fanny* at 77.[132] Ellis junior never used glass water gauges, but swore by the double cocks that he found most reliable. 'He had had boilers burst,' he admitted, 'but not from the water getting below the safety point.'[133] In the days before the Giffard injector was invented in 1858, the only way to replenish a boiler was with the mechanical pump, to work which the engine had to be running. It seems to have been a common misapprehension that too low a level of water would cause an explosion, whereas the likely outcome would be the melting of the fusible plug.

A tramroad designed for horse traction did need some adaptation for steam. There were places, it was found, where the distance between double tracks was adequate for trams to pass each other but not locomotives. William Wells, who had succeeded Hodgkinson as engineer, was allowed £50 in 1831 to rectify the matter.[134] Locomotives, too, damaged the track. In August 1830 the MCC minuted

With a view to save the breakage of tram-plates and to prevent the consequent interruption of the freighters generally, Resolved – that no locomotive steam engine be allowed to travel on this Company's tramroads that is not suspended on proper springs.[135]

Britannia, like *St David* and Prothero's *Speedwell*, weighed far more per axle than any loaded tram, but seems to have been exempt from a weight limit because it was sprung. This was the Stephenson factor at work: leaf – as opposed to steam – springs were inaugurated possibly at Heaton in 1821 and certainly at Killingworth in 1827 and on *Lancashire Witch* in 1828.[136] The rogue engine smashing the cast-iron tramplates was probably, as we shall see, from Blaina. Nonetheless both the MCC and the Sirhowy had regularly to upgrade their lines with heavier plates. In July 1831, 'notwithstanding the great number of plates that appear to be broken by the Locomotive Engines, Mr Cooke [the MCC's clerk] is requested to render them every accommodation.'[137] One is reminded of the comment by Francis Trevithick, who trained at Tredegar, that 'the writer worked locomotives on those same tramways ... in 1837, and it was then necessary to send platelayers to jump from the waggon-trains to replace broken plates.'[138] From 1842, when the MCC began to relay its lines with wrought-iron plates, the problem was greatly eased.[139]

Ellis senior's notebook shows that *Britannia* remained at work for at least four years more. On 7 June 1834,

The following is the weight of Iron – Coal Trams &c Weigh'd on the Park Machine

	Trams	Tons	C
To – Iron	23	85	3
To – Coal	4	18	10
To weight of iron trams	23	21	0
To do Coal do	4	6	18
To weight of Engeon		11	5
To weight of Tank Tram		3	0
		145	16

Whent down in 7 howers – without any accidence the Brittannia Locomotive Engine John Stephens [driver]. Sined Wm Williams Machine Man.[140]

Note that by now the weight of the engine had been increased (by its new boiler?) from the original 8 or 9 tons to 11¼.

Britannia was probably withdrawn around 1840: perhaps in 1839 when John Stephens became driver of *Fanny*.

ST DAVID, 0-6-0 Tredegar 1830

The next engine on the Sirhowy inaugurated the long series built at Tredegar works, where the shops were equipped to carry out almost any engineering project, by Thomas Ellis junior. Helping him was the 'chargeman' – that is, the fitter with immediate responsibility for construction and maintenance – named William Sambrook (1805-82),[141] who hailed from Dyffryn Clydach near Neath and moved to Tredegar about 1829. The censuses from 1841 to 1871 all describe him as 'engine fitter.'

We are better informed about *St David* than most of its successors. Its date is normally given as 1832, and only two modern publications have the correct year of 1830.[142] Soon after *Britannia*'s arrival, Homfray and Ellis must have decided to build a similar engine themselves, for in March 1830 'a steam-carriage, combining all the recent improvements in this mode of conveyance, is now in a state of readiness in the yard of this company, intended for the transmit of goods between Tredegar and Newport.'[143] Like *Britannia* – and all but one of Ellis's later locomotives on the 4ft

4in gauge – it was six-coupled and its cylinders were steeply inclined. Like *Britannia*, it had a return-flue boiler, to which an entry in Ellis senior's notebook refers.

Whight of Wrought Iron Boyler of the St David
May 1830
Boyler 1 [ton] -14 [cwt] - 3 [qrs] - 0 [lbs].
Tube New 1-3-2-0
Lower Part of Stack 2-0-18
2nd Part of Do 1-3-19
3rd Do 3-24 long weight [i.e. 120 lbs to the cwt].[144]

St David evidently came into service at some point during the summer, but on 14 October 1830 an inquest was held 'on Thomas Jones, aged 25 years, a fire-man, in the employ of the Tredegar Iron Company, who was severely scalded and bruised by the bursting of a boiler of a locomotive steam engine. He died in five hours after the accident.'[145] In this case the culprit was presumably *St David*. Getting it back into business – quite possibly this time with multiple tubes instead of the return flue – is no doubt reflected in another of Ellis senior's notes two months after the event (Fig. 2.13), 'The Steam Valves on St David 1⅞ Diar Equals to 2¾ Squar Inches,'[146] the necessary weight of 25½ lbs being amended to 32 lbs. He also noted, 'St David began to take Iron to Stricklands Decr 16th 1830,'[147] Benjamin Strickland being the Sirhowy Tramroad Company's agent at the weighing machine at Nine Mile Point.

Fig. 2.13
Thomas Ellis senior's sketch of safety valve for *St David*. (NLW, MS 5157 f.42r)

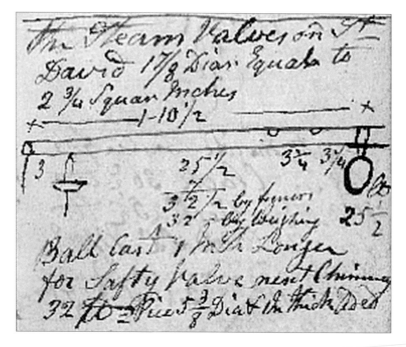

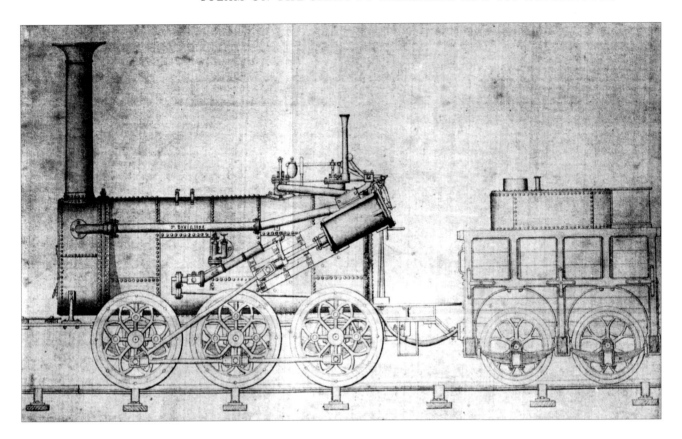

Fig. 2.14

Thomas Ellis junior's drawing of *St David*, 1848. (*Warren 1923, 154*)

Only eight years later, on 4 September 1838, the same disaster struck again.

The St David steam engine, belonging to the Tredegar Iron Co, was on her way from Pillgwenlly to Tredegar, and had passed the Court-y-Bella weighing machine about 30 or 40 yards when the boiler burst; one piece of several hundred weight was blown over the garden of F. Justice, Esq, Bellevue, to a considerable distance in the adjoining field, a man was making up the fire at the time the occurrence took place and escaped, very slightly scalded; no other accident happened by the explosion. The cause of the bursting has not been ascertained.[148]

At this date, the usual reason for boilers bursting was failure at the tube plate or the firebox end. In this case, as with *Vulcan* five years later, when large chunks were hurled great distances, it sounds like a failure of the barrel.

Again the damage was made good, and in 1848 *St David* underwent what was evidently a major rebuild. By now, and doubtless for many years past, the boiler was multi-tubular with a proper smokebox which, together with the chimney, was whitewashed every week (some say every month) to make the engine more visible to rail and road

users.[149] By now, too, and very probably from the beginning, the wheels were of an intricate and attractive 'gothic' design intended to minimise the residual stresses in a one-piece casting. Thomas Ellis's own drawing of the engine as in 1848 survived at least until 1921 when his son Charles sent a photographic copy to Stephensons (Fig. 2.14).[150]

This rebuilding may account for a flurry of interest recorded in Ellis senior's notebooks:

The Saint-David took down on the 18 April 1848

	ton	cwt	Qr	lb
	179	19	3	8
iron Brought up				
28 Bar Iron Trams	30	10	0	0
1 Columbus ditto	3	4	0	0
Sand	6	17	0	0
Oats	1	13	0	0
In 6½ hours	42	4	0	0
Geo Hunter [driver]				

do. Geo Hunter St David Apl – 22 1848

Going down	Ton	C	Q	lb
	210	9	2	21[151]

The term *columbus*, meaning a large bogie coal tram, will come in for discussion later.

St David's rebuilding was perhaps also the stimulus for the intriguing photograph of it with Thomas Ellis himself on the footplate (Figs. 2.15 and frontispiece). This picture is traditionally dated to 1854, but when it was registered for copyright at Stationers' Hall in 1901 the application read 'Photograph of St David Engine, 1846, Tredegar, copied from old glass picture,' the applicant being Charles Eastment and Son, photographers of Ebbw Vale and Tredegar.[152] We may be confident that Charles Ellis, who was then living in Sirhowy, had inherited the original from his father and commissioned Eastment to reproduce it, supplying the details given on the application form. This earlier date of 1846, however, is itself in doubt, because the locomotive has clearly been rebuilt and the year 1848 for the rebuilding appears on the engine itself in Thomas Ellis's own drawing. *St David* seems to have been the apple of his eye, perhaps because it was the first engine he built himself; and one can visualise him wanting it immortalised in this new-fangled medium.

But what was the real date? A straightforward print from an old glass negative would not qualify for copyright. The clue lies in 'copied from old glass picture.' The earliest photographic methods were the calotype, which used paper negatives, and the daguerreotype, which was on silver or silver-plated copper sheets and always protected under glass. Then in 1851 the wet plate collodion or ambrotype process was introduced by Frederick Scott Archer, with the image on glass. This was a difficult process because the chemicals had to be wet: the photographer had a window of fifteen minutes at the most in which to coat the glass, make the exposure, and develop it, which demanded a portable studio. The only way to reproduce a daguerreotype or a positive ambrotype was to re-photograph it and print the result; which is precisely what Eastment seems to have done. This would count, for copyright purposes, as a 'new' photograph. The image is too sharp at the centre to be a calotype, which in any event was on paper. It shows none of the typical signs of a daguerreotype such as the faint scratches caused by buffing the plate. Most likely, therefore, the original was a positive wet plate collodion, taken after 1851 but before Ellis's departure in 1854, the details given to Eastment by Charles Ellis being (like others of his statements) slightly astray. It is thus very early in the history of railway photography; an ambrotype is also known of a Taff Vale locomotive at Cardiff.[153]

Fig. 2.15

Photograph of *St David*, c.1852, as copied by Charles Eastment 1901. (*TNA, COPY 1/449/268*)

The uneven quality of our picture, badly out of focus towards the edges, almost certainly stems not from the original but from Eastment using, when he copied it, a lens of the wrong focal length.

There is no sign that the engines carried nameplates. None is visible on the photograph. The drawing of *St David* has the name apparently painted on the exhaust pipe, but that is not visible on the photograph either.

We know the names of a number of drivers. The most frequently mentioned, possibly because he was in a privileged position, was George Hunter (1801-70), driver of *St David* in the 1840s. As we saw, this engine, at least as rebuilt in 1848, was apparently the pride of the Tredegar fleet, and Hunter moreover was Ellis's brother-in-law. But in May 1848 he disgraced himself.

> *George Hunter*, driver of the St David's engine from Tredegar Iron Works, was fined 10s and costs, 11s 6d, for refusing to allow Mr Bebell, at the Courtybella machine, to weigh and gauge his iron; and Hunter was also further fined 20s and costs, 13s 6d, for obstructing the Canal Company's road for one hour by leaving a quantity of iron lying across the rails of the road ... Hunter had made use of very abusive and indecent language.[154]

It seems to have cost him his job, for he does not feature in the 1851 census and in 1861 was publican of the Rock Inn at Argoed. His place on *St David*'s footplate was given to the long-serving Isaac Thomas (1808-63), whose record was not wholly unblemished either; as we shall see, he had already been involved in accidents with *Speedwell* and *Lady Sale*. He is said to be the bearded man beside Ellis in the photograph.[155] When he died in an accident in the Tredegar rolling mill in 1863 the works closed down for his funeral, which was attended by over two thousand people.[156]

No further mishaps to *St David* are known, except that in 1849 its fireman, Frederick Edmonds, slipped off the footplate step and was run over, losing a foot.[157] In about 1859 *St David* was converted for standard-gauge edge rail, and is said (without confirmation) to have continued at work into the 1880s, being scrapped only in 1909.[158]

The following three locomotives, although not attested until later, are here allocated to the early 1830s in order to make up the total of eight recorded in 1835.[159]

TREDEGAR, 0-6-0 Tredegar 1830/35 (by 1836)

This is first mentioned by Ellis senior in 1836:

> Tredegar Travelling Engin 10 Inch Cylinder 20 Inch Stroke Pressure 50 lb pr square Inch – say 10 by 20 Inch 42 Stroke per Minuet or the peston passing through 140 feet pr Minuet Wheels 3ft 6in Diar ... [calculations] 5.25 Miles pr hower when the Engin works at regular power. Nov 3 1836.[160]

But at some point before 1843 *Tredegar*, like most of the other engines, was fitted with larger 12in cylinders. On a timed run in that year it hauled up to *Tredegar* a train mainly of empties weighing 38 tons at 6 mph. But on another it struggled up a gradient of 1 in 85 to 1 in 61 – probably at *Tredegar* itself, where it was stiffest – at 6.2 mph excluding stoppages or 4.4 mph including them, its wheels 'continually slipping, notwithstanding the industrious application of sand.' The engine weighed 12¾ tons, there were two tons of coal in the tender, and the load of the train excluding the 'water-tram' was only 28 tons.[161]

In 1853 *Tredegar* contrived to squash its stoker while he was unhitching trams;[162] and in 1859, on the same day that sabotage to points at Argoed resulted in a spectacular runaway which will later be described,

> another pair of points had been opened and fastened in a similar way near the Holly Bush, about five miles from Tredegar, near the Sirhowy Tramroad. The consequence was that one of the Tredegar Company's engines left the line and fell down the embankment, a depth of fifty feet. We regret to say that in this instance the accident resulted in serious injury to the fireman of the engine.[163]

Another less circumstantial account, although it turns the two acts of sabotage into one, is clear about the name of the locomotive involved. Of three trains travelling up in the dark,

> the second engine, the 'Tredegar,' after stopping to take in water as usual at the Holly Bush Inn, four miles below Tredegar, had not proceeded more than a quarter of a mile when it was found the engine and tender were off the line, owing to some persons unknown having altered the switches. The engineer, fireman and watchman jumped off, the chain connecting with the train luckily broke, and the engine and tender rolled over a precipice into a field about 30 feet deep. Happily there was no other person in the trucks.[164]

At this date, as again we shall see, the Sirhowy Tramroad had just been relaid with standard-gauge edge rails. The first locomotives for the Sirhowy Railway (which did not yet officially exist) had not been delivered, and in any event carried only numbers, not names. *Tredegar* must therefore be the tramroad engine, but no doubt recently equipped with combined wheels that fitted both plate and edge rails.

Of Ellis's locomotives between his first and his last, there are no illustrations. But because *St David* and *Bedwellty* were essentially identical in layout, it seems fair to assume that the intermediate *Tredegar* and the others were too. While this might suggest conservatism on Ellis's part, it could equally, and more probably, mean that the design was eminently fit for its purpose.

JANE, 0-6-0 Tredegar 1830/35 (by 1841)

This is mentioned only in Charles Ellis's list and in Thomas Ellis senior's notebook in April 1841, when a safety valve was designed for 'the Jane Locomotive Engin.'[165] It was named, it has been suggested, after Homfray's mother who was sister of the current Sir Charles Morgan of Tredegar.[166] Possibly so; but there was also at that time a ship named *Jane* trading into Newport.

(LORD?) RODNEY, 0-6-0 Tredegar 1830/35 (by 1848)

Powell and Charles Ellis call it the *Lord Rodney*, but there was never any such ship. There was, however, a *Lady Rodney*, a steam packet that plied between Newport and Bristol from 1823 to 1838, named after the second daughter of Sir Charles Morgan of Tredegar who had married Lord Rodney in 1819. Of the locomotive, little is recorded, and only under the name of plain *Rodney*. In April 1848 Ellis senior noted, 'All the [locomotive] Cylinders are 12 Inches D[iamete]r except the Rodney its 10 Inches Dr;'[167] the rest, it is implied, having been changed to 12in. And in 1856,

> About eight o'clock on Monday night, a sad accident occurred to a man named Thomas Davies, stoker under the Tredegar Iron Company. He was with the 'Rodney' on the Sirhowy Railway, and getting down for some purpose, attempted to get on the stage [footplate] again, while the engine was in motion, while he missed his footing. One of the wheels passed over his foot, and crushed

> it so severely, that it is feared amputation will be necessary. About eighteen months since, he had some of his toes cut off in a similar manner.[168]

It was one of these early locomotives that gave Daniel Gooch a bad fright during his apprenticeship at Tredegar in 1832-33.

> My brother William … was a little fellow, and had gone with me to the works. I missed him from the shop and went out to look for him, when I saw him standing between the rails of a road that passed the end of the shop. On going towards him, I saw a locomotive coming within a few yards of which he was taking no notice, and had just time to run and pull him out of the way. It made my heart jump, and was a very narrow escape for him. Fortunately the engines on these roads did not travel very fast.[169]

William, then aged seven or eight, went on to become manager of Swindon works.

LADY CHARLOTTE, 0-6-0 Tredegar c.1835? (by 1840)

It has been suggested that this was named after Samuel Homfray's wife, whom he had married in 1824.[170] But she was Mrs Charlotte Homfray, not Lady Charlotte. Much more likely it was again named after a ship, a brand-new steam packet of 1835 on the Bristol run which honoured Lady Charlotte Bertie,[171] who had married Josiah John Guest of Dowlais in 1833 and rapidly became a respected and popular figure. On 26 March 1840 *Lady Charlotte* was measured for a safety valve,[172] and on 29 August 1843 was perhaps involved (though the report is muddled over the names) in an extraordinary episode of pig-in-the-middle.

> Misconduct of Engineers. A dreadful accident occurred at Pie Corner, near Bassaleg, on Tuesday, owing, to the gross carelessness of the man in charge of the Fanny, Tredegar Company's engine, employed in driving coals from Tredegar Iron Works, to Newport. This engine … was followed by one of the Rumney engines to Pie Corner, where the Rumney road branches off, previous to which there is a place for feeding the engines with water. After the Tredegar engine had been supplied she moved on about two hundred yards, when she stopped, and was left by the engineer, stoker, and latch-opener, who returned to a public-house, where they were joined by the man belonging to the Rumney engine. Some labourers who

were making repairs on the road, near where the Tredegar engine stood, were annoyed at her being in their way, and one of them being more foolish than the rest, jumped up, thinking to move her on a little way, when, by letting the steam on the wrong way, with full power, she reversed with awful rapidity, driving her large iron trams with great violence against the Rumney engine, which thus moved and backed with great force against a team of horses, belonging to Mr William Hodges, of Risca, and very narrowly escaped killing every one of them. Two, however, were injured, one of which, it is feared, will never again be of any use, and the man in charge of them nearly lost his life, trying to save his master's horses. It is impossible to say what damage might have been done to property, and what lives might have been sacrificed had not the Rumney engineer got upon his engine, and put her to work against the Lady Charlotte, the engineer of which found some difficulty in stopping the rod by which the steam is regulated, that having been put out of its place by the fellow whose misconduct was the cause of the accident. Such was the power of the two engines working against each other, that the large iron trams were thrown one on the top of another. The gross misconduct of the men will, we trust, be visited in the most exemplary manner, by their employers.[173]

Charles Wilkins claimed, extraordinarily, that *Lady Charlotte* was built by Adrian Stephens, the inventor of the steam whistle, for Dowlais, and was the first locomotive there.[174] This is quite simply wrong.

FANNY, 0-6-0 Tredegar 1839

There are a few minor records. The engine was clearly new in 1839. Ellis senior notes 'Leavers for Fanney Locomotive Feby 27th 1839' and 'Fanny Locomotive Started Thursday March 7 – 1839. John Stevens John Williams John Llewellyn'[175] – the three crew members, often indiscriminately called 'engine tenders.' As we saw, John Stevens or Stephens had in 1834 been *Britannia*'s driver.[176] An undated note, probably also from 1839, reads 'John Stevens took from Tredegar to Pill 174 Tons of Iron in one Journey & took it into yard at Pill the first Week of Aprill with Locomotive 10 Dr Cylinder 20 Inch Stroke, Fanny.'[177] After the Chartists' famous march during their uprising later in the year, 'John Stevens Engineer of the Fanny Locomotive Engine in the employ of the Tredegar Iron Compy' gave evidence of what

he had witnessed.[178] The episode in 1843, when a Rumney engine and either *Fanny* or *Lady Charlotte* squashed a train of trams between them, has already been recounted. The John Williams who was fireman in 1839, described in the Tredegar censuses as born in 1814-15 in Pembrokeshire, continued in Tredegar's employ after the tramroad's conversion to standard gauge. There survives a portrait of him in old age, labelled 'Jack Williams (also known as Jack Pembroke), the first engine driver on the later Sirhowy Railway' (Fig. 2.16).[179] The 1881 census gives him as an engine driver still.

Fig. 2.16
Jack Williams, alias Jack Pembroke, fireman of *Fanny*.
(NMW, P2003-311)

LADY MARY and *PRINCE ALBERT*

The *Lady Mary* in Powell's list is otherwise wholly unattested. If genuine, it could well have existed within his memory – he was born in 1840 – but it could equally be a phantom, a simple mistake.

Prince Albert is named only in Charles Ellis's 1915 list, and there is no contemporary record. Unless another phantom, it was surely built in or soon after 1840 when the royal marriage was the event of the year and ships instantly began to be given the name.

LAURA

Likewise mentioned only once in connection with Tredegar, its fireman being the father of John Williams of the Midland Railway.[180] In view of the total silence of other sources and the presence of a *Laura* on the Rumney Railway next door, it seems that it was ascribed to the wrong tramroad. See 2.D.ii below.

DISPATCH,
0-4-0 yard engine, Tredegar 1842/43?

Listed (as a four-wheeled shunter) by only two of the sources. No more is known. Ships named *Dispatch* were plentiful. It quite likely succeeded *Hercules* (see below) as yard engine about 1842, and the number of locomotives recorded in 1843 suggests it was built by then.

LADY SALE, 0-6-0 Tredegar 1843?

Named, probably as usual by way of a ship, after Florentia, wife of Major-General Sir Robert Sale, who in the First Afghan War of 1842 was kidnapped, imprisoned at Kabul, and dramatically released. Her best-selling account of the ordeal, published in 1843, made her a national heroine. In 1846 *Lady Sale*'s driver, Isaac Thomas, was taken to court 'for driving her ladyship into the Monmouthshire Canal Company's wall, near Pye Corner, and on the wrong line of rails.' Although exonerated because none other than the MCC's engineer himself had advised him to take the wrong road, he had to pay 6s 6d costs.[181] Where the track was double, the rule of the road was to drive on the left. We know this because in 1839 the Chartists marching downhill to Newport were ordered by their leader Zephaniah Williams,

> 'Go on, two and two, along the full roads;' that is, the left hand side of the tram-road, where the full trams come down. There are two tram-roads – the full ones come down one, and the empty ones go up the other.[182]

On 18 March 1843 – around the time deduced for *Lady Sale*'s building – Thomas Ellis senior noted the weight of 'the Locomotive Engine Wheels for large Engine.' And a few months later, 'the 12 Inch Cylinder for Locomotive Engin the pattern returned from Bristol & put in Sirhowy Stables Agst 10 1843.'[183] Why the pattern had been sent to Bristol is anyone's guess; but one wonders if *Lady Sale* was Tredegar's first 'large engine' with 12-in cylinders. All of the few cylinder dimensions of Tredegar-built engines that we have are 10in before 1843 and 12in thereafter, except, as we saw, for *Rodney*. It therefore looks

as if all the locomotives bar one were given larger cylinders between 1843 and April 1848.[184]

On 15 July 1844,
> one of the locomotive engines belonging to the Tredegar Iron Company, was proceeding from Pillgwenlly to Tredegar, on arriving at Blackwood the boiler burst, the fireman was killed on the spot, and the engineer is so much scalded and otherwise hurt that there is but little hope of his recovery.[185]

Which engine this was we do not know. It could be any of those not accounted for.

BEDWELLTY, 0-6-0 Tredegar 1853

After the completion of *Lady Sale* in perhaps 1843, there seems to have been a decade-long lull in Thomas Ellis's building of engines. The reason was perhaps that from the mid-1840s it was increasingly clear that the MCC was about to take over haulage on its own lines and thereby reduce the mileage run by Tredegar locomotives. This may be why the date of 1848 (the year of the Act which authorised MRCC haulage as well as of *St David*'s rebuilding) recurs so often in Charles Ellis's lists.

The final engine, *Bedwellty* of 1853, for whose date we have only his memory to rely on, acquired a sinister reputation by killing fifteen people within six years. The late 1850s, which saw the tramroad being converted into a railway, were a messy period, both literally at the time and in historical retrospect. The background, so far as it can be unravelled, will concern us later. But in 1858 the Tramroad Company found itself embroiled in a bitter dispute with the inhabitants of Blackwood, a typical ribbon development of cheek-by-jowl houses nine miles below Tredegar, where the front doors opened straight onto the tramroad and road with no demarcation whatever between them. It had always been a black spot for accidents, and now the Company, acting – it was claimed – dictatorially and without parliamentary authority, had 'by altering the curves, destroyed the road altogether.' The black spot became yet blacker, and demands multiplied that the Company build a three-quarter-mile deviation for the tramroad to bypass the village.

In May 1858
> Two accidents happened on Wednesday, the 12th instant, on the old Sirhowy tramroad … A special engine went down to Blackwood, to

convey the parties to an inquest upon the body of Samuel Howells, killed the previous Saturday, on the same road. This train met with a goods train from Newport, and signalled to it to slacken speed, but the signal not being observed in time, the two trains ran into each other, and a tender was forced off the rails and right across the road. No-one was hurt in the accident, but the inquiry into the former one … elicited the fact that the deceased, finding himself short of fuel for his journey, went to another engine on the road, and began to supply himself with what was needful. While thus engaged, one of the engines was put in motion, and before he could place himself in a position of safety, he was crushed to death between the two. A verdict of 'Accidental Death' was returned. On the same day a cow, which had strayed on the line through some imperfect fence probably, was run down and killed.[186]

The inquest on Samuel Howells, who was killed on 8 May 1858, was the final straw. An immediate protest meeting was held in Blackwood, with a Tredegar representative present by invitation but who refused to listen. The villagers resolved to take the matter to court. That very evening another life was lost on the doorstep,[187] closely followed by the collision on the 12th.

At the resulting hearing in Chancery, Blackwood's counsel spoke forcefully

on the haughty disregard this company has shown of the rights and even the lives of the appellants in cutting up the old road and making a locomotive railway solely for their own convenience … To exhibit the reckless destruction of human life by the Company since they began to use fast locomotives, he quoted a very 'naive' affidavit of their own to the effect that only 28 persons had been killed since 1840, 26 of the cases being separate accidents resulting in death.

These twenty-eight deaths were surely on the Sirhowy Tramroad alone, not including the MRCC line. The Vice-Chancellor, convinced, granted an immediate injunction forbidding the Company to obstruct the road up the valley and to 'run locomotive engines at twenty miles an hour across parish and turnpike roads.' He directed the case to be heard at the next assizes.[188] But it never got there. An 'amicable settlement' was reached (one wonders how amicable it really was), because the Company was applying to Parliament for powers to carry out its works,

as it should have done before starting them. In 1859, after struggling through the Commons, the Bill was rejected by the Lords because it failed to protect the interests of Blackwood.[189] It was only in a second Bill of 1860, this time successful, that Blackwood's bypass was enshrined in law. But a year later work had still not begun, and a donkey and cart lost an argument with an engine.[190]

Meanwhile, in August 1858, 'the Bedwelty engine, belonging to the Tredegar Iron Company, which has already caused several deaths, has been the means of destroying again two victims.' At Argoed it lost the wrought-iron tyre from one of the tender wheels and 'the whole train ran over the embankment, and rolled to the bottom,' killing Abraham Richards its engineer (who left a wife and eight children) and Mary Lloyd, the landlady of the Argoed Arms, who was returning from Tredegar on a tram. Two more were injured.[191] Three newspapers carried restrained and factual reports, but the *Merthyr Telegraph* lashed out in its most purple prose.

An enormous monster, breathing fire and smoke through its nostrils, as did the relentless dragon slain by our patron saint of old [Monmouthshire, remember, though culturally Welsh, was then officially in England], and drinking the blood of the innocent, is ravaging the district of Blackwood. The name of our scourge is 'The Bedwellty,' and though the inhabitants have repeatedly done battle with him, they have been invariably defeated.

After describing the accident and naming the dead, it went on,

This awful monster had then devoured 12 human beings, and appeared to take no notice of his pursuers … One or two others were hurt by his headlong flight, amongst whom must not be forgotten a man who got his right leg broken for a second time, but as this happened to be a wooden one, he bore it most stoically … Arise, men of Monmouth, … stand forth and declare that this Sirhowy tramroad shall no longer be manured with the blood of our wives and children, – that our poor-house shall be no longer burdened with the victims of a selfish monopoly.

Yet within a year *Bedwellty*'s fatal score had grown by a further three. Once more the *Merthyr Telegraph* ranted, without giving further details, 'The waste of life on private railways is enormous. One engine alone on the Sirhowy line has killed

Fig. 2.17
Tredegar's *Bedwellty* in service on the standard gauge. (*Tasker 1992*)

15 persons. Three men in as many weeks have been destroyed.'[192]

The identity of a few of those whom *Bedwellty* had previously slaughtered, although the reports do not name the locomotive, may be guessed. In 1854 a man was

> engaged at Pill, attaching the engine to the columbuses of the Tredegar Company, when the bar which he carried, slipped under the place of fastening, and thus no check being placed on the motion of the advancing engine, it crushed him against the columbuses so frightfully, that he died on the following evening, of internal haemorrhage.

The inquest jury deplored 'there being no sufficient buffers to those carriages. If the man should fail exactly to fix the coupling bar of the engine, while it was in motion, he must be subjected to serious accident.'[193] Next year an engine was derailed on the Sirhowy and continued its journey on the ballast. A young man, no doubt the latchman,

> jumped off the front plate, ran about ten yards, and then fell down, when the engine passed over his body, killing him on the spot. The men belonging to the luggage-train, escaped with their lives, but all were more or less injured. The engine itself was but slightly damaged.[194]

And the year after that, an ostler at the Tredegar stables was crushed to death between two trams.[195]

Bedwellty the killer engine was adapted for the standard-gauge edge rail with which part of the line was laid about 1857; but until the rest of the tramroad was converted in perhaps 1859 it ran on combined wheels. At this sort of stage it was fitted with a heavy wooden buffer beam and spring buffers. It is said to have worked until about 1882, to be scrapped some years later (Figs. 2.17-19), although there may be confusion with *St David*.[196] By the time *Bedwellty* was photographed, if not from the beginning, it had a large dome which *St David* did not, and a Salter-type safety valve rather than the old weighted lever version. *Bedwellty* and *St David* are the only Ellis products traditionally said to have been converted for edge rail running, working at first on the revamped tramroad and, after the arrival of the Sirhowy Railway's own engines, presumably shunting at the ironworks. But we now know that *Tredegar* was also converted, and in 1862, as we saw, the works still had seven locomotives. Even in 1869 there were four carrying materials from one department of the workshops to another.[197] One suspects that several of the Ellis engines continued in this way, for purpose-built standard-gauge ones are not recorded at Tredegar until that same year of 1869.[198]

SPEEDWELL, 0-4-0 Neath Abbey 1830
HERCULES, six-wheel Neath Abbey 1831

(both ex-Thomas Prothero *c.*1835)

In addition to Tredegar's home-grown locomotives, there were two incomers to the Sirhowy. See under 2C.ii Thomas Prothero.

Fig. 2.18 *Bedwellty* in 1882. (*NMW, P77.5046*)

Fig. 2.19 *Bedwellty* derelict. (*Locomotive Magazine, Jan 1915, 11*)

2B ii. Argoed Colliery?

VULCAN, 2-2-0? Fenton, Murray & Co? 1831? (ex-Thomas Pearson 1842?)

Vulcan was the victim of an explosion at Blackwood in 1843 that was fully and widely reported.

On Saturday afternoon [22 April 1843], between five and six o'clock, a distressing accident occurred on the branch railway at Blackwood, a few miles from Newport, occasioned by the blowing up of a locomotive engine used on the line, by which two persons were killed, and two others seriously injured. The branch railway in question is the property of the Tredegar Iron Company … An engine called the Vulcan, with a train of waggons returning from Newport to the mines, stopped at Blackwood where the engine drivers and stokers got off, and went to the George public-house, which was opposite the railway, for refreshment. They had not been in the house many minutes before an explosion took place, which shook the entire village. The men, in rushing out, discovered that it was the engine on the line that had exploded, and in the carriage-road alongside of the railway, they saw two men who had been knocked down by the remnants of the boiler, which, together with the engine, was totally destroyed, and scattered several hundred feet from the place where the accident happened. One of the unfortunate persons was Mr Davis, a farmer, residing at Bultry [Buttry] Hatch, in Monmouthshire, who was in his 70th year, and the other proved to be Mr Philip Williams, a tradesman living at Blackwood. The latter was quite dead, part of the skull having been carried away, and Mr Davis, while the men were conveying him to a house in the neighbourhood, expired from the injuries he had sustained. Two other persons were afterwards discovered in a field near the railway, having been struck by pieces of the engine. They were immediately placed in safety; but it is supposed, from the extent of injuries they have received, it is impossible for them to recover. Great damage was done to several houses near the spot. All the window-frames in the George public-house were blown in, and part of the roof carried away; and the walls of the stables, and some cottages attached, were thrown down by the concussion. Some pieces of the boiler and engine were picked up nearly four hundred yards from the railway, and one was upwards of seven hundred. The explosion is reported to have resulted from the engine driver neglecting to open the valve, after shutting off the

steam, when getting off the engine. The loss of property, engine included, is estimated at 1000l at least.[199]

Another report adds that one man escaped 'who was actually sitting on the fore-plate of the Vulcan, when a large piece of the boiler flew over his head.' This was the latchman, whose occupational hazards will later come in for discussion. It also records that Samuel Homfray paid for repairing the damaged property, and that the engine was valued at £500. The inquest jury returned a verdict of accidental death.[200] This is a classic case which suggests the management winked at the common practice of the driver raising the pressure by tying down the safety valve while running and only releasing it when stopped. This time he failed to release it.

If *Vulcan*'s cause of death is clear, its identity is not.[201] Because the two accounts quoted above are independent of each other, the name must be accepted; but it is mentioned nowhere else, not even in Charles Ellis's various lists. The answer is probably that the engine was not part of Tredegar's ordinary stock, but belonged to a colliery beside the Sirhowy: it was travelling not to Tredegar but 'to the mines.' Argoed, which was owned by the Tredegar Iron Co and was probably the largest colliery feeding the Sirhowy, would fit the bill;[202] hence Homfray's payment of compensation and the engine's absence from Ellis's lists.

The Liverpool & Manchester's No. 19 was named *Vulcan*: a 2-2-0 of the Planet type (see Fig. 2.20) with 11in cylinders and 5ft driving wheels built in 1831 by Fenton Murray & Co of Leeds, subcontracting for Stephensons.[203] It was sold in 1841 for £399 to T. Pearson.[204] This was almost certainly Thomas Pearson of Hatfield Peverel in Essex, who was building a section of the Eastern Counties Railway. In 1842, having dissolved his partnership, he finished the contract, sold off the left-over materials, and in 1843 went bankrupt.[205] It is only supposition that he bought *Vulcan* and then sold it to Wales, but the circumstances fit.

It may seem strange that an industrial concern should buy so elderly (for those days) a locomotive, whose single pair of drivers of 5ft diameter would be much inferior in handling heavy loads compared to the Tredegar norm of six-coupled wheels of 3ft 6in. Yet the fact remains that Dowlais, whose requirements were closely similar, had in 1835 bought the ex-Liverpool & Manchester No. 20, *Etna*, a Planet type of 1831 virtually identical to *Vulcan* but built by

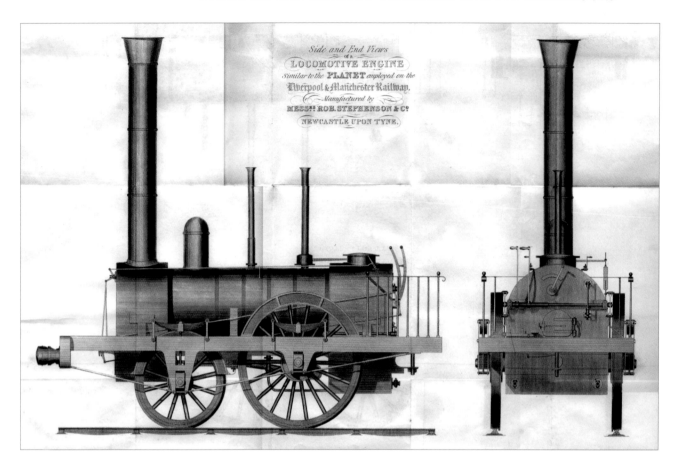

Side and End Views of a LOCOMOTIVE ENGINE similar to the PLANET employed on the Liverpool & Manchester Railway. Manufactured by MESS.RS ROB. STEPHENSON & C.O NEWCASTLE UPON TYNE.

Fig. 2.20
Stephenson's Planet type.
(*De Pambour 1836*)

Stephensons.[206] That these two sisters should finish their careers as near neighbours is no doubt the purest coincidence. There were in South Wales at least twelve further ex-main-line four-wheeled engines of 1830s vintage by Stephenson, Bury and the like – including two that we shall meet at Blaina, one on the MRCC, and four on the Rumney.[207]

Thomas Ellis senior's notebook contains an undated and unexplained entry:

'Stevinsons 10½ Inches D[iamete]r Cylinder 16 Inch Stroke. Boyler 6ft long 3ft 4in Dr. 90 Tubes 2 In Dr. Fire place 2ft 10 In by 2ft. Chimney 10 In Dr 8ft 10 In high above the Boiler. Main Wheel 5ft Dr Small Wheel 2ft 4 Inches Dr.'[208]

Of all early Stephensons, these dimensions most closely (but not exactly) match those of the four Rocket-type 0-2-2s built for the Liverpool & Manchester in 1830.[209] No. 2 *Arrow* and No. 3 *Meteor* were sold in 1840 and 1837 to unknown buyers; No. 4 *Dart* was broken up; and No. 5 *Comet* was sold in 1832 to William McKenzie the contractor.[210] There is no evidence whatever that any of them came Tredegar's way; and little likelihood either, for this class had even less power. Although Ellis's notes usually have a relevance to Tredegar, this one is probably a red herring, the details copied perhaps from an advertisement but not acted on.

For Ebbw Vale locomotives that operated on the Sirhowy Tramroad, see under Ebbw Vale, 2C iv.

2C WESTERN VALLEYS LINES

2C i. Blaina Iron Co

Unnamed, Blaina, 1830

The *Cambrian* reported in June 1830, after announcing the imminent arrival of Thomas Prothero's two locomotives, that 'Messrs Brown, of the Blaina Iron Works, have very nearly completed a locomotive engine for their own use, embracing many improvements, the particulars of which we shall be able to lay before our readers very shortly.'[211] Regrettably the newspaper failed to live up to its promise.

Little is therefore known of this engine. But it is clearly the one at which the MCC aimed its ban of August 1830 on unsprung locomotives. *Britannia*, *St David* and *Speedwell*, being sprung, were relatively innocent of smashing the tramplates, and the unsprung criminal must have been the Browns' first engine from Blaina. Thus in 1831 we find Thomas Brown writing an open letter to the MCC committee complaining that 'after our going to a considerable expense in providing tram carriages and a locomotive engine to travel your road, we were driven from it.' As a result their iron, instead of going out south down the MCC's Aberbeeg line, 'ascends a road with a heavy inclination above a mile [from Blaina to Nantyglo], then descends a steep line of road to the Canal,'[212] which would be either Bailey's Govilon Tramroad or, with a transshipment, the Clydach Railroad. The reason was surely the ban on their engine due to its lack of springs.

In view of the Browns' deep involvement in Richard Trevithick's 1804 locomotive, which was also unsprung, one wonders how closely their 1830 engine resembled it in other respects. Its boiler does indeed seem, like the Nantyglo engine of 1814, to have owed some inspiration to Trevithick. In 1837 his son Francis, as a young man of 25, spent some time at Tredegar, and said, as recorded by Francis Pettit Smith in 1862, that 'he made a great many Locomotive Engines on his Father's principle at the Tredegar Valley Iron works 25 to 30 years ago – at least a dozen of them were at work there.'[213] If correctly recorded – and Smith very likely misunderstood or misquoted him – this is a preposterous exaggeration because at best, as we shall see, Trevithick did no more than rebuild one engine. But while he was there he met William Brown of Blaina, and in 1840-1,

when beginning to take an interest in his father's career, he tried fruitlessly to get in touch again in order to ransack Brown's memory. He recalled that

> When I saw Mr Brown he was looking at the boiler of a Locomotive in which he had placed I think 5 tubes. He remarked that though a great many locomotives had been made since my Father's (for then all the iron works of any importance used them – I think the works I had to do with [Tredegar] had ½ Score) except that my Father proposed three tubes in his boiler and the one he [Brown] then looked at had 5 tubes.[214]

This somewhat incoherent record is referring to Richard Trevithick's patent of 1802, which embraced a boiler with double return flues or breeches tubes or, as Francis summarised it,

> a cylinder of wrought iron with flat ends, having three internal wrought-iron tubes. The fire-place is in the lower of the tubes, which tube extends the length of the boiler, and returns to the fire-door end as a double tube, where it joins the wrought-iron chimney.

This double return-flue arrangement was actually applied in Trevithick's London steam carriage of 1803, of whose boiler a contemporary drawing survives (Fig. 2.21),[215] and arguably, as we have seen, in the Penydarren engine of 1804 as well. In the Browns' engine, then, the flue returned similarly but as a quadruple rather than a double tube. This was perhaps one of the 'many improvements' mentioned by the newspaper. The same principle was also suggested for locomotives by the Scottish marine engineers David, James

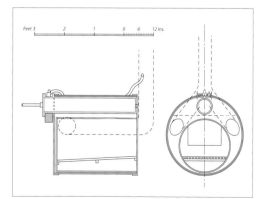

Fig. 2.21
Simon Goodrich's drawing of the boiler of Trevithick's London steam carriage in Mar/Apl 1803. Note the large fireplace and the two oval return flues uniting at the chimney foot.
(*Forward 1921*)

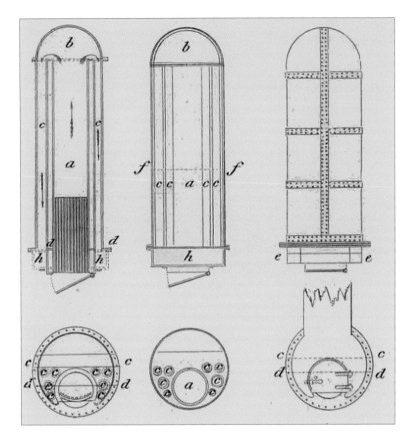

Fig. 2.22

Napier boiler, 1831.

a, firebox and flue;

b, receiver in domed boiler

end; *c*, return tubes;

h, smokebox.

(Repertory of Patent

Inventions 12 (1831), pl. v)

and William Napier in their patent of 1831 (Fig. 2.22), with about eight tubes — the number was optional — returning to a smokebox at the fireplace end from which the single chimney rose. The return tubes in the earliest Napier marine boilers of 1831-2 were 4in in diameter by 8ft long, or 5in by 9ft.[216] The idea was also applied from 1831 by Timothy Hackworth to his Wilberforce class on the Stockton & Darlington but in extreme form, with about a hundred return tubes.[217] This Hackworth version was devised independently of the Napiers'. We may guess, but do not know, that the Browns' boiler was devised independently too; and as we saw there is the possibility that it was already present in the Nantyglo rack locomotive.

Unnamed, Blaina, 1833

In 1833, 'Messrs Browne and Son, of the Blaina Iron Works, have, during the past week, put in motion one of the most complete steam carriages that has been seen in Monmouthshire. It will convey from the works to Newport 30 tons of iron per day.'[218] One presumes that this second engine had springs and that the first engine of 1830 had by now been given them. One also

suspects that both had been withdrawn from service by 1843 when there were 'only two parties who at present use locomotive engines in Monmouthshire [namely Tredegar and Ebbw Vale], with the exception of the Rhymney Iron Co.'[219]

No. 1 and No. 2, 2-2-0 Bury 1838, ex LNWR 1848

These were bought by Blaina from the LNWR (Southern Division) in probably March 1848, having originally been London & Birmingham Nos. 5 and 9 (Fig. 2.23). The LNWR valued them at £300 and £500 respectively but sold them as a pair for £1050. The cylinders were 12 by 18in, the wheels 5ft 6in and 4ft.[220] In 1849 they were described as 'old engines'[221] and are included in Simmons' list. They worked on plateway wheels until the MRCC took over locomotive haulage, and perhaps continued as yard engines thereafter.

2C ii. Thomas Prothero, freighter

Once Forman and Homfray had set the ball rolling with their Newcastle-built locomotives in 1829, Welsh engineers and further industrialists took up the challenge. One was Thomas Prothero (1780-1853), an energetic lawyer and coal-owner, Town Clerk of Newport, a man who, with a finger in every imaginable pie, was of high local influence. In June 1830 the *Cambrian* announced,

> Arrangements have recently been made by the Monmouthshire Canal Company for adopting their existing lines of Tram-road, for the use of Locomotive Engines, which are likely to become general in that district, and that nearly 1000 tons of tram-plates are now manufacturing for that purpose, at the Coalbrook Vale and Nant-y-Glo Iron Works.—Mr Prothero, one of the most extensive coal merchants in that neighbourhood, intends hauling his coal to Newport with two engines, preparing for him at Neath Abbey Iron Works.[222]

***SPEEDWELL*, 0-4-0 Neath Abbey 1830**

Next month the *Cambrian* reported the debut of the first of these two locomotives.

> The engine made by them [Neath Abbey] was landed on Mr. Prothero's wharf on the 16th instant, and on Tuesday last twenty tram-waggons, weighing fifteen tons, were attached to it, which it drew with the greatest ease, at the rate of four miles an

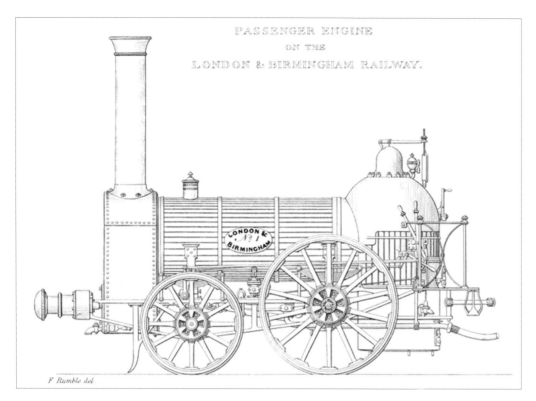

F. Rumble del.

Fig. 2.23
London & Birmingham
Railway Bury-type
passenger engine.
(*Whishaw 1842, Pl. 6*)

hour, up the tram road to Mr. Prothero's colliery, called Blaencyffin Isha [near Llanhilleth north of Crumlin], where twenty tram-waggons loaded with coal were attached to it, which it hauled with the like ease that it took up the empty tram-waggons, and returned to Mr. Prothero's wharf with its burthen in twelve hours from the time that it started from thence in the morning. The coal being heaped high above the side boards of the tram-waggons, and the road having several sharp angles, made it prudent to proceed slowly, but the engine is capable of moving with as much rapidity as any engine that has yet been made. The distance from the wharf to the colliery and back again is thirty miles, the weight of the coal was fifty tons and a half and the weight of the coal, tram-waggons, and tender, exceeded seventy tons. In the whole journey there was no want of steam, though the engine was retarded upwards of three hours on the journey by horse-teams, and other extrinsic impediments. On Friday, the 23rd instant, it performed the same task in the same time … The result of this experiment will prove of great advantage to Mr Prothero and other persons who are, like him, large freighters on the tram-roads, who may choose to avail themselves of it, as the substitution of Messrs Price's Locomotive Engines for horse power, will affect a saving in the expense of hauling to the amount of nearly 50 per cent. To accomplish the task performed by the Engine in one day, requires the labour of six horses two days.[223]

Prothero, with his many coal pits, was the largest freighter on the Western Valleys lines, in 1849 owning 550 trams. His locomotives were shedded at his 'engine yard' at Pillgwenlly.[224]

Speedwell, the first locomotive built by Neath Abbey, was a simple four-wheeler with vertical cylinders 10½ by 24in driving upwards, return connecting rods, bell cranks, and wheels 3ft 6in in diameter. The general arrangement drawings (Fig. 2.24), no doubt representing various stages in its gestation, have differences between plan and elevation in the exhaust and the safety valve, and the engraved version is slightly different again (Fig. 2.25).[225] The cylinders had metallic packing (Fig. 2.26).[226] The bell cranks, intended to avoid the pitching and hammer-blows on the track of which ordinary vertical-cylinder engines were guilty, were fairly clearly inspired by Braithwaite and Ericsson's *Novelty* which had introduced this form of drive at the Rainhill trials of October 1829. Neath Abbey had a representative there in the person of Henry Habberley Price, one of its partners.[227] Within a month or so, before details of the competing locomotives had been published, the ironworks offered the Liverpool & Manchester an engine it was building 'on Braithwaite and Ericsson's plan, but with alterations and improvements.'[228] Nor was Neath Abbey the only local party interested in the trials. William Crawshay II of Cyfarthfa was tempted to enter a locomotive, and he too offered

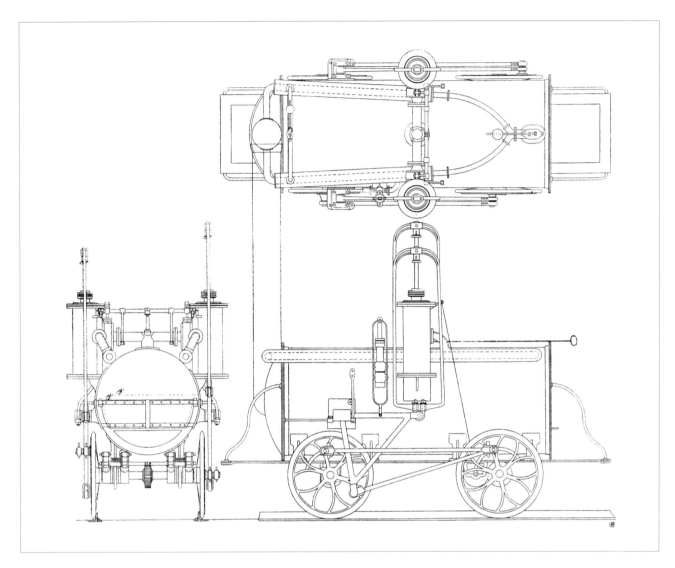

Fig. 2.24
Prothero's *Speedwell*,
Neath Abbey 1830.
(*Dendy Marshall 1937, 130,
after drawing in WGAS*)

Fig. 2.25 *Speedwell.*
(*Engineering, 15 Nov 1867*)

one to the Liverpool & Manchester.[229]

The engine that Neath Abbey then had on the stocks, although its similarity to *Novelty* hardly extended beyond the bell cranks, was surely what became *Speedwell*, the drawings for which run from December 1829.[230] The very wide fire door suggests that the boiler had twin fireplaces whose flues then united before uniting in a single chimney on the centre line. This was a breeches boiler (as distinct from the reverse arrangement, a breeches tube), precisely as found on the Stephensons' *Lancashire Witch* of 1828.[231] Very likely Price, during his visit north to Rainhill, had included an inspection of the Bolton & Leigh. Thus, if the Browns' engine incorporated a touch of Trevithick, *Speedwell*'s design incorporated not only a touch of Braithwaite and Ericsson but a touch of Stephenson too. A later drawing of *Speedwell*, undated but probably of the mid-1830s, shows a new boiler, 11ft long, with a corrugated firebox (for which see Ebbw Vale's *Abbey* below, 2.C.iv) and 33 tubes.[232]

Curiously, *Speedwell* had no crossheads or guides for the piston rods, and the steam discharged from its safety valve was fed into the main exhaust pipes, which would reduce noise that might frighten nearby horses but would make the engine steam even harder when blowing off. It might be thought that the MCC's ban of August 1830 on engines without springs was aimed at *Speedwell*, for the side elevation shows none; but they are undoubtedly present on the end elevation. Its tender, however, was unsprung and, as was the case with many trams, its wheels were splayed or inclined outwards (Fig. 2.27).[233]

But Prothero's early optimism proved sadly unfounded.

> Mr Prothero, a large coal-shipper, who purchased two excellent locomotives from the Neath Abbey Company, worked them upon the Monmouthshire Canal Company's tram-roads, and after losing a considerable sum of money by using them, found it more economical, again to resort to horse labour.[234]

Thus in about 1835 he sold his engines to Tredegar where they left their mark. In 1838 'Isaac Thomas [driver], H. Harris [fireman] and Evan Jones [latchman], belonging to the "Speedwell" locomotive engine of the Tredegar Iron Works,' ran into a mare and broke its legs, for which Samuel Homfray personally paid compensation.[235] And Ellis senior records that on 2 January 1840 *Speedwell* was given a new safety valve.[236] Thereafter it is heard of no more.

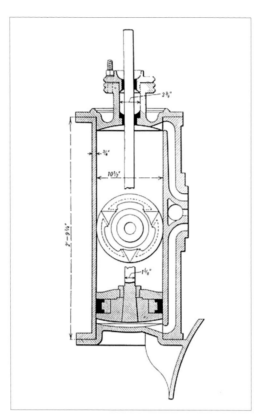

Fig. 2.26
Speedwell's cylinder.
(*Dendy Marshall 1937, 131, after drawing in WGAS*)

Fig. 2.27
Speedwell's tender.
(*WGAS, D/D NAI L/37/5*)

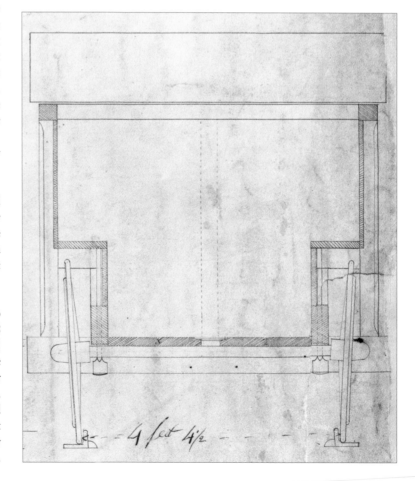

HERCULES, six-wheel Neath Abbey 1831

This is a difficult engine to interpret from the few drawings, which suggest a design date of February-March 1831. It had six double-sprung wheels (that is, with two pairs of springs per axle) and 10½in cylinders; but at that point certainty ends. One partial drawing has an extraordinary arrangement of the wheels: the front and back ones – surely the drivers – are 3ft 6in in diameter but the centre ones only 3ft 1in, the wheelbase being 7ft. Alongside is a plan of curved track of about 27ft 6in radius to the centre line (Fig. 2.28).[237] If the rail gauge was narrowed at this point, the front and rear wheels would run close to the edge of the plates but, with care, all would be well. Perhaps this design was replaced by a more conventional one before it left the drawing board. The drive has been implausibly seen as a bell crank, which would make *Hercules* a larger version of *Speedwell*.[238] But now we have better information.

Francis Trevithick records in his biography of his father that 'in 1837 the writer lived near this engine [Tredegar puddling mill], and frequently saw it at work; the blast was as useful as in the locomotives then in the writer's charge.' Again, 'he at the same time renewed a long-idle early locomotive on Trevithick's plan, that had been built by Neath Abbey. The double or breeches fire-tube in the boiler was removed to make room for thirty small tubes, such as were then coming into use for locomotive boilers.'[239] Trevithick clearly means not a a double fireplace with single flue as on *Lancashire Witch* and as we suspect on *Speedwell*, but a double return flue as on his father's London steam carriage.[240] The date of a note on its safety valve by Ellis senior, 'the Hercules Steam Clack Apl 1837,' chimes well with a boiler revamped in that year.[241] In 1841 Trevithick elaborated further.

When in Wales I met with a locomotive which was made at Neath Abbey and had been thrown aside perhaps some years because it would not work. Outside cylinders, horizontal, fixed nearly on a level with the top of the boiler, a vertical beam, and the connecting rod joining a pin on the outside face of the driving wheel. The boiler had a tube I think about 12 inches diameter passing from the fire place to the end of the boiler and turning returned again to the fire end to the chimney. This engine in its main features was but a follower of the original one [i.e. Penydarren]. The boiler was the defective part. I took out the two wro[ugh]t iron tubes and substituted about 30 2¾ or 3 inch brass tubes with some other alterations and the engine did very well. We used her for jobing [*sic*] about the furnace yard, going from 6 to 12 miles per hour on tram plates, burning coal.

Fig. 2.28

Prothero's *Hercules*, Neath Abbey 1831. (*WGAS, D/D NAI L/38/7*)

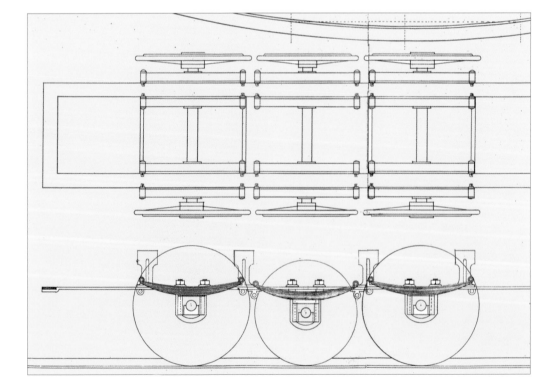

His letter included a small sketch:[242]

In 1831 Neath Abbey gave up single-flue and return-flue boilers in favour of multi-tubular ones; and, of their three previous locomotives for the 4ft 4in gauge built in 1830-1, both *Speedwell* and Ebbw Vale's *Lark* had bell cranks. This leaves *Hercules* as the only known candidate for the return-flue rocker-beam engine described by Francis Trevithick. As far as can be told, it was the first application of such a drive to any locomotive anywhere, but unlike later examples it had the chimney at the cylinder end because of the return flue. If the wheel arrangement of the Neath Abbey drawing was proceeded with, we have the strange set-up of smaller carrying wheels between the outer driven wheels, which would presumably be classified as 0-2-2-2-0. I know of no British parallel, although Jules Petiet tried some 0-2-6-2-0s on the Chemin de Fer du Nord in 1862, without success. On the matter of fuel, no doubt all the early Welsh-built locomotives were coal-burners, but probably all those in the Monmouthshire valleys by English makers, including *Britannia*, burnt coke.

Thus, as rebuilt by Trevithick, *Hercules* returned to work. Two years later it was in a different sort of trouble: 'To damage sustained by Hercules Engine 1839.'[243] It had evidently run into a horse-drawn tram, and it cost £5 1s 6½d to repair the horse, its harness, and the shafts. The accident apparently happened near Bassaleg (that is at Pye Corner, the junction with the Rumney Railway), which suggests that *Hercules*' duties were not limited to shunting in the yard.

2C iii. Martin Morrison, freighter

Morrison, of Crumlin and Newport, was proprietor of a number of collieries and like Prothero a major freighter on the MCC: in 1849 he had 250 trams.

Unnamed, 0-6-0 Neath Abbey 1832

The few drawings of parts are all dated November 1832,[244] and there is an engraved general arrangement of an engine of 1832 which is very likely Morrison's (Fig. 2.29).[245] It was another rocker-beam with 10½in cylinders, closely similar (but not identical) to Ebbw Vale's *Perseverance*, of

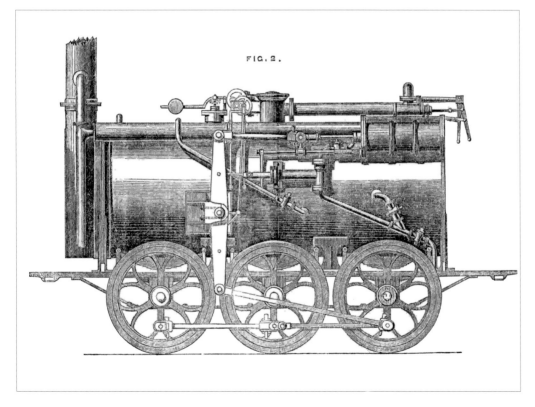

Fig. 2.29
Morrison's Neath Abbey rocker-beam engine, 1832. (*Engineering, 15 Nov 1867*)

which more shortly. It had a hinged chimney, which implies that it had to pass under a bridge. At this date overbridges were rare on tramroads, only two being known in the Western Valleys: the Big Bridge at Ebbw Vale and a cast-iron one at Coalbrookvale on the Aberbeeg Tramroad which was too low for locomotives without lowering chimneys.[246] By 1849 Morrison owned no locomotives, and it may well be this engine that was up for sale in 1836 at Nantyglo,[247] near which Morrison had a colliery (Fig. 2.30)[248] With 10½ in cylinders it was surely by Neath Abbey. Nothing more can be said with any certainty, but conceivably it was bought by Ebbw Vale and named *Abbey* (see 2C iv. below), just as Prothero's engines were bought by Tredegar.

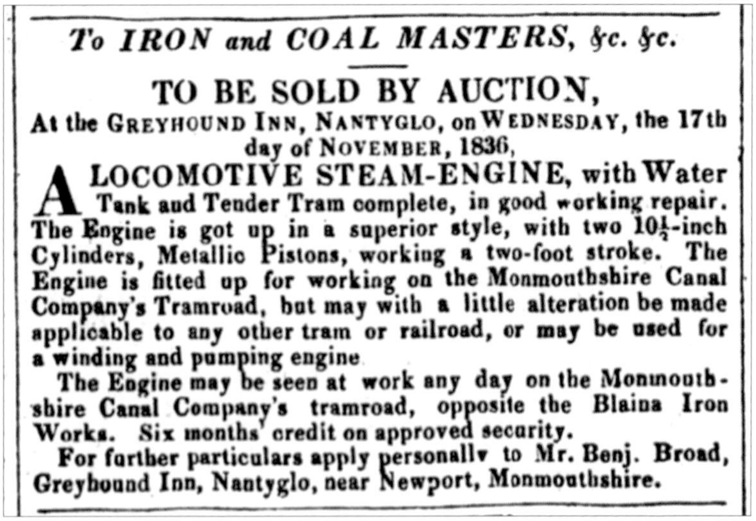
To IRON and COAL MASTERS, &c. &c.

TO BE SOLD BY AUCTION,

At the GREYHOUND INN, NANTYGLO, on WEDNESDAY, the 17th day of NOVEMBER, 1836,

A LOCOMOTIVE STEAM-ENGINE, with Water Tank aud Tender Tram complete, in good working repair. The Engine is got up in a superior style, with two 10½-inch Cylinders, Metallic Pistons, working a two-foot stroke. The Engine is fitted up for working on the Monmouthshire Canal Company's Tramroad, but may with a little alteration be made applicable to any other tram or railroad, or may be used for a winding and pumping engine.

The Engine may be seen at work any day on the Monmouthshire Canal Company's tramroad, opposite the Blaina Iron Works. Six months' credit on approved security.

For further particulars apply personally to Mr. Benj. Broad, Greyhound Inn, Nantyglo, near Newport, Monmouthshire.

Fig. 2.30
Sale advertisement, perhaps for Morrison's engine.
(*Cambrian, 12 Nov 1836*)

2C iv. Harford Brothers / Harford Davies & Co / Ebbw Vale Iron Co

The evidence for Ebbw Vale's engines is disappointingly scanty. The first arrived in 1831. But whereas for most other concerns a reasonably complete list can be worked out with fair confidence, that is not the case here. The works had no dominant figure such as Tredegar had in Thomas Ellis, nor a dutiful son like Charles Ellis to blow his trumpet for him; and the Neath Abbey collection is meagre, *Perseverance* apart, in its Ebbw Vale drawings.[249]

LARK, 0-6-0? Neath Abbey 1831 or 1832

Little is known. The few Neath Abbey drawings that belong to it are dated from November 1830 to July 1831,[250] and from a number of components it shared with the slightly later Gloucester & Cheltenham's *Royal William* of 1832, (Fig. 2.31) it seems clear that it too was an 0-6-0 with bell-crank drive and cylinders 10½ by 24in. How long it lasted, we cannot tell.

HAWK, 0-6-0 Neath Abbey 1832?

There seems to be only one relevant Neath Abbey drawing, undated, for the frame of an 0-6-0 with cylinders probably 10½ by 24in and 3ft 9in wheels.[251] But when the Bodmin & Wadebridge Railway's second locomotive, *Elephant*, was on order in 1835, Nathaniel Tregelles Price of Neath Abbey drafted specifications for its boiler, which was to be 12ft by 4ft 6in.

> The firebox and tubes to be constructed in a very similar manner to that of the locomotive engine called the 'Hawk' belonging to Harfords Davis and Company of Ebbw Vale but the tubes are to be copper 2½ inches diameter ⅛ inch thick and 18 to 20 inches long ... screwed into the bottom of fire tube (Fig. 2.32).[252]

Hawk too clearly resembled *Royal William*, both in its bell-crank drive and in its vertical water tubes, seventy in number.[253] Vertical water tubes have the advantage over horizontal ones in being less prone to collect sediment. No exact date is known, other than that it must be 1835 or earlier. One suspects that, like *Royal William*, it was 1832. It was reportedly still at work in 1849.[254]

In 1818, as we saw, the Ebbw Vale and the Sirhowy Ironworks, on either side of the ridge between the Ebbw Fawr and Sirhowy Rivers, came together under the ownership of the Harfords. For smelting, each was self-sufficient, but at no stage did Sirhowy manufacture wrought iron. The two works therefore operated in tandem, linked by the circuitous Rassa Railroad and, perhaps from 1818,[255] by a new but still circuitous private line. The natural route to Newport for iron made at Ebbw Vale was down the MCC Western Valleys line past Crumlin, and that for Sirhowy iron, as had been the case before the Harfords took over, was down the Sirhowy Tramroad.

In 1832, in order to circumvent the roundabout route, a mile-long tunnel was completed through the ridge.[256] This may have been the work of Zephaniah Williams, later of Chartist fame, who was the Harfords' mineral agent at the time.[257] Both portals are now buried,[258] but at the Ebbw Vale end the keystone bore the inscription 'James

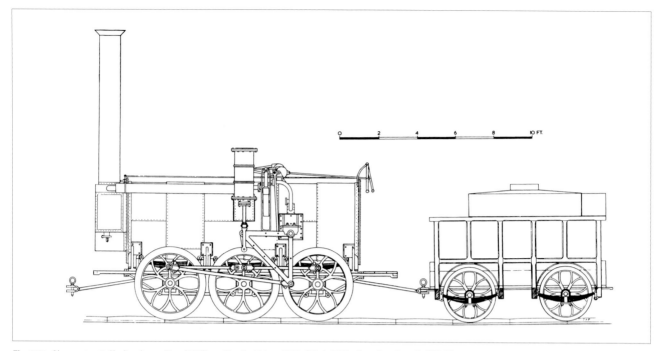

Fig. 2.31 Gloucester & Cheltenham, *Royal William*, Neath Abbey 1832. (*Bick 1987, after drawings in WGAS*)

Harford Tunnel. 1832.' The new route made it easy to transport Sirhowy pigs to Ebbw Vale for processing and to bring finished products back for export; although, the connecting line being of 2ft 9in gauge, anything that came back through the tunnel had to be transshipped to the 4ft 4in. But this manoeuvre was now feasible again because the Sirhowy Iron Company – meaning the Harfords – had at last made its peace with Tredegar and the Sirhowy Tramroad Company, and the rail link from Sirhowy to Tredegar had been restored.

According to the Act of 1802, the tramroad company had to charge tolls at no less than the current rate on the MCC lines, which fluctuated according to the market price of iron and coal and to what the canal company thought it could get away with. Thus in 1831, a time of depression in trade, the MCC – and therefore the Sirhowy – charged 1½d per ton per mile for coal, compared to 1d on the Rumney and many other tramroads, much to the disgust of the freighters.[259] But in 1833 the Sirhowy Iron Co negotiated lower rates for itself on the Sirhowy Tramroad. The MCC, claiming that this infringed the Act, applied to the courts for an injunction, but the case was dropped following an agreement whereby the Sirhowy Tramroad repaid the MCC £1,250 in tolls.[260] By 1843 a good half of Ebbw Vale iron was going out down the Sirhowy,[261] all of it hauled by Ebbw Vale locomotives.

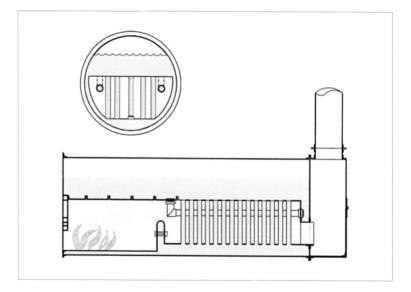

Thus we find in Ellis senior's notes, 'March 1st 1833 the two Ebb [*sic*] Vale Engines first began to work on Tredegar Road,'[262] and they rapidly made their presence felt. A few weeks later a young man with the resounding name of Zorobabel Jenkins was travelling from Sirhowy to Newport on an Ebbw Vale locomotive when he slipped off and was killed by the trams.[263] A few months later still,

As one of the steam-engines belonging to Messrs Harford was proceeding with its train of carriages through Tredegar Park on Friday last, from some

Fig. 2.32
Boiler of Bodmin & Wadebridge *Elephant*, closely similar to that of Ebbw Vale's *Hawk*. (*John Stengelhofen, after drawings in WGAS*)

cause or other, it tilted over and was precipitated over the precipice with great violence into the park. One of the men sustained considerable injury, but it is hoped not to be of sufficient extent to endanger his life. The steam carriage is, as may be naturally expected from a heavy body being thrown from such a height, much fractured.[264]

In 1835 there were still two Ebbw Vale engines on the Sirhowy.[265] At this early stage we do not know which they were – in 1843 the works had six,[266] some of which continued to use the MCC line – but before long two names are recorded.

PERSEVERANCE, 0-6-0 Neath Abbey 1832

Many – maybe all – of the Ebbw Vale engines were built by Neath Abbey; it was by no means uncommon for one Quaker firm to give discounts to another. This engine, originally intended to be called *Industry*, was renamed during construc-

tion, just as Dowlais' *Success* was confusingly renamed *Perseverance* at the same time. Curiously, *Perseverance* was the motto of the Sirhowy Tramroad Co. The boiler had a domed front but was surely multi-tubular (Fig. 2.33).[267] As on *Hercules* the cylinders, 10½ by 24in,[268] were mounted horizontally high on the boiler, and via a rocker beam they drove six-coupled wheels 3ft 9in in diameter. The chimney was hinged for lowering; not for the tunnel to Sirhowy for which, even with the chimney down, the engine was much too big, but probably to pass under the Big Bridge at Ebbw Vale. *Perseverance* was the first of what seems to have become almost a standard class of Neath Abbey 0-6-0 rocker-beam engines with wheels 3ft 9in or 3ft 10in in diameter, to which we may also assign Morrison's engine already described, Ebbw Vale's *Abbey* next to be discussed, Victoria's *Alert* of 1841 (2C v.), Rhymney Iron Co's *Bute* and *Rhymney* of 1839 (2D ii.), and the mysterious *Goliath* of 1846 (2E).

Fig. 2.33

Ebbw Vale's *Perseverance*, Neath Abbey 1832. (*WGAS, D/D NAI L/27/6*)

Perseverance is recorded in only one accident, in 1836 when 'the engine tender, with the Perseverance locomotive, of Ebbw Vale Works, fell off the carriage, by Sirhowy mill farm, near Tredegar,' and lost a leg.[269]

From 1831 Ebbw Vale had a locomotive shed at Newport,[270] which may account for a complaint in 1847 that in the unlighted George Street the public was in danger after dark from 'two powerful engines' belonging to Ebbw Vale.[271] Perhaps they were on their way home to bed, for it seems that night running was in general discouraged.[272] They were maintained at the works, with spares supplied from Neath Abbey.[273]

ABBEY, 0-6-0 Neath Abbey 1836?

Despite three contemporary records, there is some uncertainty about this engine. In 1839 three Bedwellty men were taken to court for assaulting its Ebbw Vale crew – David Morris, Daniel Roberts and William Thomas – on the footplate. The attack took place when they were 'about four miles from Tredegar, while in charge of the Abbey engine, the property of Messrs Harford and Co.' The offenders were sent to gaol.[274]

Then on 9 April 1841

the boiler of one of the locomotive engines, plying between Tredegar and Newport, and belonging to Messrs Harford, Davies & Co. of Ebbw Vale Iron Works, burst when passing the Tredegar furnaces, and instantly killed the engineman, who was standing before the fire-place, and severely scalded another person who was standing with him at the time. The unfortunate deceased whose name was David Morris, had wedged down the safety valve of the engine, with the view of getting up sufficient steam to take the load up the inclined plane, leading to Sirhowy Works, at once, instead of performing two journeys as usual. The boiler, although of a very superior construction, could not bear the additional pressure, which was supposed from the time, to have attained about 700lbs on the square inch, burst into the fireplace, and blew the tender backward, tearing the hook asunder of an inch and a half in diameter, which connected it to the engine. The reaction of the steam jerked the whole body of the engine forward the almost incredible distance of 50 yards, clear of the ground, testifying too plainly to the enormous pressure which had then madly been got up, and a melancholy warning to others, who almost daily jeopardise their lives in a similar manner.[275]

This was the fourth burst boiler on the tramroad in eleven years, and two years later the score had grown to six. In order to tackle the final gradient without splitting the train, it was common practice to build up pressure, if necessary by abusing the safety valve. David Morris had driven for Ebbw Vale for five years and the *Abbey* had been his engine two years earlier; so it was evidently *Abbey* that exploded. Five years back from 1841 takes us to 1836, and this may hint that *Abbey* was new in that year. There is indeed a small handful of Neath Abbey drawings dated 1836 which seem to refer to an 0-6-0,[276] but there is no certainty.

David Morris's father protested at the accusation of recklessness:

Finding that the engine was not in a proper state of repair, the wheels and springs especially, the deceased and his surviving brother made repeated complaints to Mr Godfray [Ebbw Vale's engineer], that they were afraid an accident would occur from its dilapidated state. Mr G. then remarked it would last another fortnight, when another engine should be procured.

For his pains, David Morris had been given a month's notice. But there was a witness, the father added without further detail, who could testify that his son had not tampered with the safety valve.[277]

We last meet the *Abbey* in 1849 when Captain J. L. A. Simmons of the Railway Inspectorate was conducting trials on the MCC's Western Valleys line. One of the locomotives he employed was Ebbw Vale's *Abbey*. It was described as Neath Abbey-built, six-coupled with cylinders 10¼ (surely a mistake for 10½, the Neath Abbey standard) by 24in, wheels 3ft 10in, weight 13 tons, and pressure 65 psi.[278]

An engraving of the boiler of a Neath Abbey engine of about 1836 – by no means necessarily of this engine or even of an Ebbw Vale one – is worth including (Fig. 2.34). There are 22

Fig. 2.34
Neath Abbey boiler with corrugated firebox crown. (*Engineering, 15 Nov 1867*)

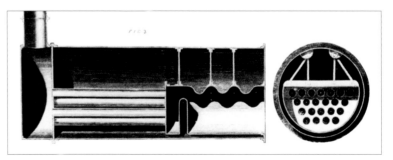

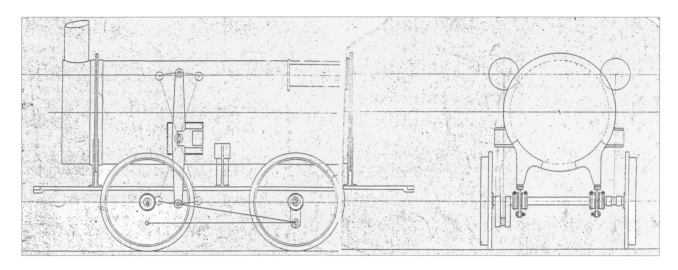

Fig. 2.35
Sirhowy yard engine,
Neath Abbey 1832.
(*WGAS, D/D NAI L/53/66,
53/55*)

horizontal fire tubes and a corrugated crownsheet to the firebox, a feature intended to stiffen a thin plate. Structurally it would work well, but sediment collecting in the corrugations would cause overheating, and apart from the reboilered *Speedwell* and *Royal William* no other Neath Abbey engine is known to have had it. There is also a midfeather forming a small combustion chamber between firebox and rear tube plate. Weaver wonders if its purpose was to improve the combustion of the volatiles driven off from a coal fire, a pioneering precursor of the brick arch of later locomotives.[279]

Fig. 2.36
Ebbw Vale-Sirhowy tunnel,
Ebbw Vale portal.
(*Jones 1971, 23*)

Sirhowy yard engine, 0-4-0 Neath Abbey 1832

This was another Neath Abbey engine with rocker beam, built according to the drawings of January-May 1832 for the Sirhowy Iron Co rather than the usual Harford Davies & Co, which must locate it on the Sirhowy side of the ridge (Fig. 2.35). It was of 6hp with very small cylinders (about 7 by 16in) and the cranks positioned between the wheels and the frames.[280] Being four- rather than six-wheeled and with cylinders so small, this was surely not for 'main line' use but a yard shunter, the counterpart of Tredegar's later *Dispatch*. The 'combined' wheels of 3ft 1¾in overall diameter were designed for use on either plate or edge rail, in the former case running on the wheel flange. This feature will be discussed, along with comparable devices, in Part 3.

Tunnel engine, 0-4-0 Neath Abbey 1832, 2ft 9in gauge (2F i. in Locomotive Summary)

The tramroad through the new tunnel was narrow gauge (Fig. 2.36), and Neath Abbey designed for Harford Davies & Co a small 6-hp four-coupled locomotive with combined wheels 3ft 1in in diameter that once again could run either on plate or edge rails. There are two drawings. One, of 31 December 1831, is in outline only, but includes the profile of the tunnel, 8ft wide and 8ft high, which gives very generous clearance. It notes that the engine was to be delivered in three months and gives the gauge as 'Breth of the Road outside the Creas 2 feet 9' (Fig. 2.37). This was surely written by someone from Tyneside, where crease meaning flange was standard parlance, but is recorded nowhere else in South Wales. The boiler was to be multi-tubular, for it had a smokebox from which twin chimneys, 17ft 5in high, could fold down as on Dowlais' *Perseverance*; and the horizontal cylinders, once again about 7 by 16in, were to be inside the frames and under the footplate.[281] The other drawing is fully worked up and marginally different in detail (Fig. 2.38).[282] It shows how the connecting rod to the cranked front axle was hooped to clear the rear axle.

There is a single drawing of a new design, undated but surely of 1832, which shows another four-coupled 6hp engine with cylinders about 7 by 16in, but for plate rails only and with a rocker beam (Fig. 2.39). It closely resembled the yard engine of the same date but differed somewhat in dimensions, and the drive was as usual outside the wheels, not inside. The single chimney, 15ft 9in high above the rails, was hinged, and a rod into the smokebox perhaps operated the damper.[283] If

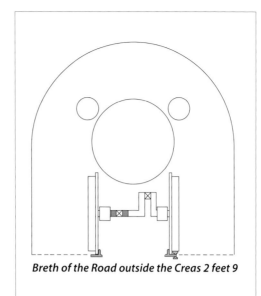

Breth of the Road outside the Creas 2 feet 9

Fig. 2.37
Ebbw Vale tunnel locomotive, Neath Abbey 1831 design, end elevation. (*after drawing in WGAS*)

Fig. 2.38
Ebbw Vale tunnel locomotive, Neath Abbey. 1831 design, plan and side elevation. (*WGAS, D/D NAI L/58/3*)

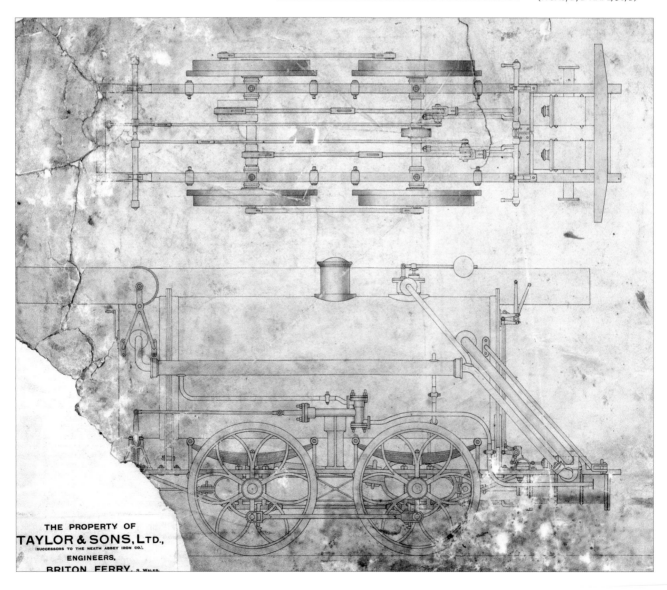

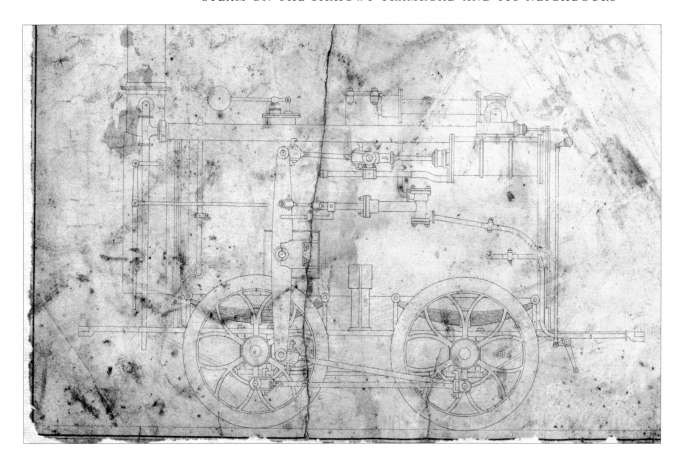

Fig. 2.39

Ebbw Vale tunnel
locomotive, Neath Abbey,
1832.
(*WGAS, D/D NAI L/28/6*)

the engine entered the tunnel with a full head of steam, the fire banked up and the damper closed, it should be capable of making the passage without running out of steam or asphyxiating the crew. This version, one presumes, was built, although there is no direct evidence; but it does make up the tally of six engines which Ebbw Vale had when put up for sale in 1844.

ALERT? 0-6-0, Neath Abbey 1841?

The bankrupt Ebbw Vale company, along with Sirhowy and Victoria, was bought in 1846 by the Darbys of Coalbrookdale. Simmons' list of 1849 still credits Ebbw Vale with six engines (those running on MRCC metals, not including the tunnel line). *Alert* is mentioned only once, as at work for Ebbw Vale in 1849,[284] and it is suggested below that it was acquired in 1846 with the Victoria Ironworks plant.

It is not clear when Ebbw Vale's use of the Sirhowy Tramroad came to an end. A further quarrel with the MRCC over the high level of tolls was patched up in 1852,[285] and next year some of its iron was still going down via Nine Mile Point.[286] But by 1859, with the MRCC lines

fully converted, Ebbw Vale's iron had left the Sirhowy, although coal traffic continued from Sirhowy's pits to the west of the ridge.[287]

2C v. Monmouthshire Iron & Coal Co, Victoria Ironworks

ALERT? 0-6-0, Neath Abbey 1841?

The upstart Victoria Ironworks founded in 1836 had its own engine by July 1843, when it was lent for trials to the MRCC;[288] and when next year the works were put up for sale it still had one locomotive and tender.[289] It does not however feature in Simmons' list of 1849. One therefore wonders if, under the name of *Alert*, it had by then passed into the hands of Ebbw Vale.

Nothing certain is known of it beyond the name. But in the Neath Abbey collection are a few drawings of components and a general arrangement, without place or customer's name (Fig. 2.40) but all dated 1841,[290] of another rocker-beam engine of 4ft 4in gauge and of the now familiar type with 10½in cylinders.[291] It was apparently identical to the engine of 1832 which we have attributed to Morrison on the Western

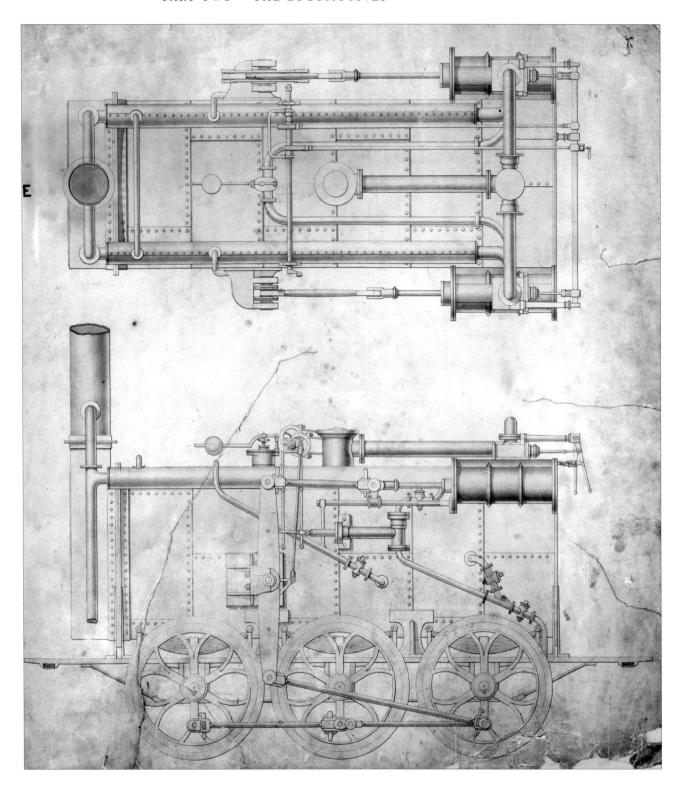

Valleys lines (see 2.C.iii), and quite possibly to other six-wheel rocker-beam locomotives of the standard class. The gauge puts it in either Taff Vale or the Western Valleys system, the latter being much the more likely. It is therefore suggested that it was Victoria's (and later Ebbw Vale's) *Alert*.

2C vi. Monmouthshire Railway & Canal Co

This particular tale, with the Western Valleys tramroads on the brink of becoming railways and their locomotives becoming more orthodox, is an appendix, almost, to the main story. Even

Fig. 2.40
Probably Victoria Iron Co's *Alert*, Neath Abbey 1841. (*WGAS, D/D NAI L63/2*)

before its creation in 1848, with the intention of handling all the haulage on the system from 1 August 1849, the MRCC ordered relatively straightforward locomotives, sixteen of which began life with plateway or at least combined wheels.[292] There were sheds for stabling and repair at Court y Bella and Aberbeeg.[293]

No. 1, *DOCTOR*, Grylls & Co 1847

The first of the MCC's locomotives was a product of Grylls and Stubbs of Llanelli, whose background is explored later under the Rumney Railway (Brithdir Colliery, 2.D.iii). No. 1 was an 0-8-0 tender engine with cylinders 16 by 16in and 3ft wheels, and a monster for its day: one 'of the largest and most powerful class of locomotives manufactured in Europe,' of which a further example was built in the same year for the Llanelly & Llandilo Railway.[294] These were the first eight-coupled engines in Britain, and the last until 1864.[295] When No. 1 was shipped from Llanelli on 19 October 1847,[296] it was reported that 'it is called the Newport,' perhaps the makers' shorthand for 'the engine for Newport.' By January 1848, however, it was sporting a new name, though it is far from obvious what had inspired it.

> A fine powerful eight wheel-engine, called the 'Doctor,' has recently arrived, and several experimental trips made from Newport to Nantyglo and Ebbw Vale. We are informed the results were highly satisfactory. Several other engines are expected shortly for the same purposes [i.e. to enable the MCC to become carriers].[297]

Satisfactory, as it turned out, was far from the appropriate word. *Doctor*'s weight of 20 tons (compared to about 13 tons for Ellis's Tredegar locomotives) was too great for the track, and its wheelbase of 9ft 6in (compared to *Britannia*'s 7ft 4in) too long for the curves. In the summer of 1848, Grylls and Co having by then gone bankrupt, it was sent to the Uskside Iron Co at Newport for various deficiencies to be put right at the substantial cost of £415. The verdict then was, 'She is of very rude construction and will always be attended with great expense to keep in working order; when she will work, she will take a very heavy load.'[298] But, fresh out of the shops, it instantly disgraced itself and sorely embarrassed the MCC committee who were on a tour of inspection. As James Brown put it, in his self-appointed role as a gadfly to pester the management,

> With a view to becoming carriers, they built twenty model waggons, the result of which proved a total failure in every respect. The next essay of their 'apprenticed hands' was to order a locomotive, which turned out, if possible, a greater failure than had the waggons … The 'Doctor' had become unmanageable. After having taken the committee, on their way to Nantyglo, as far as Blaina, it had run away with the engineer and stoker. The committee actually relay nineteen-twentieths of their roads, and, when the work is completed, find out that they are so close to each other, as not to admit of trains passing.[299]

All this is corroborated by the newspaper reports.

> As the 'Doctor' engine was returning from Nantyglo iron-works on Wednesday last [30 August], after conveying the committee of the Monmouthshire Canal Company on a tour of inspection, when near Abertillery, suddenly became unmanageable, and started off at a fearful rate down towards Aberbeg. At this point there is a sharp curve [34ft radius], round which the 'Doctor' had difficulty to get at the best of times, and this serving as a check to the speed [a rare case of friction between wheels and flanges being an advantage], one of the hauliers fortunately succeeded in putting a bar of iron as a sprag into one of the engine wheels, and thus brought the 'Doctor' to a stand. The engine-men, with much presence of mind, kept their position on the engine and tender, but Mr Edwards, of Risca, a valuable agent of the company, imprudently jumped off, but fortunately escaped with a slight sprain of the ankle.[300]

And, later, the company itself admitted,

> Many miles of tramplate were laid down… But this was done with so little judgment or regard to the necessary distance between the up and down lines, that it was afterwards found necessary to take up and relay the whole of them.[301]

All this incompetence gave Brown ammunition for further digs at the committee,[302] who reacted to their humiliation by ordering *Doctor* off the road. At that, Uskside took umbrage, thinking that aspersions were being cast on their repairs. In July 1849 *Doctor* was 'driven to the dock, where

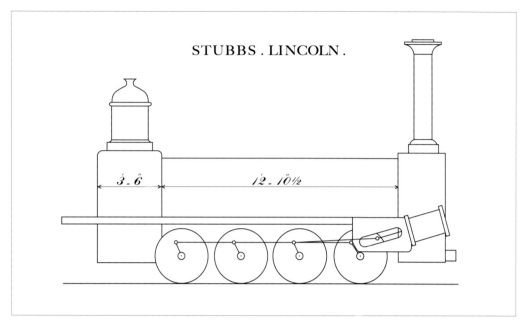

STUBBS . LINCOLN .

3 . 6   *12 . 10½*

Fig. 2.41
MRCC *Doctor*, Grylls &
Stubbs 1847.
(*Clark 1855, . vol. 2, diagram
pl. 6 part 2, no. 37*)

chains were absolutely fastened to the cylinders, and by these fastenings, No. 1 Engine was employed to land the heavy engines of Stothert and Slaughter [Nos. 6-8] from the Trows in which they were brought.'[303] It has been said that it may have been converted to an 0-6-2,[304] but the company, finally washing its hands of it, condemned it in March 1850[305] and advertised it for sale in April as eight-coupled.[306] It was finally sold in December 1852 or January 1853 to Thomas Powell the coalowner, but which of his many pits it served is not known.[307] An outline drawing is in Clark's *Railway Machinery* (Fig. 2.41) labelled 'Stubbs, Lincoln,' Lincoln being an obvious mistake for Llanelli. Clark describes it only as 'designed to run on mineral lines in Wales.'[308]

Nos. 2-5, Neath Abbey 1848

Nos. 2-5 were identical 0-6-0s with cylinders 15 by 24in, 4ft 1in wheels and very large domes,[309] and seem to have been modelled on a current design by E. B. Wilson & Co of Leeds (Fig. 2.42). Their wheelbase of 11ft 10in, however, was considerably greater than *Doctor*'s, and their weight of 19 tons was barely less. This fault was early recognised. An internal report of 1850 asked and answered the question:

> Are the present engines of the company the best adapted for the traffic and the gradients?[310] *They are adapted for the traffic and gradients, but are too heavy for the road.*[310]

Fig. 2.42
MRCC Nos. 2-5, Neath
Abbey 1848.
(*IRR, 121 (1990), 126 after
WGAS, D/D NAI L/33*)

No. 2 (which, along with *Abbey*, showed its paces to Captain Simmons in 1849) seems to have been named *Ebbw Vale*.[311] Even this late generation of locomotives took almost as heavy a toll of life and limb as did its predecessors. No. 2 killed its guard or brakesman in a shunting accident in 1850.[312] No. 4 is said to have been sold in July 1856 to the 'Rhymney Road Co,'[313] but there is no record of such a sale in the Rhymney accounts, and No. 4 was still on the MRCC in 1859 when it failed to whistle at a Newport level crossing and mowed down a boy.[314]

Nos. 6-8, 0-6-0 Stothert & Slaughter 1849

The remaining engines need not detain us long. Nos. 6-8 were 0-6-0s by Stothert & Slaughter of Bristol, which were delivered in July 1849.[315] No illustration can be found. In the course of a few months in 1850 No. 6 knocked down a haulier, No. 7 cut off the legs of its own guard, and No. 8 ran over a young brakesman who was detaching trams from the train which was running (illegally) at 12 mph.[316] From 1850 all trains had by bye-law to be accompanied by a guard or brakesman.[317]

Nos. 9-10, 2-4-0 WT Sharp Brothers 1849

Among the earliest four-coupled tank engines anywhere, they were built by Sharp Bros of

Manchester (works numbers 604 and 606) with cylinders 13 by 18in and 5ft driving wheels (Fig. 2.43).[318] One of them hauled an inspection train for Captain Simmons in October 1849.[319] In 1851 No. 9, on an up train, was hit by a runaway tram at Abertillery, and the impact detached the last tram from its train which ran back downhill to Aberbeeg where it hit No. 3 on the next up train. Much the same happened in 1859 when No. 9 lost its coupling at the same place and three trams with 30 tons of iron ore ran back for four miles before meeting some timber trams which they comprehensively smashed.[320] This was a steep and curvaceous stretch that saw an undue number of accidents.

No. 11 *AEGEON*, 0-4-0? Maudslay 1838?, ex-Waring & Sons 1849

This was a relative antique bought in September 1849 via Stothert & Slaughter. It has been suggested that it was a Bury-type goods engine built in 1838 by Maudslay, Sons & Field as the London & Birmingham's No. 82, which did not have a name (Fig. 2.44);[321] if so, the cylinders were also 13 by 18in and the wheels, before they were replaced with flangeless ones, 5ft in diameter. This was sold by the LNWR in 1847 to Waring & Sons, contractors for the East Lincolnshire Railway. Being so dissimilar to the rest of the

MRCC stock, it seems likely that it was intended for relatively light work such as hauling works or maintenance trains. Its appearance inaugurating the first passenger service in 1850 rather supports the notion.

Nos. 12-13, 0-6-0 Sharp Brothers 1850

In 1851, in the absence of signals despite the line being open for passengers, No. 12 ran into an engine that was taking on water at Aberbeeg.[322]

Nos. 14-15, 0-4-0 WT Stothert & Slaughter 1850

Soon converted by the MRCC to six-wheelers by adding 'straining wheels.'[323] In 1852 someone tried to sabotage No. 14 by pouring oil into the tank.[324]

No. 16, 4-4-0 Stothert & Slaughter 1850

A very early application in Britain of the leading bogie, and apparently an unsatisfactory one.[325]

The 1848 Act laid down that from 1 August 1849 the company should ban horse haulage in favour of traction by its own locomotives. On that day two empty trains were dispatched from Newport, one behind a Neath Abbey engine to Blaina, the other behind a Stothert & Slaughter to Ebbw Vale. The journey of 20-odd miles took each of them six hours, and the return train from Ebbw Vale with 210 tons of iron needed extra assistance to move it downhill. 'The engines several times got off the tram-plates,' explained the press release, 'which will account for the long time taken in the journeys.'[326] The embarrassing fact was that the track was inadequate for their weight and their wheelbase. Tredegar and Ebbw Vale therefore had to be asked to carry on with their own engines, and other freighters continued with horse power. It was not until 13 May 1850 that improvements to the track allowed the MRCC engines to take over, and one of the new locomotives was reported as hauling 130 of the old trams at 10 mph.[327] It was only on 23 December 1850 that the Western Valleys lines began to be opened for passenger traffic, with an inaugural train to Blaina hauled by No. 11 *Aegeon*.[328]

A service from Aberbeeg to Ebbw Vale was expected to follow shortly. But when Captain Laffan the Railway Inspector visited in 1851 he refused permission, and further work had to be done;[329] and on his second visit on 10 Jan 1852 the company suffered the ultimate embarrassment, for his inspection carriage was derailed.[330] Passengers could not travel on the Beaufort line until 19 April 1852, with an omnibus service provided to take them on from Ebbw Vale to Tredegar.[331]

In hindsight, Brown's criticisms of the MRCC in the 1840s were fully justified. The directors were indeed an unsatisfactory bunch, indecisive,

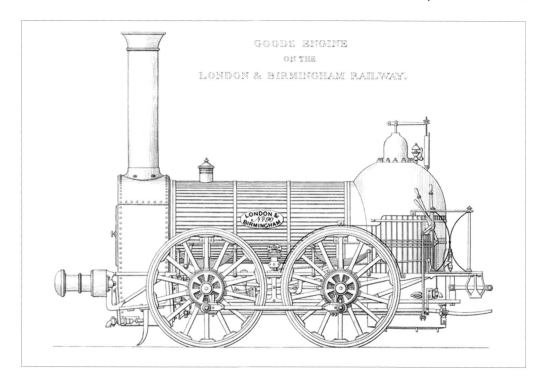

Fig. 2.44
London & Birmingham Railway Bury-type goods locomotive, 1838. (*Whishaw 1842, Pl. 6*)

alternately dilatory and over-hasty, skimping on their infrastructure, diverting their energies into promoting the Newport & Pontypool Railway, insisting on excessive dividends, and misguided at this critical juncture in their choice of civil and mechanical engineers. On the Sirhowy, Thomas Ellis had grown up and trained on home ground at Tredegar. His counterparts on the MRCC, by contrast, were outsiders. Edmund Scott Barber was an imported mining engineer and lasted only from 1846 to 1848 when he perhaps lost his job over the double-track fiasco. Henry Colson, the locomotive superintendent who purchased the inappropriate *Doctor* and the four Neath Abbey engines, had no experience of mineral lines, having come from the London & Brighton and the London & Croydon atmospheric railway.[332] He lasted from 1847 to 1850. At least their successors David Jones (a former contractor) and William Craig (previously at

Neath Abbey) were more competent;[333] and in 1850, during a marathon eight-hour meeting, a palace revolution deposed the MRCC chairman and clerk and most of the directors.[334] It did not, however, end the back-biting.

All of these MRCC locomotives would have worked between Newport and Risca, and some of them – we cannot tell which – would have worked from there to Nine Mile Point. All began life with plateway wheels, or at least combined wheels. At regular intervals between 1853 and 1859 Nos. 2-16 were converted for standard-gauge running, and most were subsequently sold off.[335] After 1850 it seems that all new MRCC engines were built for edge rail only.

The first engines delivered in 1859 to the Sirhowy Railway (as opposed to the Sirhowy Tramroad) were built for standard gauge and seemingly never had combined, let alone purely plateway, wheels.[336]

2D RUMNEY RAILWAY

The Rhymney Valley being somewhat out on a limb and its population sparser, it received considerably less attention from the press than did the Western Valleys. Our primary sources are the Neath Abbey drawings and the Rhymney Iron Co's accounts which, though invaluable, are short on detail. There are also William Lewis Meredith's reminiscences, published in 1913 when he was 70, but they are unreliable. Our understanding of Rhymney's locomotives is therefore largely a matter of deduction.

2D i. Rumney Railway Co

Ballast engine, unknown builder, by 1855

Although, like the Sirhowy, the company never supplied the haulage, it did own one locomotive. In 1855 'the little ballast engine' is mentioned as the property of the Railway Company as distinct from the Iron Company.[337] This was clearly a works engine for permanent way trains and, at this time when the great conversion from plate to edge rail was under way, it seems reasonable to suppose it could run on either type.

2D ii. Rhymney Iron Co

It is abundantly clear that, if the Rumney Railway was late in being built, it was also late

in acquiring locomotives. The catalyst was the creation of the Rhymney Iron Co in 1835, which next year appointed Josiah Richards from Dowlais as its engineer.[338] With him he brought as assistant John Phanuel Roe (1815-88), a young and surely talented Irishman who had joined Dowlais in 1835 as draughtsman. In 1839 he stepped into the shoes of Richards himself, who had died from falling off the top of an engine house under construction,[339] and Roe became Rhymney's chief engineer. He deserves to be better remembered than he is.

Of the ironworks' locomotives, some bore names and some only numbers. The rationale behind the number series is not clear, but it certainly included both those on the Rumney and those on the Rhymney Limestone Railway (RLR: see 2F iii). First and last the iron company had at least fourteen engines: ten on the Rumney and four on the RLR. Six were built by Neath Abbey and four were bought second-hand. These purchases all feature in the accounts, but the remaining four locomotives do not, and it is clear that they were built in-house. An inventory of stock in 1848 lists eight engines to date, but gives only their name or number and valuation, not their builders or dates. Technical details of the home-built locomotives are therefore almost non-existent, and there are no images of them; but presumably all were designed by Roe, who left Rhymney in 1851 to become Nantyglo's chief engineer.[340] Meredith names Edwin Richards, son of the Josiah who fell off the engine house, as Roe's successor as locomotive engineer from 1849 to 1853, when he moved to Tredegar.[341] But he was born only in 1830, and though listed in the 1851 census as engineer at Rhymney, in 1861 he was merely an engine driver at Tredegar. Meredith seems to have over-rated his status.

AMELIA, 0-6-0 Neath Abbey 1838

It was John Roe who from 1837 'organized a locomotive line between Rhymney and the shipping berth at Newport,'[342] and he did so with gusto: five new engines by Neath Abbey in little over a year. The name of his first was a nod to the Rhymney Iron Co's senior partner, William Thompson, who had married Amelia, daughter of Samuel Homfray senior; and their only child was another Amelia. The price was £725 16s 3d,[343] delivered in July 1838 by boat up the Neath Canal to its terminus at Pont Walby, where it cost £4-odd to crane it ashore. From there it had to be hauled up the incline on Tappendens' Tramroad to Hirwaun and thence on its own wheels to Rhymney by a poor and steep road, no easy task with a load of at least a dozen tons. The accounts have two entries: 'Paid W Baker for haulage of Locomotive £24,'[344] and (a matter of nine man-days of work) 'Haulage of Locomotive from Hirwain, £2 0s 6d,' the latter representing the Rhymney team that accompanied the procession.[345] This was precisely how Dowlais and Charles Jordan had been transported in 1836 and 1838 to Dowlais, also by William Baker (but for £21, the distance being less), using specially cast hoops 6in wide that fitted round the wheels. These engines too were escorted by ironworks men.[346]

Amelia was another with bell-crank drive[347] but cylinders 8½ by 20in, smaller than Neath Abbey's standard but the same as all the Dowlais engines except Perseverance.

LAURA, 0-6-0 Neath Abbey 1838

Laura, costing the same as Amelia, seems to have been its sister engine and was delivered very shortly afterwards, A couple of months so later, however, there was an incident that sounds to have been serious, although it was not mentioned in the local press. The accounts record on 17 and 29 December 1838, 'Neath Abbey Co for Repair of Locomotive Laura broken at Blaina Wharf'

£86 16s 7d, 'men's time with Locomotives' £84 6s 6d, and 'Repairing the Laura' £61 16s 7d.[348] Amelia and Laura together were valued at £1,400 in 1848, slightly below their cost.

Laura is mentioned in a brief note of 1905 about the Tredegar engines on the Sirhowy: 'The driver of "St David" was named George Hunter [this is correct]. Mr John Williams, late of the Midland Railway locomotive department, St Pancras, to whom we owe these particulars, states that his father was fireman of the sister engine "Laura".'[349] This must be a simple mistake: there is no other hint of a Laura on the Sirhowy, and John Williams' father is known as a Rumney driver.[350]

ALDERMAN, 0-4-4-0 G Neath Abbey 1838

A highly distinctive engine. 'Then,' says Meredith, placing it out of order, 'Mr John Roe made the great "Alderman," vertical cylinders [in fact inclined] on to a crank shaft, geared with three wheels to two carriages so as to enable the sharp curves to be negotiated.'[351] Likewise Roe, according to his obituary, 'designed and constructed, to the best of his own belief, the first eight-wheeled double-bogie locomotive to haul heavy traffic. The engines had an intermediate shaft, which was connected to the bogies, so as to allow freedom of movement.'[352]

Not quite the first double bogies, if that is how the Wylam and Whitehaven engines – and Stewart's – are to be interpreted; but it was the first of its generation. It surely owed a major debt to the projected Neath Abbey rack-and-adhesion double bogie of 1831 intended for Dowlais (Fig. 2.45),[353] which was not built as such; but Roe would have had every opportunity to see its plans in the Dowlais drawing office. His 0-4-4-0 for the Rumney Railway, much simpler in the absence of the rack drive and the double folding chimneys, was built by Neath Abbey, all the drawings being dated October 1837 to June 1838, (Fig. 2.46).[354] It was delivered not to Hirwaun but by sea to Newport: 29 September 1838, 'Landing Locomotive at Blaina Wharf, 12s' (the wharf was rented from Blaina until 1841 when Rhymney built its own) and 'Assisting same, £23 19s 9d.'[355] Once ashore it could be put straight on the tramroad and hauled (or even steamed) up to Rhymney. The cylinders were again 8½in and the boiler about 10ft 3in by 4ft 1in. Each bogie, of about 3ft 1½in wheelbase, had coupled wheels, the inboard axles being driven from a central crankshaft by a gear wheel with concave

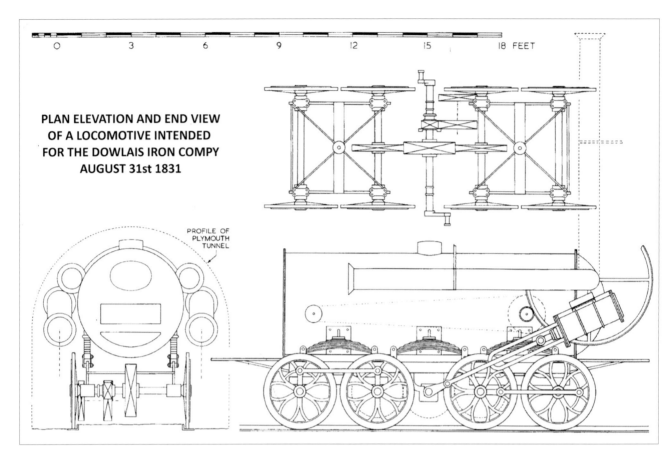

PLAN ELEVATION AND END VIEW
OF A LOCOMOTIVE INTENDED
FOR THE DOWLAIS IRON COMPY
AUGUST 31st 1831

PROFILE OF
PLYMOUTH
TUNNEL

Fig. 2.45
Proposed double-bogie
engine for Dowlais, Neath
Abbey 1831.
(*Rattenbury and Lewis 2004,
64 after drawings in WGAS*)

Fig. 2.46
John Roe's Alderman 0-4-4-0
for Rumney Railway, Neath
Abbey 1838.
(*Engineering, 15 Nov 1867,
456*)

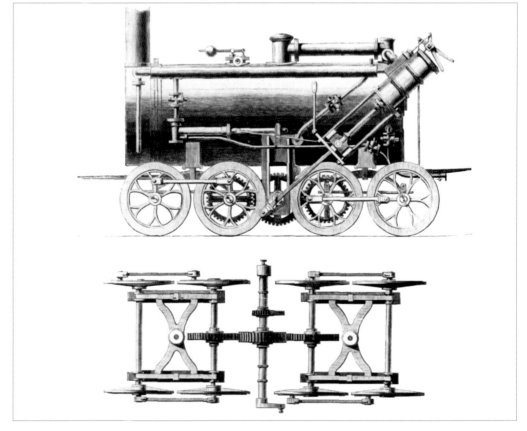

teeth. Equalised suspension was cleverly supplied by inverted springs between the bogie axle boxes and the bolsters connecting the boiler brackets.

Thereafter we only hear of it in three entries in the Rhymney works journal: in September and December 1851, 'Raising Bute & Alderman £3 0s 6d' and 'Getting Alderman on Road 5s 6d,' and in March 1852 'Haulage of Alderman 3s.'[356] This sounds like the aftermath of a collision, although it is not recorded in the press. The name must be another nod to William Thompson, chairman of the Rhymney Iron Co, who was commonly referred to as Mr Alderman Thompson. He died in 1854.

The Rumney's sharp and numerous curves were no doubt the reason for the bogie design. But after *Alderman* nothing certain is heard of the principle, and perhaps it did not live up to expectations.

BUTE, 0-6-0 Neath Abbey 1839

Little is known. *Bute* is heard of by name in 1848, when the driver and fireman left it and its train blocking the main line at Pillgwenlly while they drank in a nearby beer-house; in 1851 when it seems to have been in a collision (see under *Alderman* above); and again in 1852 when it badly injured its latchman;[357] But it was invoiced by Neath Abbey on 20 March 1839 for £829 10s 0d including a 1¼ per cent discount.[358] The cylinders were 10½in diameter and the few drawings, dated between November 1838 and January 1839, suggest a six-wheeled rocker-beam design like the Ebbw Vale engines we have met.[359]

There is a minor mystery in a sandstone slab in the National Museum covered in polished blacklead like the lintel of a domestic fireplace.[360] On it is carved a four-wheeled tender locomotive named *Bute 1*, more like a toy than a Neath Abbey product, which is pulling two four-wheeled passenger carriages. At one end is the date 1853 (Fig. 2.47). The accession record made in 1932 reads,

This stone was the work of William Lewis, Twyn Gwyn Farm, Ynysddu, Mon (now deceased) who worked at the Mynyddislwyn Quarries in the year 1853, where the stone was hewn, when about 20 years of age. It is a supposed copy of the first engine on the Sirhowy Railway which he named Bute 1st. We his daughters wish to present it to the Cardiff Museum.

Mynyddislwyn Quarry was in the Sirhowy valley, and the 1851 census has William Lewis,

stone quarry labourer, born in 1834/5. But in 1853 the Sirhowy Railway still lay in the future, and the Sirhowy Tramroad had neither an engine named *Bute* nor a passenger service. The MRCC had a passenger service but no *Bute*. The Rumney had a *Bute* but no passenger service. The Rhymney Railway did not yet exist; but its Bill was submitted to Parliament in 1853, though it is far from clear why a young quarryman should be promoting an unbuilt railway in a different valley.

RHYMNEY, 0-6-0 Neath Abbey 1839

Again no technical details are known beyond 10½in cylinders. The only mention of its name is in the inventory of 1848, but what must be this engine was invoiced by Neath Abbey on 3 August 1839 at the same price as *Bute*, and was surely a sister engine.[361] Both were delivered, via Hirwaun again, by William Baker in September and October.[362] They were together valued in the inventory of 1848 at £1,750 or almost exactly their cost.[363] One of these first four Rhymney locomotives we have already met playing pig-in-the-middle with a Tredegar engine at Pye Corner in 1843, and in 1847 two unnamed locomotives collided, without injury.[364]

There is another minor mystery in a crude Neath Abbey sketch of a hand-cranked roller and gears, entitled 'sundry wheels for [lowering] stack of Locomotive Engines for Dowlais & Rhymney 1840.'[365] The Dowlais engine was *Charles Jordan*, which had to pass through Plymouth tunnel on the Merthyr Tramroad.[366] But no Rhymney engine is known to have had a hinged stack, nor is any overbridge or tunnel known.

SUPERB, ex-Cleave 1843

For nearly three decades from 1839 Rhymney bought nothing more from Neath Abbey. But on 12 October 1843 the accounts record it paying £444 7s 6d in cash to 'Cleave [or C. Leave ?] for Locomotive *Superb*,'[367] and three months later

Fig. 2.47
Carved stone depicting locomotive *Bute*, 1853. (*NMW, 32.186*)

2s 6d for 'Drawing Engine on Plates,' possibly getting it on the road.[368] Meredith tells a quite different story, that *Superb* was built by Neath Abbey for Ebbw Vale and bought second-hand by Rhymney; but there is nothing whatever to confirm this, and no other hint of a *Superb* at Ebbw Vale. In June 1848 it was being reboilered: the Rhymney inventory includes in the boiler-makers' shop

> Boiler Plates, 4½ tons @ £14 p ton
> Locomotive Boiler Sheet complete £40
> 2 Tube plates 84 Holes drilled in each Plate for 'Superb' £43 4s 0d

and its list of locomotives ends with *Superb* valued at its cost price.[369] Who or where Cleave was we do not know. We might expect a contractor, but the only known one of that name, Henry Cleave, had a contract on the London end of the London & Birmingham in 1835, which might be too early.[370] The only hint of a locomotive named *Superb* on any railway at this time concerns Dr William Church's experimental engine which exploded at Bromsgrove in 1840, but its subsequent (rebuilt) career rules it out, and there is doubt even over its proper name.[371]

No. 4, 2-2-0 Bury 1838, ex-LNWR 1847
No. 5, 2-2-0 Hick & Co 1840, ex-LNWR 1847

During the 1840s, the output of the Rhymney Iron Co leapt ahead: in 1839 it had three furnaces in blast, by 1849 nine.[372] Although we have no figures for coal, output from the valley was burgeoning too. Hence, presumably, the rapid enlargement of the locomotive stock in the decade following 1838 when six further engines were acquired. In this Rhymney differed from Tredegar, where there was a decade-long lull between 1843 and 1853.

In August 1847 the Rhymney accounts record 'Paid L & N W Railway Co for 2 Locomotives, £1250' and 'Freight 2 Locomotives from Gloster, £24 1s.'[373] These were Bury-type passenger engines, just like the two we have met at Blaina (Fig. 2.23). No. 4 was built in 1838 by Bury as the London & Birmingham's No. 8, No. 5 built in 1840 by Benjamin Hick & Co of Bolton as the Aylesbury Railway's No. 1. The cylinders were 12 by 18in and the wheels 5ft 6in and 4ft with a weight of nearly 8 tons.[374] It was not until the South Wales Railway of 1852 that the first line from England penetrated Wales, and meanwhile Gloucester was

the railhead. The £24 for freight refers to haulage by road, for all we know by William Baker again.

This pair seems never to have borne names, only numbers. Late in 1847 'one of the new engines' (unspecified) burst its boiler at Pillgwenlly, without injury,[375] and the inventory of June 1848 brackets Nos. 4 and 5 together with a combined value of £1,250 – cost price again.[376] In 1850,

> The Rhymney Iron Company's engine, No. 41, was proceeding from the works to Newport, and when near Ruederron [Rhiwderin], the latchman, William Powell, suddenly, while perhaps trying to regain his seat at the head of the tender, after opening a latch, fell under the engine, and was not missed until they arrived at Pie Corner. The driver and others immediately went back in search of the poor fellow, and at about a distance of two hundred yards from the engine, they saw on the road, to their horror, one half of Powell's body, which had actually been cut in two; and the portions separated.[377]

Engine numbering never reached anywhere near 41, and this is a misprint for No. 4. The Rhymney works journals, listing the cost of coffins bought that year, include one 'for William Powell, Haulier killed by No. 4 Locomotive, 15s.'[378]

No. 6

All we know for certain is its presence in the 1848 inventory as 'New Engine No. 6,' valued at no less than £1,000, more than any other, which might possibly suggest another double-bogie engine, this time home-built.[379]

Thus in June 1848 the inventory, by omitting *Alderman*, lists nine engines, and next year Simmons' table gives only six. Possibly some had been retired, but a discrepancy remains. Nos. 8-10 did not run on the Rumney, but on the narrow-gauge RLR (see 2F iii).

Unnamed 2-2-0, Bury 1845 ex-LNWR 1854

It seems that after the beginning of 1855, when the conversion of the Rumney to combined rail had been achieved, the Rhymney Iron Co engines had fully-fledged standard-gauge wheels. Thus a number of locomotives involved in accidents after that date probably fall outside our scope.[380] But in 1854 the company acquired a further second-hand four-wheeler by Bury.[381] Built originally for the Manchester & Bolton Railway, it was bought by Rhymney in 1854 for £700 plus carriage from

Manchester (£17 12s), expenses (£3 7s 10d), a fee to William Fairbairn (£6 13s which was not paid), and Sharp Stewart for an 'engine crank' (£72).[382] It was probably converted for plateway running; but yet another engine from the LNWR, a Maudslay which arrived in 1859, almost certainly was not.

In the 1840s and 50s, some locomotive components were bought ready-made: springs from H. J. Thrupp and the Uskside Iron Co of Newport, crank axles for the inside-cylindered engines from Stothert & Slaughter of Bristol, boiler plates in small quantities from Tredegar and in large (£79-worth) from Coalbrookdale, and in 1852 '6 Loco Wire Caps' which sound like spark arresters.

The Rumney story was not composed entirely of mysteries and accidents. In 1854 we hear of a somewhat miserly prosecution by the Railway Company who charged a haulier 'with wasting the water provided for the company, for the engines running on the line, and with having injured the tramroad itself by reason of the water having washed away the ballast.' The haulier claimed he was just as entitled to take water for his horses as engine men did for their locomotives; but he was over-ruled.[383] The inventory of 1848 includes (under the heading of Trams) '9 Water Tanks for feeding Loco' at £8 apiece and '24 Iron Pipes ditto' at 10s 6d.[384] No doubt fed by streams, these were presumably located at intervals beside the line.

In 1848 there was even, for once, positive cause to smile.

Man versus Steam. On Tuesday evening a comical adventure was witnessed near Bedwas Church – a race between Mr John Jones and the locomotive called 'Bute' – distance three hundred yards, for a sovereign a side. It was won by the former by about twenty yards. What next! There were nearly 200 spectators present. Wonders will never cease. Here we have a man distancing a locomotive steam-engine in the contest of speed![385]

2D iii. Brithdir Colliery

BRITHDIR, 0-4-0? Grylls & Co? 1846/7

This is surrounded by some mystery. A report of February 1847 in the *Monmouthshire Beacon* introduces the story.

A locomotive on a new patent principle, has commenced to run on the tram road between Newport and Tredegar Iron Works, to convey passengers as well as luggage trains, at a speed of 20 miles an hour, a feat hitherto deemed by engineers impracticable on tram plates (no[t] rails), with short curves incessantly occurring, as is the case on the tram road in question. Heavy bets were thus decided on its practicability, and the novel principle of its construction has elicited the applause of all scientific engineers.[386]

A patent principle new in 1847, whose emphasis was on speed, points to that of John Isaiah Grylls and William Stubbs. They were partners in the South Wales Ironworks at Llanelli, the latter also being locomotive superintendent of the Llanelly & Llandilo Railway,[387] and they had an inordinately high opinion of their own products. When in 1846 they reported to the *Mechanic's Magazine* that they had sold a powerful 0-6-0 to Ireland, the editors wisely exercised caution.

The correspondent who has furnished us with the preceding states that the makers are patentees of an improved locomotive, which will achieve 'a speed of 120 miles an hour, with greater precision and certainty than the present engines perform 60!' He will excuse us for declining to insert such a statement as from ourselves, until we have some proof of the fact affirmed.[388]

Grylls and Stubbs' patent of 2 June 1846 covered a variety of topics of which most, like recessed boilers to allow 12ft driving wheels (inconceivable on a plateway), need not concern us. But another of their 'improvements' may well be the same as our 'locomotive on a new patent principle.' It had two cylinders mounted between the driving axles, one driving backwards and one forwards, and an elongated combustion chamber between firebox and tubes (Fig. 2.48).[389] While the patent drawing

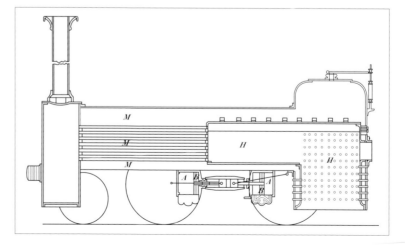

Fig. 2.48
Stubbs and Grylls patent locomotive 1846/7.
(Repertory of Patent Inventions 9 (1847), pl. XVIII)

shows an 2-4-0, our locomotive need not have had the same arrangement, for an 0-4-0 would better suit sharp curves. Conceivably the engine reported in the *Beacon* was that advertised for sale at Llanelli as second-hand in September 1846, but without further detail this is only surmise.[390]

We hear no more of this engine plying between Newport and Tredegar, but four months later the *Monmouthshire Merlin* published a flowery account of a trip up the Western Valleys from Newport to a colliery at Llanhilleth owned by Reginald Blewitt, where a new mine pump was being demonstrated.

> The proprietors of the Brithdir Colliery very kindly provided for the transit of their friends to the scene of attraction, having set apart their fine locomotive, the Brithdir, to which were attached a few of the patent iron trams, constructed by the engineer, Mr John Hughes [note: no such patent existed], who has brought the locomotive referred to, to its present state of perfection ... On this line, where persons are wont to travel at funereal pace, where canvas-covered omnibi plod primitively to town with their market-going coteries – and where sluggish ceffyls [horses] haul a protracted extension of black diamond freighted trams which, like huge snakes, 'drag their slow length along,' – upon this line did the Brithdir and its adjuncts career away ... being apparently so pleased with its performance as frequently to whistle aloud, only stopping at 'partings,' or in taking a bumper at the pumps, at a rate which, when no breakers appeared a head, was set down in the log at thirty knots an hour – evidently shewing, that by proper locomotives and a double line of tram way upon the approved principle, great things can be effected, even without organic changes.[391]

The corresponding but briefer and more prosaic report in the *Monmouthshire Beacon*, the *Merlin*'s main rival, reads:

> On Monday last Mr John Hughes, of Pillgwenlly, engineer, with a party of gentlemen, proceeded on the line of railway belonging to the Monmouthshire Canal Company, between Newport and Tredegar, with a steam-engine, by way of an experimental trip, prior to that company turning carrier, pursuant to their act of parliament. The engine acted well, but we have not heard its speed. All who witnessed it are unanimous in awarding their meed of praise to the builder. This engine was erected at Newport, and we hope to see many of the same sort erected here.[392]

The *Beacon* is certainly wrong in sending this engine to Tredegar, because the *Merlin*'s list of those attending firmly places the event at Llanhilleth. But it seems likely that these reports of February and June 1847, with their emphasis on speed, refer to the same engine. True, their '20 miles an hour' and 'thirty knots an hour' must be taken with a very large pinch of salt. Although by 1847 the MCC's rails were wrought iron, conversion to standard gauge lay in the future, and the speed limit on the Western Valleys lines was still 10 mph.[393]

Brithdir Colliery was not in the Western Valleys proper, but near the Rumney Railway, on the west bank of the River Rhymney a mile south of New Tredegar and served by a 400-yard branch. Its proprietor was William George until in 1849-50 the pit and its plant were sold, although no locomotive is mentioned in the notices.[394] John Hughes (1814-89) was a Merthyr man whose father (another John) had been a foreman at Penydarren in 1804.[395] He became a partner in the Uskside Iron Co at Pillgwenlly, the largest of the Newport engineering works, and in later life played a major role in introducing industry to Russia by founding the great ironworks at Yuzovka (Hughesovka) in Ukraine, which grew into the present Donetz. Uskside is said elsewhere to have produced no locomotives until 1849;[396] and whereas the *Beacon* has *Brithdir* built by Uskside, the *Merlin* says it was brought by Hughes 'to its present state of perfection,' which could very well mean that he merely tinkered with it. Brithdir Colliery was a customer of Uskside.[397]

All in all, then, the evidence suggests that we are dealing with a single engine on temporary loan from the Brithdir Co through the good offices of John Hughes, and that it was built not, as the *Beacon* claimed, by Uskside but, even though their name is nowhere associated with it, by Stubbs and Grylls.

2D iv. Marshall Knowles & Co, White Rose Colliery

Charles B. Marshall and William Knowles, who were large coal proprietors based in Newport, owned the White Rose Colliery at New Tredegar.[398] It is notoriously difficult to track the dates, owners and even the precise location of Victorian coal mines, and we cannot be sure that Marshall & Knowles were the successors of the Brithdir Company or, if so, whether they inherited the locomotive *Brithdir*.

Three engines (including *ROSE* ? 0-4-0), unknown builders, by 1854

The firm is first recorded at the beginning of 1853 when one of its engines blew up on the Rumney, injuring the driver, fireman, latchman and a platelayer.[399] At the end of 1854 the firm was advertising for an engineer to maintain three locomotives and 100 coal and coke waggons at their shed at Bassaleg.[400] Next year, after a derailment at points suffered by a Rhymney engine at Bedwas, Marshall & Knowles' engine safely passed the spot; 'but the tire of their wheels was deeper than that of the Rhymney Iron Company's.'[401] This must mean that whereas at least one of the Rhymney Iron Co engines had ordinary shallow-flanged wheels, Marshall & Knowles' engines had deep-flanged combined wheels. One night a year later again, a drunk lay down across the track at New Tredegar, where his legs were severed as 'a party of gents were returning to Rhymney on one of Marshall's engines.' The inquest jury felt that 'neither Marshall's nor any other engine should be on the road but on the time specified in the rules.'[402] In the same year, £200-worth of damage was done to the Rhymney Iron Co's trucks by Marshall's engine.[403] And finally in 1861, as a result of the dissolution of Marshall and Knowles' partnership, two locomotives were offered for sale: *Star*, 0-6-0ST, cylinders 14 × 20 in, wheels 4 ft 3 in, weight about 18 tons, and *Rose*, 0-4-0 tender engine, cylinders 14 × 18 in, wheels 4 ft 6 in, about 15 tons, both specified as 'suited to a Narrow guage Railway,'[404] whether that means they were already standard gauge or suitable for conversion to it. *Rose*, as a tender engine at a time when saddle tanks were all the rage on industrial lines, could well be old enough to have been built with combined wheels. Most probably all Marshall & Knowles' engines down to 1855 had combined wheels, but the later ones, like the Rhymney Iron Co's, did not. Some of their locomotives ended up pumping at collieries.[405]

2D v. Messrs Prothero, Pengam or Bassaleg?

Unnamed, 0-4-0 Maudslay 1839, ex-LNWR 1853

Thomas Prothero of Newport died in 1853 and his coal empire was inherited by his three sons. In November 1853 the LNWR sold to Messrs Prothero the former London & Birmingham No. 84, an 0-4-0 built by Maudslay in 1839 and identical to the MRCC's *Aegeon*. The price was £600.[406] There is no certainty that the new owners were our Protheros, but it is likely enough. The LNWR was to deliver it to Birmingham, from where it could make its own way down the newly-opened Newport Abergavenny & Hereford. This was well before the conversion of the Rumney was complete, and one would expect it to be given plateway or combined wheels. There is no doubt that the Protheros had a locomotive by 1857 when a new engine of Crawshay Bailey's named *Dart* ran off the road at Twyn Shon Evan near Bedwas, and a few minutes later an engine belonging to Messrs Prothero, pulling a train of Thomas Powell's trucks, ran into it. Seven or eight of the trucks and Prothero's engine were considerably damaged.[407] Which of the numerous Powell and Prothero pits the engine served is not stated, but there were several clustered around Pengam. It is however on record that the Protheros had second-hand Bury engines – indistinguishable from Maudslays – at Bassaleg, where perhaps they were shedded.[408]

2E TRAMROAD UNKNOWN

GOLIATH, 0-6-0? Neath Abbey 1846

There are five Neath Abbey drawings of parts for *Goliath*, all dated February 1846,[409] but giving no destination or customer's name. It was evidently yet another engine with rocker-beam drive and the cylinders were 10½ in, but the gauge cannot be determined, although the name implies considerable size. There is therefore no certainty that it is relevant to us, but the chances are that it was built for somewhere in the Western Valleys, possibly a branch of the Rumney.

2F INTERNAL AND LIMESTONE TRAMROADS

Limestone was used in great quantities – roughly a ton for every ton of iron produced – in the blast furnace as a flux to encourage impurities in the ore to coalesce as cinders or slag. At the heads of the valleys it outcrops just north of the ironworks. The earliest furnaces in our area – Sirhowy, Beaufort and Ebbw Vale – all drew their supplies from Trefil quarries by way of the edge-railed Trevil and Rassa Railways of 1796, which fall outside our scope. From about 1803 new limestone feeders were normally tramroads.[410]

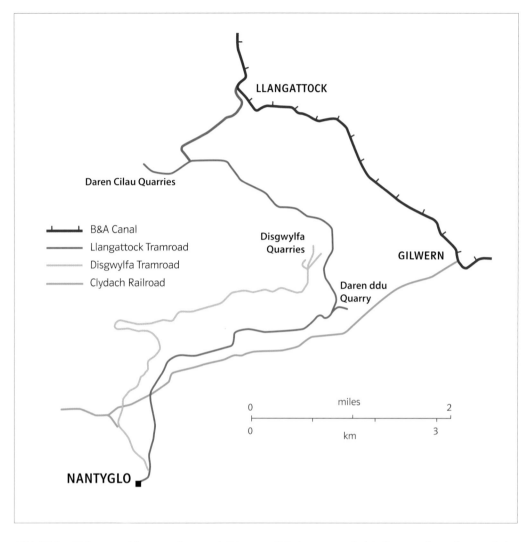

Fig. 2.49
Llangattock Tramroads.

2F i. Ebbw Vale tunnel locomotive, see 2C iv.

2F ii. Bailey's Llangattock Tramroad

In 1821 Nantyglo had built Bailey's Tramroad from the works to the B&A at Govilon, and in 1828 (probably in July), it had acquired direct access to the MCC's Aberbeeg Tramroad.[411] The rack-rail link to the Clydach, therefore, was now no longer so vital, and the need for steam haulage on it, we might deduce, became correspondingly less important. At the same time Nantyglo, hitherto supplied from Disgwylfa quarries, began to obtain its limestone from a different source, Daren Cilau quarries to the north. These already had (from 1815) a tramroad which dropped northwards down inclines to kilns on the canal at Llangattock, from where the lime was distributed for agricultural purposes (Fig. 2.49). Its gauge was 3ft 6in over the flanges. On 24 April 1828 the Baileys obtained permission from the

B&A to extend this line southwards round the mountain to Nantyglo, and in August 1828 it was being surveyed. The resulting line, for most of its five miles, was virtually level, with locomotive working seemingly intended from its inception.[412]

Unnamed, 0-4-0 G? Nantyglo? c. 1814, converted Tredegar 1830 (see 2A ii. above)

On 7 December 1830 this Llangattock line was opened, to carry not only limestone south to the works but also surplus coal north to the canal for sale in Brecon and its hinterland.

> The Nantyglo and Llangattock Railway, which has just been completed, at an enormous expense, by those spirited and liberal individuals, Messrs J and C Bailey, was opened on Tuesday last. The first coal carried along it, amounting to twenty-five tons, was distributed among the poor of the parishes of Llangattock and Crickhowell.[413]

It was steam-operated from the start. Only a week after the opening, it was reported, 'Mr Homfray, of Tredegar, and Mr Bailey, of Nantyglo, have received "Swing" letters, imperatively calling upon them to destroy their respective locomotive engines,'[414] 'Swing' being the name of the current Luddite-like anti-mechanisation movement. Bailey's engine, as already suggested, was Nantyglo's old Blenkinsop-type rack engine, rebuilt from edge to plate rail.

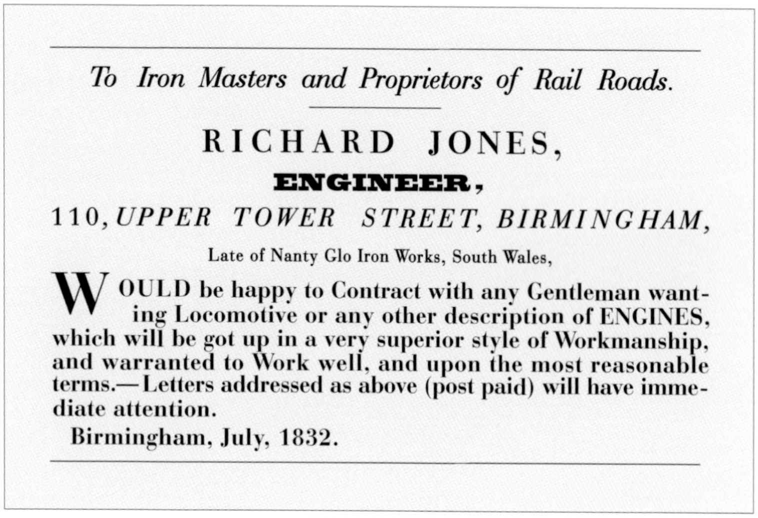

Unnamed, 0-4-0 Richard Jones 1832

The number of Nantyglo engines grew slowly. At the end of July 1832 Richard Jones, engineer of Birmingham and 'late of Nantyglo ironworks,' addressed an advertisement to 'Ironmasters and Proprietors of Rail Roads' offering to build locomotives for them (Fig. 2.50).[415] Within a fortnight he responded to an enquiry from Dowlais,

I will supply you with a Locomotive Engine to the weight you want, working upon four wheels & Springs with Metallick pistons and fitted up in a superior style of Workmanship, deliver'd at Bristol and put to work for the sum of 350 pounds. I would advise you to have one of 4½ tons, including water in Boiler and the cistern to carry water to suply the Boiler. I am now making one for Mr Bailey of Nantyglo to the above weight, if your road will bear that weight it will be preferable to the other, the price will be the same. I will warrant it to keep a sufficient supply of Steam and draw as much as any Engine in the Kingdom of its weight on the same road.[416]

This Nantyglo engine, assuming it was completed, is the only one Jones is known to have built. Birmingham directories of 1835 do not include him, and presumably by then his business had failed.

In 1834 it was noted,

There is also a tramroad and inclined plane for conveying limestone from the Darren rocks to the canal, and Messrs Bailey have recently established a steam-carriage and tramroad for the carriage of coal from their mines in Monmouthshire to the wharf near the village of Llangattock.[417]

But next year disaster struck.

Last week a dreadful event took place near Nantyglo, by the bursting of the boiler of one of the steam

engines employed in conveying a train of waggons with lime stone from Llangattock to Nantyglo; three labouring men were killed. The principal engineer was absent, and it is generally supposed that the ignorance of the deceased unfortunate men, in the management of the engine, led to the catastrophe.[418]

Which engine this was we have no way of telling, but the cause of the accident was evidently tampering with the safety valve: the report on the inquest says the boiler burst through 'the steam not having been allowed to escape in the usual manner.' The verdict was accidental death, and a deodand of £1 was levied on the carriage.[419] This was one of only two such cases on any tramroad in our area, the other being in 1843 when, after a Nantyglo haulier's death, deodands of 1s each were imposed on the horses, the tram and the load of iron that killed him.[420] The ancient system of deodands – confiscation of equipment that caused deaths – was abolished in 1846.

SAMPSON, 0-6-0? Lloyds, Fosters & Co, 1839

It was seemingly four years before a replacement came.

A locomotive engine intended to ply on the Messrs Bailey's Railroad from Nantyglo to Llangattock passed through this town [Hereford] on Tuesday last [22 October 1839], on its way to the former place. This piece of machinery, while remaining in the town, attracted general observation: it came from the Old Park Foundry, Wednesbury, Staffordshire, being manufactured by Lloyd, Foster and Company, well known as eminent makers, the

To Iron Masters and Proprietors of Rail Roads.

RICHARD JONES, ENGINEER,
110, UPPER TOWER STREET, BIRMINGHAM,
Late of Nanty Glo Iron Works, South Wales,

WOULD be happy to Contract with any Gentleman wanting Locomotive or any other description of ENGINES, which will be got up in a very superior style of Workmanship, and warranted to Work well, and upon the most reasonable terms.—Letters addressed as above (post paid) will have immediate attention.
Birmingham, July, 1832.

Fig. 2.50
Richard Jones, late of Nanty Glo Ironworks, advertises. (*MM, 11 Aug 1832*)

engine, which is named "Sampson" is of 40 horse-power, and appears a handsome and massive piece of mechanism, being calculated to perform feats in drawing burthens in its train, which some time back would seem improbable. Its weight alone is 8 tons, and including the carriage and tender, the weight is upwards of 19 tons.[421]

Lloyds, Fosters & Co were a Quaker firm, whose proprietors included both Sampson Lloyd – descended from the founder of Lloyds Bank and himself later an MP and chairman of the bank – and a cousin of his, Sampson Foster.[422] They built stationary engines,[423] and are credited with only three other locomotives, all of much later date, for their own standard-gauge works system. Virtually nothing is known of these.[424] In the 1850s Thomas Powell the coalowner bought a number of the improved model trams and the MRCC bought wheels from them.[425]

Unnamed, Neath Abbey, 1841

Perhaps *Sampson* did not live up to expectations, for only two years later the Baileys commissioned another engine. In the Neath Abbey collection is an unscaled drawing of a tender. It has been torn

Fig. 2.51

Gravestone of Joshua Morgan, Llanelly, 1871 'died from injuries caused by the *Cymro* engine'.

off a larger drawing.[426] The normal Neath Abbey scale of one inch to the foot gives a between-wheel gauge of 3ft 6in. The only surviving caption reads 'for Mr Bailey;' but a summary catalogue of the collection compiled in 1935, when this drawing was perhaps more complete than now, adds 'for 10½in engine' (the standard Neath Abbey cylinder size) and the date of 1841.[427] This drawing is identical in every detail to one of the tender for the Gloucester & Cheltenham's *Royal William* of 1832 (Fig. 2.31).[428]

CYMRO BACH, 0-4-0 Uskside, 1849/50, and *CYMRO*, 0-4-0 Uskside, *c.* 1860

'*Cymro Bach* [Little Welshman],' said a newspaper in 1856, 'was the name of the first engine that started on the line made for carrying limestone, about six years ago, from Llangattock, Crickhowell, to the Nantyglo works,' whose driver had just died.[429] Dating, therefore, from about 1850, it was hardly the first on the line, and about 1860 it was joined by another named simply *Cymro*. Between them, like many another tramroad locomotive, they left behind a dismal trail of death and injury. A man's hand was mutilated in 1853. In 1859 not only was a woman run over ('the sixth person who has been killed on the line, and none of them had any right to be there'), but an engine driver was crushed between the trams. And there is at Llanelly (near Llangattock, not the Carmarthenshire one) the gravestone of Joshua Morgan, latchman, 'who died of injuries caused by the *Cymro* engine' in 1871 (Fig. 2.51).[430] In 1874 a man was hit on the head while firing *Cymro Bach*.[431] In 1881 a boy lost a foot by foolishly trying to climb aboard an engine in motion by way of the connecting rod. And at the last, in 1889, 'For sale, the Llangattock Tramroad, together with Locomotives and about 60 limestone Trams.'[432] This shows that we are still dealing with two engines.

What was their origin? In 1849, the *Merlin* reported, John Hughes of the Uskside Iron Foundry at Newport had just built his first locomotive, *Blaenafon*, for Blaenavon's 3ft 3in-gauge plateway. This was designed by Thomas Dyne Steel (1822-98), the Blaenavon Company's engineer. 'We understand,' the *Merlin* went on, 'that another engine, from the same model, is already in progress:'[433] this was for Bailey's Llangattock Tramroad. Blaenavon's first small engine was followed about 1860 by a larger one also designed by Dyne Steel and built by Uskside. In 1864 the Severn & Wye Railway's engineer

Fig. 2.52

Bailey's Llangattock Tramroad, *Cymro*, Uskside c.1860? in Cudworth & Johnson's yard at Wrexham. (*George Alliez collection*)

G. W. Keeling was sent on a fact-finding tour of various steam-operated lines, and at Brynmawr he found a tramroad 'of similar gauge to Blaenavon, and worked by locomotives [note the plural again] similar to the smaller engine seen there.'[434] It therefore appears that *Cymro Bach*, like the smaller Blaenavon engine, was an 0-4-0 built in 1849/50 by Uskside, weighing nearly 8 tons and capable of 8-10 mph and of pulling 50 tons up 1 in 60; and that in about 1860 Dyne Steel, who in 1859 had become Crawshay Bailey's agent and 'converted the Llangattock Tramway from Brynmawr to Llangattock into a locomotive road' by laying heavier chaired rails,[435] commissioned another engine, *Cymro*, of the same sort.

Sadly, there is no certain illustration of either, and no record of what became of them after they were sold in 1889. But the dealers Cudworth & Johnson of Wrexham had an engine named *Cymro* with cylinders 10 by 14 in, which was used by the contractors for the Wrexham-Ellesmere railway of 1892-5. Some say it was bought from Green's Foundry at Aberystwyth, was auctioned in 1897, and finally departed for Littlehampton or Shoreham.[436] Thus it may have been our *Cymro*, regauged and much tinkered with (Fig. 2.52).

The Llangattock Tramroad commands imposing views of the Vale of Usk, and it is no surprise to hear of excursion trains on it. In 1856 a party of geologists travelled to the quarries 'in a nicely carpeted number of trams attached to the Cymro-bach engine.'[437] In 1861 the Beaufort Volunteers, en route to the Breconshire Review at Llangorse, made the first part of their journey by rail to Llangattock.

> The corps marched to the lower end of the town [Brynmawr], where a special train awaited them. The word 'all right' being given, a contest took place between the bandsmen, who were in the front carriage, and the 'great iron horse.' The latter soon made himself a conqueror, for he not only overpowered their music with the noise of steam and whistle, but soon half-smothered and blinded them with smoke, dust, &c.[438]

What is more, the Sunday Schools of the eleven chapels in mid-Victorian Brynmawr laid on annual treats for the children.

> Some chartered the *Cymro* engine and trams, which were white washed for the occasion, and into these the young folk piled, and were driven to Llangattock, where they had a trip on the canal, a picnic, and returned by tram.[439]

Some such occasion, we may deduce, whether the passengers were Volunteers or schoolchildren, gave birth to the famous song *Crosher Bailey had an engine*, which is first mentioned in 1863.[440] The engine in question must have been either *Cymro Bach* or *Cymro*.

2F iii. Rhymney/Bute internal lines

When Tredegar and Rhymney furnaces were established in 1800, each rapidly acquired its own system of internal tramroads and of feeders from nearby coal and ore mines and from Trefil limestone quarries (Fig. 2.53). These were laid at the same time as the Sirhowy Tramroad was being built towards the south, and can be traced back at least to April 1803 when

> fifteen little waggons coupled together were hauled by two quite moderately sized horses; however, we were told that on the best tramroads two such horses could pull nineteen such waggons, each loaded with 15 hundredweights.[441]

William Lewis Meredith claimed, on the authority of his grandfather's papers, that these tramroads originated in 1798,[442] but he was probably confusing the Tredegar-Trefil with the edge-railed Trevil Ralroad. In fact both the 2½-mile Tredegar-Trefil line and a 2-mile branch westward across the watershed to Rhymney were authorised by the Sirhowy Tramroad Act of 1802. Both formed a single system with the same 3ft gauge; but in 1815 the 3ft 6in-gauge Brynoer Tramroad and its end-on continuation Hall's Trefil Tramroad were built, running north from Rhymney and past Trefil to Talybont on the B&A. They took over the carriage of limestone from Trefil to Rhymney.[443] Rhymney had to wait many years for its own exit tramroad; meanwhile much of its iron was sent overland to Merthyr for processing at Cyfarthfa works, but the rest had to go out via Tredegar and down the Sirhowy until 1828 when the Rumney Railway materialised as a direct link to Newport. Thereafter, although Rhymney's internal narrow gauge survived, it had no presence on the eastern side of the watershed.

The gauge of these lines – especially of the Tredegar-Trefil – has been variously given as 2ft, 2ft 6in, 2ft 10in, 2ft 11in, 2ft 11¼in, 3ft and 3ft 6in. The first two of these figures and the last,

Fig. 2.53

Tredegar-Trefil-Rhymney tramroads.

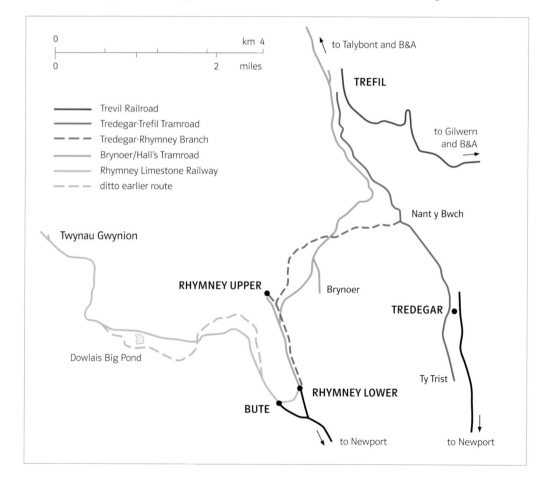

however measured, have no justification. Thomas Ellis senior very specifically records the gauge as 3ft: 'The Guage [sic] of Mr Rosser Thomas Tram Road [at Brynoer, leading off the Rhymney branch] 2-9 between the Flanches 3-0 over the flanches Octer 27th 1828 this is for Casting a Machain for Wayaing.'[444] His dimensions are confirmed by the German engineers who visited Bute in 1826-7 as 32in Prussian measure (2ft 9in English), which must be inside the flanges.[445] Drawings for 'Forman's Engine' and a later Rhymney locomotive, both shortly to be discussed, give the same gauge of 3ft over the flanges. All refer to this connected Tredegar-Rhymney-Trefil system which, until Homfray's original attempt at a Sirhowy Tramroad was widened in gauge in 1804, also extended the best part of ten miles further south.

Unnamed, 0-6-0 ('Forman's Engine') Robert Stephenson 1829

In 1828 two engines were ordered from Robert Stephenson & Co of Newcastle. One, known to the builders only as 'Forman's Engine' or 'No 14 Travelling Engine', was ordered early in December by William Forman, who was still, with William Thompson, a partner in Penydarren Ironworks as well as in Tredegar. The other ('Humphrey's Engine', 'No 15 Travelling Engine' or, later, *Britannia*) was ordered by Tredegar quite separately and later in the month. Whether Forman had made his own overtures to Stephensons or was working hand in hand with Homfray, we do not know.

The original plans for Forman's engine (Fig. 2.54), undated but attributable to late 1828 or early 1829, show an 0-6-0 with twin vertical boilers after the fashion of *Twin Sisters* then being built for the Liverpool & Manchester.[446] Its wheels were to be 3ft in diameter and set 3ft 1½in apart for running on rails of 3ft gauge, with cylinders steeply inclined and valve motion driven via crank and rocker arms by a gear wheel on the rear axle. But the design was drastically changed, for an outline drawing dated July 1829[447] shows a horizontal boiler. According to another Stephenson source the flue, probably a single non-return one, was elliptical in section, perhaps to increase the heating surface and to minimise distortion fractures due to expansion.[448] The inclined cylinders, 7 by 20in, were mounted on the boiler

Fig. 2.54
Bute, 'Forman's Engine' 1829. (*Rattenbury and Lewis 2004, 54 based on Stephenson works drawings*)

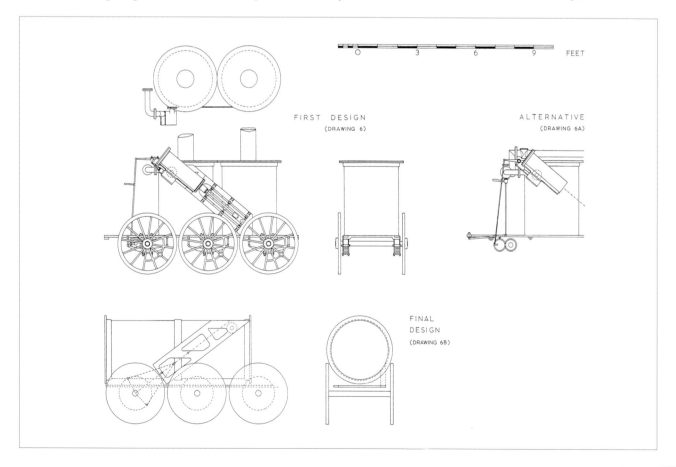

back, the frames were of flat bar 3in by 1 in, and the wheels were 3 feet in diameter. Stripped down to its components for re-assembly on arrival, it was shipped from Newcastle in July 1829, together with *Britannia*, to Tredegar's Pillgwenlly wharf at Newport. It cost £375 plus £19-odd for freight, packing and extras.

On the drawings this engine is named simply 'Forman's Engine' and in the Description Book 'Forman's Wales'.[449] Only the Ledger has 'Willm Forman Penydaren' as the address on the invoice,[450] for which reason it has generally been ascribed to Penydarren.[451] But this is now seen to be wrong. There is no other evidence whatever for a 3ft gauge there, whereas there certainly was at Rhymney and Bute. Above all, Forman was not only a partner in Penydarren (where he lived in Penydarren Place), but also managing partner of Bute; hence that firm's current title of Forman & Co. This explains why Forman's engine was delivered to Newport (convenient for Bute) rather than to Cardiff (convenient for Penydarren).

What work Forman's engine did at Bute is open to debate. By this date the Rhymney-Trefil connection on the 3ft had already been abandoned, and Hall's Trefil Tramroad was the wrong gauge. One wonders if it was intended for Bute's limestone tramroad from Twynau Gwynion quarries to the west, which was built to the right gauge at just the right time (1826-7)[452] and, as we shall shortly find, was certainly locomotive-worked at a later date. The difficulty is that its gradients, with long stretches at worse than 1 in 30, seem impossibly heavy for a locomotive of 1829. Most likely, therefore, this was simply a yard engine, perhaps even, in the spirit of cooperation between the works, shared with Rhymney.

After a brief and presumably unsuccessful spell at Bute, however, it did end up at Penydarren. In 1832 – after Forman's death in 1829 – it went back to Stephensons to be rebuilt as an 0-4-0 on the 4ft 4in gauge, and under the new name of *Eclipse* it ran, again briefly and it seems unsuccessfully, on the Merthyr Tramroad.[453]

2F iv. Rhymney Limestone Railway

Whereas for half a century Rhymney drew most of its limestone from Trefil, around 1826 the new Bute furnaces were given their own quarry at Twynau Gwynion to the west, which had previously been leased to Dowlais and was served by a steeply-graded tramroad about four miles in length (Fig. 2.53);[454] in 1836 there were 92 iron

trams on it.[455] Finally in 1852 Rhymney gave up Trefil and thereafter relied solely on Twynau Gwynion This brings us back to John Phanuel Roe, whose obituary mentions how he built locomotives for the Rumney Railway,

besides largely introducing locomotive haulage in other directions, notably upon the Company's limestone road, previously worked by horses, where, after bettering some of the curves and steep portions, suitable locomotives were successfully worked on grades of 1 in 28; shoe or skid brakes, acting on the rails, were used.[456]

This must have been before Roe left Rhymney for Nantyglo in 1851. As well as serving the limestone quarries, the Bute tramroad passed a number of small coal pits.[457] We first hear of it in its upgraded form in June 1850 when a drunk was mowed down by a runaway train of nine 3-ton limestone waggons whose coupling had broken and whose brakesman had lost control.[458] By the end of that year there was a locomotive on the line near Dowlais Big Pond, above the worst of the gradient, where a horse pulling a trap on the turnpike road shied at the noise of an engine and bolted.[459] At exactly the same time the Rhymney works journals begin to record coal supplies to locomotives on the Limestone Road.[460] Further improvements to the route followed, with large deviations that eased the gradient to an average of about 1 in 30 on the lower half – a stretch known as 'the incline' although it was never rope-worked – reducing to 1 in 78 where the plateau was reached. This, at least from 1857, was known as the Rhymney Limestone Railway (RLR), even though it was still a tramroad. By 1858 there were two locomotives in steam at the same time, one for coal and one for limestone.

No. 8, 0-4-0?, Rhymney *c.*1850

Although not recorded until much later, this engine's number would seem to place it at the beginning of steam haulage on the RLR, presumably designed by Roe and built at Rhymney. The number sequence of Nos. 8-10 rather suggests that all three were built at virtually the same time. In 1860/1 No. 8 killed a collier, whose coffin was debited in the accounts to 'Coal Works' rather than 'Limestone Road,' implying that costs of the coal and limestone traffic on the RLR were kept separate.[461] No technical details are known.

No. 9, 0-4-0?, Rhymney c.1850?

Again no details are known. But No 9's demise hit the headlines. In August 1859 it was being attached to a train of empty coal trucks on a spoil bank on the 'Bute Side Railway' about a quarter of a mile from the Rhymney Railway station, which firmly locates it on the RLR somewhere near Old Dyffryn coal pit; the gauge was therefore 3ft. There was an explosion of immense violence, which flung fragments not only of the boiler but of John Raymond the driver (whom we will meet again), to a distance of 300 yards. The stoker, Robert White, was also killed instantly, but the latchman, David Phillips, was sheltered by the tender and survived unscathed. The inquest heard that water had been within ¾in of the top of the gauge glass, but the pressure, which should have been 80 psi, was over 100. The inquest verdict was accidental death owing to the recklessness of the driver. The press agreed, with the exception of the 'accidental,' and exposed some more home truths about the management of the Rhymney Iron Co.

> The engineer and his second very improperly and against the expressed wish of the coroner, elbowed their way into court to overawe the witnesses, their servants, and to defend themselves. Not content with this, the second had the audacity to interrupt the proceedings.

On a previous occasion, he testified, he had caught the driver putting on an extra 20 psi of steam, and had cautioned him. One newspaper thought the boiler had been in a sound state; but it was widely known, it revealed, that the driver was 'naturally brutal, and continually muddled with brewery beer,' and deranged enough to slaughter cattle wantonly. He had recently sworn to kill his pointsman 'and was only prevented by the man throwing himself on his belly under the carriages till they passed, after which he quitted his employment in the utmost horror.' The paper argued that the company, aware of all this, was equally to blame for not dismissing the driver.[462] The completeness of No. 9's destruction suggests that it was not rebuilt.

No. 10, 0-4-0?, Rhymney c.1850?; and probably others

Again, no technical details are on record. One hazard on the RLR was the local habit of hitching rides on the engine, even inside the ironworks precinct. In particular, east of the point where the line crossed the Dowlais-Rhymney road, trains were treated almost as buses. 'People going between Dowlais and these works often jump up for a ride, which is the most dangerous practice, and causes an enormous loss of life.'[463] On one occasion the driver gave a lift as far as Dowlais Big Pond to two policemen and an Irishwoman under arrest;[464] on another, an engine was derailed while carrying, it seems, no fewer than nine people on the footplate.[465] In 1859 a Rhymney carpenter was killed by No. 10 in unknown circumstances, and so too was an elderly Rhymney overseer while trying to climb on board the moving engine.[466] He missed his footing and 'went under the break and was there crushed into a lifeless mass,' which confirms that the main brakes still bore on the rail. Although the inquest verdict was accidental death, the *Merthyr Telegraph* argued that the Company ought to fine not only offenders who hitched rides but also drivers who permitted them. Apropos a recent accident, the paper had made

> some severe remarks at the time, which were indifferently relished by the agents, who it appears did not intend it to reach headquarters. Unfortunately for them Mr Hutchins, chairman of the Court of Directors, takes the *Telegraph*, so that the cat was let out of the bag, and scratched certain parties severely.[467]

The number of deaths and injuries around this time prompted another paper to rant,

> It seems surprising, seeing so many are killed on this [limestone] road, that the company's agents do not put a stop the practice of jumping up on railway carriages, often in mere wantonness. We observed a train laden with coal passing from the brewery to the works without any one in charge.[468]

Another hazard on the RLR was the steepness of the gradient. In 1858 the latcher of a coal engine 'was with his own engine, and perceiving another locomotive running down the incline he hastened to uncouple his engine,' but his clothes caught on some projection and he was crushed between the buffers.[469] Likewise, a few months later, the brake failed on a coal train descending the incline, and several waggons of a limestone train were smashed. Both trains had locomotives, but they had been detached.[470] Much the same happened two months later again, with brake failure as usual to blame. 'Besides the small breaks furnished to each truck, which are of little use except on a level, a more powerful break is managed from behind by means of a screw rod turned by a small wheel.' It transpired that the last time the brake had been released, the nut carrying the linkage had fallen off the end of the thread, and nobody had noticed. The runaway hit the engine of a coal train waiting at the incline foot with empties, 'shivering the tender to pieces, doubling up part of the engine, and driving the trucks laden with empty trams over the embankment.' Of the three brakesmen, two abandoned ship but the third stayed on board, suffering nasty injuries. 'This is the third collision on this road during the short period of its use,' the press complained, which shows that the final improvements to the RLR had taken place in perhaps 1858.[471] In 1862 much the same happened again, and four trams ran for a mile and a half before being derailed by catch points.[472]

Thus the first RLR locomotive was in place by 1850, and before long there were at least three, and in the following years there were very likely more.

Unnamed, 2-4-0T Neath Abbey 1867

At least one further engine was added after 1859. A Neath Abbey drawing (Fig. 2.55) dated January

1866 shows a design for an 0-4-2ST with slightly inclined cylinders 8 by 16in, wheels 2ft 6in and 2ft, swivelling couplings, and radial trailers on volute springs.[473] Intended for very sharp curves – one of 26ft radius is drawn in – this was probably the first attempt at a new design which came to fruition next year with a 2-4-0T designed by William Moyle, the Rhymney Iron Co's current engineer, with details worked out by L. Thomas, chief draughtsman at Neath Abbey (Fig. 2.56). It was to replace horse traction on a line 'in the proverbially execrable condition of most tramways about ironworks,' part of it laid on longitudinal sleepers. The rolling resistance on the level was in places as much as 60 lbs per ton, the equivalent of 1 in 45 on a normal railway. The coupled wheels were 2ft 8in in diameter on a base of 3ft 6in (the springs of the rear ones cleverly arranged clear of the firebox), the leading wheels 2ft on a short-radius pony truck, total wheelbase 7ft 1in. The wheels themselves were of William Bridges-Adams' then-fashionable design with springs between the wheel centre and the tyre (Fig. 2.57). There was (uniquely on a plateway engine?) a steam brake. The cylinders, steeply inclined, were 8 by 16in, the normal working pressure 60 psi, and the weight 9¾ tons.

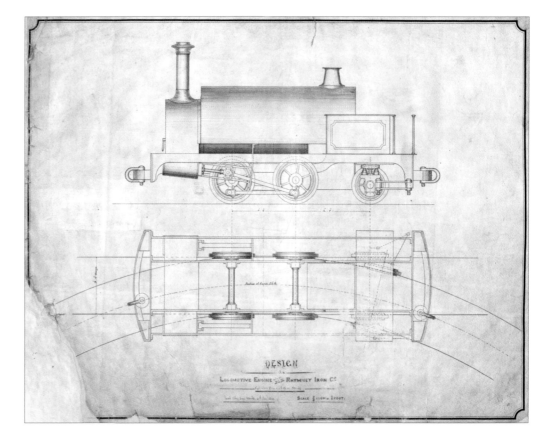

Fig. 2.55
RLR, proposed 0-4-2ST, Neath Abbey 1866. (*WGAS, D/D NAI L/39*)

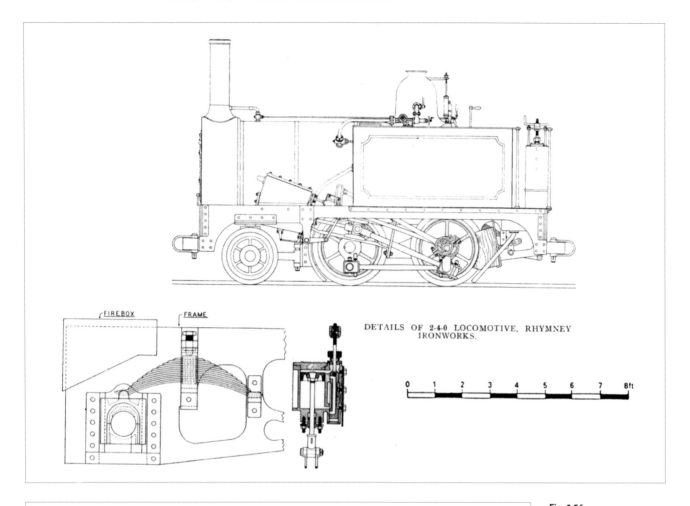

DETAILS OF 2-4-0 LOCOMOTIVE, RHYMNEY
IRONWORKS.

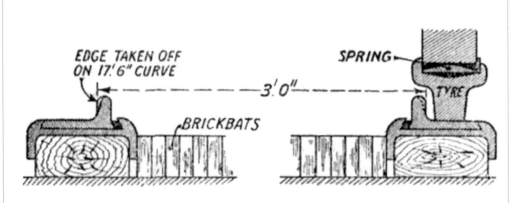

Fig. 2.56
RLR, Neath Abbey 2-4-0T,
1867, with details of rear
springs and steam brake.
(*Locomotive Magazine*
46 (1940), 215)

Fig. 2.57
RLR wheels and track, 1867.
(*Engineering, 13 Sep 1867*)

On test at Neath Abbey it easily took 35 tons up a gradient of 135 in damp conditions, but was intended for long grades of up to 1 in 25 and curves down to 17 ft 6 in radius.[474]

How well it worked we do not know, but it cannot have lasted long, for by 1875 at the latest the RLR was connected to the Brecon & Merthyr and converted to standard gauge.[475] Rhymney Ironworks closed in 1891.

2F v. Tredegar-Ty Trist and Tredegar-Trefil

In 1834 the Trefil-Tredegar line was extended a mile southwards from the furnaces to the new Ty Tryst coal pit. Both these tramroads, when they reached Tredegar, were level with the furnace tops whereas the Sirhowy was at their foot. Later, the 3ft gauge shrank a trifle. In the 1850s the cast-iron plates of the Trefil line were replaced by wrought iron, and thereafter the gauge is given as 2ft 11in or 2ft 11¼in over the flanges. Perhaps the inside gauge was retained and the thinner flanges brought the outside gauge down.

Trefil is a remote village, claimed to be the highest in Wales, and the narrow-gauge tramroad was as much its lifeline for provisions as the Sirhowy Tramroad was Tredegar's. Local people, not so very long ago,

> can also remember 'the carriage' – a home-made tram with built-in seats – being hitched on to the limestone train every Saturday morning to bring the women of the village down to the town and take them back when the shopping was done.'[476]

It was said, when plateways were first introduced, that one advantage they had over edge railways was that unflanged wheels could run on ordinary roads. So, in theory, they could; and very occasionally, if the wheels were broad enough, they did. But South Wales knew the damage they wreaked on road surfaces. In 1855 a man was fined for 'defacing the highway road,

in Castle-street, Tredegar ... by taking a narrow-wheel loaded tram over the same.'[477] Castle Street branches off Commercial Road, along which ran the tramroad to Ty Trist.

Two unnamed 0-4-0s, Tredegar c.1853

The sequence of Tredegar's six four-coupled engines on the 2ft 11in gauge is well-known and uncontentious.[478] The first two were built at Tredegar by Thomas Ellis. Two of the lists, which are hardly reliable, give their date as before 1848. Certainly it was before he left in 1854 but perhaps, because they are not otherwise attested until 1855, not so long before. A surviving photograph of one in a partly-dismantled state (Fig. 2.58), which must date to about 1900,[479] shows steeply-inclined cylinders at the back of the boiler exactly as on his 'main-line' engines. What we know about them and their successors derives almost entirely from press reports, which again record a woeful number of accidents, especially to children because these lines not only ran along

Fig. 2.58
Tredegar-Ty Tryst Tramroad, Tredegar 0-4-0ST c.1853, as dismantled in c.1900. Note the Fletcher Jennings locomotive just visible on the left. (*NMW, 1997-247/2*)

the streets, but their empty trams offered the perennial temptation of a free ride to youngsters, whether at play or returning from work.

Thus in 1855 an eleven-year-old boy was killed. According to a witness at the Ash Tree pit, part-way between Tredegar and Ty Trist, the engine was coming by, and the deceased ran after it, to get up on the hitching, between the two trams, when he fell under, and the wheel went over his leg … The little fellow was working in the pit, and was running after the trams, to get a ride homeward.'[480]

There is then a six-year silence in the local press on locomotive-related accidents, followed by no fewer than eight reports in nine years. In 1861 Isaac Jones, aged 12, fell under the wheels, and Robert Thomas Jones told the inquest,

I am brother of the deceased, and was coming with him from work on Saturday night, about 6 o'clock, when the accident happened. We were returning from the new pit, and a train of empty cinder trams came up. There were about 20 trams, which were drawn by a locomotive on a railway. Being the quickest runner, I succeeded in getting on the foremost but one. He followed, and attempted to get on the last tram but one, and as the trams were yet hot from the molten red hot cinder, he put his cap on the iron, to save his hands, while he mounted. In doing this, his hands slipped, and he fell on the line, the last two trams passing over him. I saw him fall and beckoned the engine-man to stop …We have no business riding on these trams; but we get up when we are tired. The Company does not send trams for us now, as it used to do.

Evan Lewis, stoker, deposed,

One of the men on the tender hallooed out, 'There's a boy under!' and the train stopped in six yards. It would be a job to put a guard's van behind the carriages, and that would not prevent people from getting up. There are guards on the big engine. These cinder trams are very dangerous, because they tip up when pressed on behind. It was by this tipping of the platform that Jones lost his life. I don't think we could prevent people from climbing up.[481]

This was on the line from the slag tip half a mile north of the furnaces.

In 1865 a driver was prosecuted for stealing coal by kicking it off the tender en route to Ty Trist for an accomplice to pick up, and a six-year-old was run over by a locomotive at Ash Tree Pit.[482] Next year an engine heading for the colliery toppled over and trapped the driver underneath.[483] Further youngsters were killed in 1867 and 1869 (when the inquest jury recommended the line be fenced), and another toddler, 'as is the practice with hundreds of others, strayed along the tramroad, on which the engine travels from Tytrist-pit to the yard,' and was run over.[484] Tredegar works – as distinct from the Sirhowy Railway – acquired its first standard-gauge engines (apart from the converted Ellis ones) in 1869-70,[485] and at some point the Ty Trist line was relaid to standard gauge. But the narrow-gauge plateway there was still at work in 1875.

As the engine, which is a small one, was taking a number of empty trams from the works to the Ty Trist coal pit, along the Park-row, one of the empty trams was full of boys and girls … The engine travels at a rapid speed. The trams generally go along in a jerking fashion, and a nine-year-old boy was shaken off and run over.[486]

It was at this point that 'the objectionable occupation of the streets by tramways' was rectified by building a new system of railways.[487]

These two Tredegar-built locomotives began life with tenders, but by the end they had saddle tanks, as well as low and close-set buffers. In 1865, as we shall see, they were joined by two conventional engines intended particularly for the Trefil line. Whether the old ones ever ventured north to Trefil or the newcomers south to Ty Trist is a moot point. It was said in 1869 that from Ty Trist, 'four small tank locomotives, running on tram plates, 2ft 10in gauge, convey coal and mine to the furnaces, and coal to the yard depot, where it is screened. These locomotives also convey limestone from the Trefil quarries to the blast furnaces.'[488] But the evidence rather suggests that the original pair hauled only coal and ore and cinders and the newer pair only limestone.

Two unnamed 0-4-0 STs, Fletcher Jennings 1865

The Trefil limestone quarries to the north that were tapped by Tredegar and Rhymney lie at a lower level than those tapped by Sirhowy, Beaufort and Ebbw Vale, at around 1,400ft on the bleak moorland where the counties of Monmouth and Brecon met.[489] The overall gradient from Tredegar, which stands at about

Fig. 2.59
Train on Trefil-Tredegar Tramroad with MT&AR Blaen y Cwm viaduct ('Nine Arches') behind, engraving by J. Newman published 24 Jan 1865. (*Jones 1969*)

Fig. 2.60
Trefil-Tredegar Tramroad, Fletcher Jennings standard Class A 0-4-0ST. (*Lowca Engineering Co catalogue*)

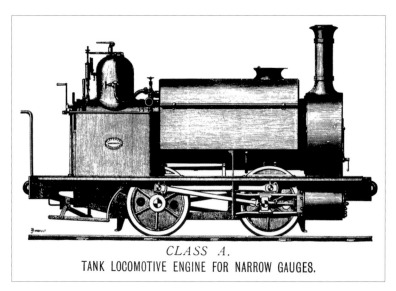

CLASS A.
TANK LOCOMOTIVE ENGINE FOR NARROW GAUGES.

1000ft, up to Trefil was therefore roughly 1 in 33. For the first half of its long life, the Trefil limestone tramroad was horse-operated. It still was so at the beginning of 1865 when an engraving was published of the Merthyr Tredegar & Abergavenny Railway's new Blaen y Cwm viaduct with the tramroad in the foreground (Fig. 2.59). Later in that year, however, two conventional four-coupled saddle tanks arrived, of a type designed for sharp curves and steep gradients (Fig. 2.60). They were built by Fletcher Jennings of Whitehaven, a manufacturer popular at South Wales ironworks. They were the makers' Class A, the works numbers were 51-52, the cylinders 8 by 16in, the wheels 2ft 6in, and the weight about 8 tons empty. That they were the first on the Trefil line is implied by the statement in March 1866 that 'a few months ago an engine was installed to run between Tredegar yard and Trefil to haul limestone.'[490] About 1900 one of them was still languishing dismantled in a shed alongside one of the Tredegar-built locomotives (Fig. 2.61).[491]

Unnamed 0-4-0 VB, Fletcher Jennings 1872

They were followed in 1872 by another Fletcher Jennings, this time a curious one built to Fletcher's patent with a vertical thimble boiler, that is with water-filled cones projecting inwards into the firebox (Fig. 2.62). The works number was 100, the inside cylinders 6 by 10 in, the wheels 2ft. Only three of this class were ever built, and the fact that Tredegar bought yet another engine the very next year suggests that this one was not a success. It certainly looks exceedingly top-heavy.[492]

Unnamed 0-4-0 ST, Vulcan Foundry 1873

The final arrival was a Vulcan Foundry four-coupled saddle tank, number 681 of 1873, with 10in cylinders and 3ft wheels (Fig. 2.63). Vulcan

CLASS D.

was a builder already known at Tredegar, for the Sirhowy Railway had bought six of its standard-gauge engines from 1859.[493] This narrow-gauge one was the last plateway locomotive ever made for Britain. Its nearest rival was a Neath Abbey engine built for Cyfarthfa in 1871,[494] but two plateway locomotives were built for New Zealand in 1881-2 by Dorset Iron Foundry of Poole, one of which worked until at least 1921.[495] There was still plenty of work for the Vulcan, however, for in the record year of 1890 the line carried more than 35,000 tons of limestone,[496] and even though Tredegar ceased making iron in 1901, the tramroad continued. This engine, as rebuilt at Tredegar in 1905 (according to the plate on its cab side) hauled its miscellany of wooden and iron trams of various shapes and sizes until 1915 when too many quarrymen had gone to war for the tramroad to be sustained, and the lease was surrendered and the line closed (Fig. 2.64).[497]

We have no information about these engines in use beyond the expected list of accidents. A few examples out of many will suffice. In 1867,

Several complaints have been made of the hurried driving through the streets lately: in Church street some casualties have occurred to little children,

Fig. 2.61
Trefil-Tredegar Tramroad, Fletcher Jennings 51 or 52 of 1865, as dismantled in c.1900. Note saddle tank dismounted behind and rear of an Ellis locomotive on the right.
(*NMW, 2016-62*)

Fig. 2.62
Trefil-Tredegar Tramroad, Fletcher Jennings vertical boiler locomotive of 1872.
(*Lowca Engineering Co catalogue*)

Fig. 2.63
Trefil-Tredegar Tramroad, maker's photograph of Vulcan Foundry 681 of 1873. (*Merseyside Maritime Museum*)

Fig. 2.64
Trefil-Tredegar Tramroad, Vulcan Foundry engine as rebuilt in 1905, at work in 1911. (*NRM, GWR A1003*)

who run after the coal train in dozens, and on one occasion the engine from the Trefil brought about sixty trams, and came to a halt across the road at the end of Collier's-row. The Rev E. Leigh was proceeding to town and waited some time to cross the road. As the engine could not move the train,

some trams were unhitched and as Mr Leigh was in the act of passing between, the engine started, and he narrowly escaped being thrown down. Summonses were taken out, and the driver and stoker were taken before the magistrates … and were fined for the offence.[498]

Fig. 2.65
Trefil-Tredegar Tramroad
at Nantybwch in 1910. Nine
Arches viaduct beyond.
(*Jones 1969*)

In 1872 a Tredegar resident was walking to Trefil when he caught up with the engine while it was taking on water, and climbed into a tram that already held some men and women. In the next tram was a boy of eight who, after the train restarted, jumped out and was killed on the spot. The latchman elaborated,

I was in front of the engine looking out for any stones which might be thrown in the road. Deceased got in at Tredegar before we started. People frequently ride up on the trams. We have no rules saying we are not to allow any one to ride in the trams … When we got beyond the curve, near the Crown Brickyard, I heard the women scream, and we stopped the engine directly. We were going very slowly, the steam being only up to 70 lbs. Anyone could have got out easily enough. We generally stop to let women get out, and on that evening we should have stopped a little way further to put some flour down. Thomas Davies had charge of the engine, and he stops wherever he chooses.

The coroner remarked that 'the boy jumped out carelessly, as boys often will do.' [499]

Only two months later,

as the last lime-stone train was coming from Trefil quarries, a very serious accident befell William Lewis, stoker (and brother to the driver, David Lewis). It appears that William was in the act of turning one of the latches or points, and slipping down his arm was run over by the loaded trams.[500]

In 1887 ('Larking with an engine,' says the headline), three butcher's boys from Tredegar had been delivering meat at Trefil and were given permission to ride on the engine.

On reaching a public-house called the Mountain Hare [Mountain Air] the train was brought to a stand, and the men in charge went into the public-house, leaving the three boys – Holms, Evans, and Johnson – on the engine. While the men were inside the tavern another lad jumped upon the engine and turned on the steam, which he afterwards failed to turn off again. The train, starting over the top of a slight incline, travelled at a terrible pace, heedless of curves and points, until it reached the Crown, where it came to a sudden stand, causing the engine to become a complete wreck. The boy Evans had the presence of mind to jump off directly the engine started. Johnson received a nasty cut, and Holms escaped unhurt with the exception of fright. The lads had a miraculous escape.

The train had run nearly half a mile to Nantybwch, where the stiff gradient can be seen in Fig. 2.65. David Lewis, the driver, indignantly denied that he and his crew were in the pub, and insisted they were releasing the brakes.[501]

In 1909 Samuel Evans, aged six, 'with other boys, was riding in the last tram and fell out, and the train passed over his body. The engine driver said it was impossible to keep the boys out of the trams.'[502] Thus this litany of tragedies on the 2ft 11in gauge ended as it had begun in 1855, with boys being boys.

Locomotive Summary

Except where stated otherwise, all ran on 4ft 4in-gauge plateways.
Engines changing hands within the area are listed under both old and new owners.

A. EXPERIMENTAL PERIOD

A i. TREDEGAR IRON CO, *works yard or feeder tramroads, gauge 3ft 0in*

				cyl. dia.	
'Tram Engine'	1803/4?	Tredegar?	0-4-0 G	4¾"	Trevithick design, possibility only

A ii. NANTYGLO IRON CO, *branch of Clydach Railroad, gauge 3ft 8in edge*

–	1814/15	Nantyglo?	4-wheel	8"?	rack, reb Tredegar 1830 to 3ft 6in plate for Llangattock

A iii. SIRHOWY TRAMROAD, *Gellihaf branch?*

–	1816	W. Stewart	0-4-4-0 G?	*c.*9"	

B. SIRHOWY TRAMROAD

B i. TREDEGAR IRON CO

Britannia	1829	Stephenson	0-6-0	10"	wdn *c.*1840? boiler burst 1830
St David	1830	Tredegar	0-6-0	10/12"	boiler burst 1830 and 1838, reb 1848, conv *c.*1859, wdn 1880s, scr 1909
Tredegar	1830/5?	Tredegar	0-6-0	10/12"	conv *c.*1859
Jane	1830/5?	Tredegar	0-6-0	10/12"	
(Lord ?) Rodney	1830/5?	Tredegar	0-6-0	10"	
Lady Charlotte	*c.*1835?	Tredegar	0-6-0	10/12"	
Speedwell	1830	Neath Abbey	0-4-0	10½"	bell crank, ex-Prothero *c.*1835 wdn *c.*1842
Hercules	1831	Neath Abbey	6-wheel	10½"	rocker, ex-Prothero *c.*1835 reb 1837, wdn *c.*1842
Fanny	1839	Tredegar	0-6-0	10/12"	
Lady Mary		Tredegar			existence unconfirmed
Prince Albert	1840/1	Tredegar			existence unconfirmed
Dispatch	1842/3?	Tredegar	0-4-0	?	yard engine
Lady Sale	1843?	Tredegar	0-6-0	10/12"	
Bedwellty	1853	Tredegar	0-6-0	12"	conv *c.*1859, wdn *c.*1882

B ii. ARGOED COLLIERY (*Tredegar Iron Co*)?

Vulcan	1831?	Murray?	2-2-0	11"?	ex-Pearson 1842? boiler burst 1843

C. MONMOUTHSHIRE CANAL CO WESTERN VALLEYS LINES

C i. BLAINA IRON CO

–	1830	Blaina		?	
–	1833	Blaina		?	
No. 1	1838	Bury	2-2-0	12"	ex-LNWR 1848
No. 2	1838	Bury	2-2-0	12"	ex-LNWR 1848

C ii. THOMAS PROTHERO, *freighter*

Speedwell	1830	Neath Abbey	0-4-0	10½"	bell crank, to Tredegar *c.*1835
Hercules	1831	Neath Abbey	6-wheel	10½"	rocker, to Tredegar *c.*1835

C iii. MARTIN MORRISON, *freighter*

–	1832	Neath Abbey	0-6-0	10½"	rocker, sold 1836?

C iv. HARFORD DAVIES & CO / EBBW VALE CO / SIRHOWY IRON CO

Lark	1831	Neath Abbey	0-6-0?	10½"	bell crank
Perseverance	1832	Neath Abbey	0-6-0	10½"	rocker, on Sirhowy from 1833
Abbey	1836?	Neath Abbey	0-6-0	10½"	rocker, on Sirhowy from 1833 boiler burst 1841
–	1832	Neath Abbey	0-4-0	*c.*7"	rocker, yard engine?
Hawk	1832?	Neath Abbey	0-6-0	10½"	bell crank
Alert?	1841?	Neath Abbey?	0-6-0?	10½"?	rocker, ex-Victoria 1846?

C v. MONMOUTHSHIRE IRON & COAL CO, *Victoria*

Alert?	1841?	Neath Abbey?	0-6-0?	10½"?	rocker, to Ebbw Vale 1846?

C vi. MONMOUTHSHIRE RAILWAY & CANAL CO

No. 1 *Doctor*	1847	Stubbs & Grylls	0-8-0	16"	reb Uskside 1848, wdn 1849, for sale 1850
No. 2 *Ebbw Vale*?	1848	Neath Abbey	0-6-0	15"	
No. 3	1848	Neath Abbey	0-6-0	15"	
No. 4	1848	Neath Abbey	0-6-0	15"	
No. 5	1848	Neath Abbey	0-6-0	15"	
No. 6	1849	Stothert	0-6-0	?	
No. 7	1849	Stothert	0-6-0	?	
No. 8	1849	Stothert	0-6-0	?	
No. 9	1849	Sharp Bros	2-4-0WT	13"	
No. 10	1849	Sharp Bros	2-4-0WT	13"	
No. 11 *Aegeon*	1838?	Maudslay?	0-4-0	13"?	ex-Waring & Sons, 1849
No. 12	1850	Sharp Bros	0-6-0	?	
No. 13	1850	Sharp Bros	0-6-0	?	
No. 14	1850	Stothert	0-4-0WT	?	
No. 15	1850	Stothert	0-4-0WT	?	
No. 16	1850	Stothert	4-4-0?	?	Nos. 2-16 conv to standard gauge 1853-9

D. RUMNEY RAILWAY

D i. RUMNEY RAILWAY CO

–	by 1855	?	0-4-0?	?	'little ballast engine'

D ii. RHYMNEY IRON CO

Amelia	1838	Neath Abbey	0-6-0	8½"	bell crank
Laura	1838	Neath Abbey	0-6-0	8½"	bell crank
Alderman	1838	Neath Abbey	0-4-4-0 G	8½"	double bogie
Bute	1839	Neath Abbey	0-6-0	10½"	rocker
Rhymney	1839	Neath Abbey	0-6-0	10½"	rocker
Superb	?	?	?	?	ex-Cleave 1843 reb Rhymney 1848
No. 4	1838	Bury	2-2-0	12"	ex-LNWR 1847
No. 5	1840	Hick & Co	2-2-0	13"	ex-LNWR 1847
No. 6	c.1847	Rhymney	0-4-4-0 G?	?	double bogie? 'new engine' 1848
–	1845	Bury	2-2-0	14"?	ex-L&YR 1854

D iii. BRITHDIR COLLIERY

Brithdir	1847	Stubbs & Grylls?	0-4-2?	?	

D iv. MARSHALL & KNOWLES, *White Rose Colliery, Brithdir*

–	by 1853	?	?	?	boiler burst 1853
–	by 1854	?	?	?	
Rose	by 1854	?	0-4-0	14"	

D v. MESSRS PROTHERO, Pengam or Bassaleg?

–	1839	Maudslay	0-4-0	13"	ex-LNWR 1853

E. TRAMROAD UNKNOWN

Goliath	1846	Neath Abbey		10½"	rocker

F. NARROW GAUGE

F i. HARFORD DAVIES & CO, *Ebbw Vale-Sirhowy tunnel, gauge 2ft 9in*

–	1832	Neath Abbey	0-4-0	c.7"	rocker

F ii. NANTYGLO IRON CO, *Bailey's Llangattock Tramroad, gauge 3ft 6in*

–	1814/15	Nantyglo?	0-4-0 G	8"?	reb Tredegar 1830 from edge rail rack loco
–	1832	Richard Jones	?	?	
Sampson	1839	Lloyds Fosters	?	?	
–	1841	Neath Abbey	?	10½"	
Cymro Bach	1849/50	Uskside	0-4-0	?	sold 1889
Cymro	c.1860	Uskside	0-4-0 ST	?	sold 1889

F iii. FORMAN & CO / RHYMNEY IRON CO, *internal lines, gauge 3ft 0in*

–	1829	Stephenson	0-6-0	7"	to Penydarren 1832

F iv. RHYMNEY IRON CO, *Rhymney Limestone Railway, gauge 3ft 0in*

No. 8	1850	Rhymney	?	?	
No. 9	c.1850?	Rhymney	?	?	boiler burst 1859
No. 10	c.1850?	Rhymney	?	?	
–	1867	Neath Abbey	2-4-0 T	8"	

and probably others

F v. TREDEGAR IRON CO, *feeder tramroads, gauge 2ft 11in*

–	c.1853	Tredegar	0-4-0	?	later ST, wdn c.1875
–	c.1853	Tredegar	0-4-0	?	later ST, wdn c.1875
–	1865	Fletcher Jennings	0-4-0 ST	8"	
–	1865	Fletcher Jennings	0-4-0 ST	8"	
–	1872	Fletcher Jennings	0-4-0 VBT	6"	
–	1873	Vulcan Foundry	0-4-0 ST	10"	reb 1905, sold/scr 1915

Notes to Part Two

1   Reynolds 2003, Lewis 2019b.

2   Rattenbury and Lewis 2004.

3   WGAS, D/D NAI.

4   Report of the Commissioners for Railways for 1849, Appendix 74, 157-178 = *PP* 1850, vol. xxxi, 179.

5   See in general Ince 1990 and Ince 2001.

6   Reynolds 1986, 64; Reynolds 2003, 174.

7   Denman 2000, 19.

8   NRM, 1903-102.

9   Guy et al 2019, App. 2.

10   The formula for the horsepower of a single-cylinder engine is

$$\frac{\text{(Total pressure on piston in psi)} \times \text{(distance piston travels in feet per minute)}}{33{,}000}$$

For Penydarren, cylinder 8¼in by 4ft 6in; for Tram Engine, 4¾in by 3ft. Assume maximum boiler pressure is 40psi. In the absence of indicator diagrams, generalise that effective pressure in cylinder is 50% of boiler pressure, which allows for cut-off of steam at an indeterminate point part way through the stroke, but multiply by 2 because it is a double-acting engine.

Distance piston travels per minute = stroke in feet × 2 × rpm.

Thus for the Penydarren engine nominal hp is

$$\frac{384{,}840}{33{,}000} = 11.66$$

For Tram Engine it is

$$\frac{85{,}070}{33{,}000} = 2.58$$

Deducting a conventional 10% for frictional losses gives about 10.6 and 2.3 brake horsepower respectively. I am indebted to Jennifer Protheroe-Jones for the formula.

11   Letter from William Menelaus to John Hackworth, 27 Jan 1872: Young 1923, 21.

12   Letter from William Llewellin to William Menelaus, 24 Nov 1855: Trevithick 1872, vol. 1, 176.

13   *Engineering*, 27 Mar 1868, 278. John Phanuel Roe (1815-88), after an apprenticeship under John Llewellin's brother, moved in 1835 to Dowlais as draughtsman and assistant engineer, and shortly thereafter to Rhymney as chief engineer. We shall meet him again.

14   NRM T/1903-102.

15   Forward 1952.

16   Oeynhausen and Dechen 1971, 67.

17   For further discussion see Guy et al 2019, App. 2.

18   Van Laun 2000, 174, 176, 179.

19   Rattenbury and Lewis 2004, 29, 62 and n.175.

20   The evidence for the exact gauge is set out under 2F.ii below.

21   Svedenstjerna 1804, 104; translation, 59.

22   *Engineering*, 27 Mar 1868.

23   *MPICE*, 8 (1849), 30.

24   Obituary of Field in *MPICE*, 23 (1863-4), 488-92.

25   Forward 1921; Clements 1970, 35.

26   *South Wales Daily News*, 2 Sep 1886. 'Cheviot' is identified as Turner in *South Wales Daily News*, 1 Jan 1891. He moved to Cardiff in 1862 from his home town of Berwick where he was a customs clerk (*Evening Express*, 16 Dec 1895).

27   *Western Mail*, 27 May 1887.

28   Wilkins 1888, 162, 187.

29   *Weekly Mail*, 3 Mar 1895.

30   *Weekly Mail*, 31 Aug 1895, repeated verbatim in Wilkins 1903, 134. This last was noted but dismissed by Dendy Marshall 1953, 19.

31   Aberconway 1927, 271.

32   Trevithick 1872, vol. 1, 190.

33   Trevithick 1872, vol. 1, 222 dates it, less reliably, to about 1800-01. Dickinson and Titley 1934, 71 give 1804. Powell 1902, 24 says it was at first for blowing the blast furnaces but was moved to power the rolling mill which came into use in 1807. On 31 March 1805 Homfray was intending to put up a 42 hp Trevithick engine at Tredegar which is probably the one in question (Eyles 1970-1, 156-7). This is the last date at which we hear of Trevithick's presence at Penydarren, and possibly at Tredegar too.

34   Ellis told Francis that 'the Mill and Puddling engine at Tredegar was made by Mr Aubrey Engineer at Penydarran and My Father,' i.e. that Aubrey was engineer at Penydarren but that the engine was built, as one would expect, at Tredegar (NRM, 2002-8348/74/2, 26 Dec 1868). This ties in with Aubrey's and Ellis senior's known careers. Francis, however, in quoting this letter, twists it to 'the mill and puddling engine at Tredegar were made by Mr Aubry and my father at Penydarran' (Trevithick 1872, vol. 1, 222).

35   NRM, 2002-8348/74/3 (4 Mar 1869). Taken down In 1858, says Powell 1902, 24.

36   Andrieux 1815; Dendy Marshall 1953, 29-54; Bye 2003; Guy 2001, 122-3; NEIMME, Watson/1/6 doc.61; Winstanley 2014, 122-5, 128.

37   NEIMME, Watson/3/13 doc.116; Watson/3/112 docs.10, 17; transcribed in Forward 1930.

38   Reynolds 2017.

39   NEIMME, Watson/1/6/53 doc.61.

40   *MM*, 27 Mar 1830.

41   *Repertory of Arts, Manufactures and Agriculture*, 2nd series, 33 (1818), 19.

42   Newcastle City Library, 6749-53; Guy and Reynolds 1999.

43   *HT*, 20 Nov 1858.

44   In 1859 he recalled that construction of his Govilon tramroad from Nantyglo was completed on 6 September 1821 (*HT*, 10 Sep 1859). This is probably a journalistic mistake: it was actually on 6 December (*HJ*, 19 Dec 1821).

45   *HT*, 4 Oct 1862.

46   *GJ*, 10 Dec 1810.

47   *GJ*, 16 Jul 1810.

48   *GJ*, 25 Nov 1811.

49   Rattenbury 1980, 49, 68, 70-1, 75, 80.

50   Van Laun 2001, 45, 134.

51   Science Museum, 1881-57.

52   *CT*, 24 Aug 1889.

53   *Silurian* 26 Jun 1852.

54   NRM, 2002-8348/73 (in 1854).

55   *Mining Journal*, 2 Oct 1858, copied in Trevithick 1872, vol. I, 178.

56   NRM, 2002-8348/66/2, Francis Trevithick to John Enys, 1841.

57   NRM, 2002-8348/72/2, William Brown to Richard Edmonds, 6 Jun 1853.

58   NLW, MS 5157 f.23v.

59   NLW, MS 5157 f.42v.

60   For Hackworth's and others' spring valves, see Gibbon 2001, 208-15.

61   NLW, MS 5156 f.20v.

62   NLW, MS 5155.

63   *Cambrian*, 23 Sep 1815; *GJ*, 8 Jan, 5 Feb 1816; *London Gazette*, 30 Jan 1816.

64   *Practical Mechanic and Engineer's Magazine*, 4 (Oct 1844), 24; copied in Dendy Marshall 1953, 99-100; a similar account in *Practical Mechanic and Engineer's Magazine*, 4 (Nov 1844), 57-60.

65   Paar 1963, 119.

66   Increased to 3ft 8in in 1843: Paar 1963, 38.

67   NRM, T/1903-102, p 28 and Smith's expenses sheet. His transcription and sketch differ slightly from Trevithick's in NRM, 2002-8348/87; Trevithick 1872, vol. I, 179. See also Liffen 2018.

68   Paar 1965, 66, 69.

69   For all these, see Guy 2001 and Rees 2001.

70   Rees 2001, 156, which combines the two Whitehaven drawings as published by Mulholland 1978, 178-9 and adds the missing valve drive.

71   Together with a less important follow-up of 13 Feb, TNA, RAIL 1014/4/28, quoted in Barrie and Lee 1940, 18 and Dendy Marshall 1953, 101.

72   Meredith 1913, 228.

73   *Morning Chronicle*, 19 Sep 1811; *GJ*, 4 Oct 1813;

74   Barrie and Lee 1940, 18.

75   Rattenbury and Lewis 2004, 64. It materialised next year as *Perseverance*, without the bogies but still with the rack drive.

76   Reynolds 1986.

77   Reynolds 2019.

78   Rowson 2019.

79   For his locomotives, see Forward 1951, Dendy Marshall 1953, 61-76, and especially Guy 2001, 123-5, 134-7.

80   *Repertory of Arts and Manufactures*, 2nd series 24 (1814).

81   *Cambrian*, 21 Jan 1815.

82   NLW, MS 5160 f.65v. Son of Maurice Ellis, he was baptised at Eyton-upon-the-Weald-Moors nearby. He was described in 1804, just after moving to Tredegar, as 'carpenter.'

83   *MM*, 31 Mar 1849. Jones 1969, 52 has him training at Garnddyrys (the Blaenavon Company's forge) and elsewhere, but quotes no source.

84   *MB*, Sep 1853.

85   Powell 1902, 64-5.

86   *CMG*, 22 Sep 1854, 17 Feb 1855, 24 Oct 1857; *MM*, 14 Mar 1857.

87   *MM*, 25 Dec 1858.

88   *Swindon Advertiser*, 31 Jun 1865.

89   NRM, 2002-8348/74/2 (26 Dec 1868).

90   *MM*, 1 Jan 1870.

91   Though he was on the committee of the Tredegar Literary Institution, and at Swindon helped establish a Welsh church (*MM*, 29 Dec 1849; *Seren Cymru*, 4 Nov 1864).

92   *MM*, 31 Mar 1849. In 1851 Ellis took out his only patent (no. 13,535), for improvements in rolling iron.

93   *MM*, 30 Mar 1850.

94   Many references in Trevithick 1872.

95   Copy in NRM, 1985-1107.

96   Madison 2015; *MM*, 30 Nov 1867.

97   *MT*, 26 Jul 1862.

98   *MM*, 29 Aug 1858, 27 Jul 1861; *MT*, 26 Jul 1862.

99   *MM*, 7 Aug 1874; obituaries in *Weekly Express*, 10 Feb 1902, *PIME* 1902, 197.

100 Powell 1902, 64-5.

101 NLW, MS 5155-5160A, donated by Iwan Morgan in 1944; in Charles Ellis' possession from 1868 or earlier until 1921 or later (NRM, 2002-8348/74/2; Warren 1923, 32, 154-5).

102 'The late Sir Daniel Gooch – an interesting local relic,' *Western Mail*, 19 Oct 1889.

103 'An old colliery locomotive,' *RM*, 9 (Nov 1901), 422.

104 'Early coal-winding engines,' *Monmouthshire Evening Post*, 22 Feb 1912 with correction 23 Feb.

105 'The Sirhowy Railway,' *Locomotive Magazine*, 21 (Jan 1915), 9-11.

106 Present whereabouts unknown. Good copy in NWM 2003-152/2. First published in Warren 1923, 154.

107 First published in *RM*, 9 (Nov 1901), 422. Frequently reproduced.

108 That of *St David* apparently first published in Jones 1965. Frequently reproduced.

109 'An old mineral locomotive,' *Locomotive Magazine*, 11 (Mar 1905), 49.

110 Jones 1965, Jones 1969, 53-4; Tasker 1992, 18-20; Byles 1982, 16-17; Hill and Green 1999, 154-6; Reynolds 2000; Lewis 2001.

111 Lewis 1835, vol 4, s.v. Tredegar; NLW, MS 5155; *PP* 1850, vol. xxxi, 198; Morris 1868, 19; Shore 2017, 34.

112 Guy and Reynolds 1999 (of 1818).

113 Elsas 1960, 171 (of 1821).

114 NRM, 2002-6348/74/1 (letter to Francis Trevithick, 22 Jun 1854).

115 Warren 1923, 32. But he is muddled, ascribing the information about the Newcastle visit (32 n. 5 and 154 n. 1) to Charles Ellis's letter of 1912 to the *Monmouthshire Evening Post*, which in fact deals only with the winding engine at Gellihaf. Warren's source seems rather to have been a letter, now lost, from Charles Ellis to Robert Stephenson & Co of 8 Jul 1921 (Warren 1923, 155 n.2).

116 NLW, MS 5158.

117 NLW, MS 5159 f.13r: 'Mr Daniel Gouch began to Work with Thos Ellis Senior Febry 6th – 1832 Left Jany Pay 1834'; Gooch 1892, 16, 20.

118 *Brecon & Radnor Express*, 30 Aug 1917. George ended up as divisional engineer of the Cambrian Railways.

119 So the Stephenson Description Book (NRM, ROB/2/4/1, f.3). But even at the time there was confusion about the numbers. Elsewhere in the Stephenson papers they are given as Nos. 14 and 16: Dendy Marshall 1953, 142-3.

120 Dendy Marshall 1953, 143.

121 Stephenson ledger, NRM, ROB/4/1 f.205, 31 Jul 1829.

122 Warren 1923, 154.

123 TNA RAIL 500/6, 16 Sep 1829.

124 TNA RAIL, 500/ 6, 3 Nov 1829.

125 Barrie and Lee 1940, 19.

126 *MM*, 26 Dec 1829.

127 *Locomotive Magazine*, 21 (Jan 1915), 10.

128 *MM*, 27 Mar 1830.

129 *MM*, 3 and 10 Jul 1830. The boy cannot be found in the burial records of neighbouring parishes. Byles 1982, 18 gratuitously names this engine as *St David*.

130 NLW, MS 5157 f.43r.

131 *Cambrian*, 31 Jul 1830.

132 NLW, MS 5155-60, various.

133 *MT*, 6 Dec 1856.

134 TNA, RAIL 500/7, Nov 1831.

135 TNA, RAIL 500/6, 24 Aug 1830.

136 Dendy Marshall 1953, 117-18.

137 TNA, RAIL 500/7, 26-8 Jul 1831.

138 Trevithick 1872, vol. I, 165.

139 Hadfield 1967, 148.

140 NLW, MS 5160 f.23r.

141 *Locomotive Magazine* 11 (Mar 1905), 49. The John Sambrook it names must be a mistake, William being the only candidate in the censuses.

142 Barrie and Lee 1940, 33; and Byles 1982, 17 who says, certainly in error, that it was supplied by Stephensons in kit form.

143 *MM*, 27 Mar 1830.

144 NLW, MS 5156 f.20v.

145 *MM*, 23 Oct 1830. Jones 1965, 42 and 1969, 53 (who introduces a fictitious date of March 1830) and Tasker 1992, 20-1 are muddled about these explosions of 1830. Ten boiler explosions are recorded on our tramroads between 1830 and 1859, or 12½ per cent of all the engines.

146 NLW, MS 5157 f.42r.

147 NLW, MS 5157 f.41v.

148 *GMBG*, 8 Sep 1838.

149 *RM*, 9 (Nov 1901), 422; Meredith 1906, 255; *Locomotive Magazine*, 21 (Jan 1915), 10.

150 Warren 1923, 154-5; Jones 1965 fig. 3, apparently signed by Ellis; another photographic copy in NWM, 2003-152/2. The present whereabouts of the original is unknown.

151 NLW, MS 5159 f.69.

152 TNA, COPY 1/449/268.

153 Rowson 1995-6, 314.

154 *CMG*, 13 May 1848.

155 http://image.slidesharecdn.com/homfrayt railsculpturesfinalwithnotes-131105064228-phpapp02/95/homfray-trail-sculptures-final-with-notes-46-638.jpg?cb=1383634070

156 *MM*, 5 Mar 1863.

157 *MM*, 7 Apl 1849.

158 Jones 1969, 54.

159 Lewis 1835, vol. 4, s.v. Tredegar.

160 NLW, MS 5158.

161 *MM*, 29 Apl 1843.

162 *MB*, 4 Jun 1853.

163 *Western Daily Press*, 7 Feb 1859.

164 *HT*, 12 Feb 1859.

165 NLW, MS 5155.

166 Jones 1965, 42.

167 NLW, MS 5159 f.69.

168 *MT* 14 Jun 1856.

169 Gooch 1892, 19-20.

170 Jones 1965, 42; Tasker 1992, 20.

171 *Cambrian* 14 Mar 1835.

172 NLW, MS 5155.

173 *MM*, 2 Sep 1843.

174 Wilkins 1903, 123.

175 NLW, MS 5155, 5159 f.69.

176 NLW, MS 5160 f.23r.

177 NLW, MS 5159 f.20r.

178 Newport Reference Library, Chartist Collection 14_102_01, chartist.cynefin.wales/scripto/transcribe/2518/3100.

179 NWM, P2003-311.

180 *Locomotive Magazine*, 11 (Mar 1905), 49.

181 *MM*, 10 Oct 1846.

182 *MM*, 30 Nov 1839.

183 NLW, MS 5155.

184 NLW, MS 5159 f.69.

185 *MB*, 20 Jul 1844.

186 *MM*, 22 May 1858.

187 *CMG*, 15 May 1858; *HT*, 15 May 1858.

188 *MT* 26 Jun 1858; *HT*, 3 Jul 1858.

189 *MM*, 30 Jul 1859.

190 *HT*, 1 Mar 1862.

191 *MM*, 28 Aug; *Welshman*, 3 Sep; *Pembrokeshire Herald*, 3 Sep; *MT*, 4 Sep 1858; Moore 2017.

192 *MT*, 2 Jul 1859.

193 *MM*, 10 Feb 1854. Similar cases in Cambrian, 9 Jun 1838, and *MT*, 10 May 1856.

194 *MM* 18 Aug 1855.

195 *MT* 10 May 1856.

196 Charles Ellis in *Locomotive Magazine* 21 (Jan 1915), 11 says it worked until 1883, but a photograph dated 1882 shows it apparently disused (NWM, P77.5046, our Fig. 2.17). Jones 1965, fig. 5, in reproducing this photograph, says it is of *St David*. But it is clearly *Bedwellty*.

197 *Western Mail*, 20 Nov 1869.

198 Hill and Green 1999, 156.

199 *HJ*, 10 May 1843.

200 *MM*, 29 Apl 1843.

201 It was not built by Vulcan Foundry, for there is no candidate in that company's works list.

202 *Silurian*, 31 Oct 1840.

203 De Pambour 1836, 34, 243.

204 Thomas 1980, 244.

205 *Essex Herald*, 11 Jan, 11 Oct, 1 Nov 1842; *Bell's New Weekly Messenger*, 20 Aug 1843.

206 Thomas 1980, 244; Rattenbury and Lewis 2004, 71.

207 Others at Llanelli, Llansamlet, two more at Rhymney, and a second at Dowlais (de Havilland 1994, 38-9; Potts and Green 1996, 69; Hill 2007, 53, 57, 113).

208 NLW, MS 5155.

209 NRM, ROB/2/4.1 (Description Book), f.5; de Pambour 1836, 182; Warren 1923, 232-4.

210 Thomas 1980, 244.

211 *Cambrian*, 5 Jun 1830.

212 *MM*, 12 Feb, 12 Mar 1831.

213 NRM, T/1903-102, f.17.

214 NRM, 2002-8348/66/4, Francis Trevithick to John Enys, 25 Mar 1841.

215 Forward 1921.

216 No. 6090, 4 Mar 1831; *Repertory of Patent Inventions* 12 (1831), 261-3 and pl. V; Napier 1904, 76.

217 Young 1923, 248-54; Warren 1923, 294-7.

218 *BM*, 20 Jul 1833.

219 *MM*, 29 Apl 1843.

220 Jack 2001, 100, 106.

221 Hill and Green 1999, 139.

222 *Cambrian*, 5 Jun 1830.

223 *Cambrian*, 31 Jul 1830.

224 TNA, RAIL 500/7, Nov 1834.

225 WGAS, D/D NAI L/31-7, Dendy Marshall 1937, 130, and engraving in *Engineering* 15 Nov 1867. The details are discussed by Weaver 1983, 90.

226 Dendy Marshall 1937, 131, dated 22 Dec 1829.

227 *Cambrian*, 17 Oct 1829.

228 Thomas 1980, 151.

229 Rattenbury and Lewis 2004, 58-9.

230 Rattenbury and Lewis 2004, 58-9.

231 Warren 1923, 144.

232 WGAS, D/D NAI L/38/8.

233 WGAS, D/D NAI L/37/5.

234 *MM*, 29 Apl 1843.

235 *GMBG*, 24 Feb 1838.

236 NLW, MS 5155.

237 WGAS, D/D NAI L/38/7. Other drawings are l/36/1-3.

238 Bick 1987, 64, with no support from the drawings.

239 Trevithick 1872, vol. 1, 224, 165.

240 Trevithick 1872, vol. 1, 178.

241 NLW, MS 5155.

242 NRM, 2002-8348/65, Francis Trevithick to John Enys, 26 Dec 1840.

243 NLW, MS 5155.

244 WGAS, D/D NAI L/52/1-2, L53/3-4.

245 *Engineering*, 15 Nov 1867, 453 and Weaver 1983, 91. Weaver errs in thinking the wheels to be 3ft and hence the cylinders to be 8½in. They were actually 3ft 10in and 10½in.

246 *MM*, 14 Apl 1849.

247 *Cambrian*, 12 Nov 1836.

248 *MM*, 12 Feb 1831.

249 Hill and Green 1999, 97, admit the same difficulty.

250 WGAS, D/D NAI L/23/4, L/26/1-5, L/28/1, L/29

251 WGAS, D/D NAI L/53/22.

252 Bodmin & Wadebridge minute book, 19 Sep 1835: Messenger 2012, 147.

253 Dendy Marshall 1953, 210.

254 Hill and Green 1999, 94, who call it, most improbably, an 0-4-0.

255 Hill and Green 1999, 83; van Laun 2001, 127 prefers 1813 , but this line is not shown on the OS draft survey of that year.

256 *MM*, 28 Jan 1843; Jones 1971.

257 Jones 1969, 56.

258 At SO 1607 1018 and 1472 0980 (van Laun 2001, 230).

259 *Cambrian*, 19 Feb 1831.

260 Hadfield 1967, 137-8; *GMBG*, 2 May 1835.

261 *MM*, 29 Apl 1843.

262 NLW, MS 5159 f.13r.

263 *GMBG*, 6 Apl 1833

264 *Cambrian*, 7 Dec 1833.

265 Lewis 1835, s.v. Tredegar.

266 *GMBG*, 8 Jul 1843.

267 WGAS, D/D NAI L/27/6. Other drawings L/27/1-5.

268 Weaver 1983, 91 is wrong over the dimensions.

269 *GMBG*, 9 Jul 1836.

270 TNA, RAIL 500/7, Nov 1831.

271 *MM*, 27 Mar 1847.

272 Although in 1847 Rhymney paid £4 14s 6d 'for Lamps for Loco' (GlamA, DRH/55 f.175).

273 WGAS, D/D NAI L/14/1, 14/12, 27/1-6a, 53/22.

274 *GMBG*, 17 Aug 1839; *MM* 19 Oct 1839.

275 *Cambrian*, 24 Apl 1841.

276 WGAS, D/D NAI L/4/2, L/22/1, L/28/2, L/53/57.

277 *MM*, 29 May 1841.

278 *MM*, 14 Apl 1849. Transcribed with comments in Steggles 2009.

279 *Engineering*, 15 Nov 1867, 453; Weaver 1983, 91-2.

280 WGAS, D/D NAI L53/55, L53/66; see also L/44/1-6.

281 Rattenbury and Lewis 2004, 66.

282 WGAS, D/D NAI L/53/5, L58/3.

283 WGAS, D/D NAI L/28/6, L28/6a.

284 Hill and Green 1999, 94.

285 *CMG*, 21 May 1853.

286 *MM*, 12 Aug 1853.

287 *MM*, 30 Jul 1859.

288 *GMBG*, 8 Jul 1843.

289 *MM*, 30 Dec 1843, 9 Mar 1844.

290 WGAS, D/D NAI L/52/6-14, L/63/2.

291 WGAS, D/D NAI L/63/2.

292 Hill and Green 1999, 285-6 summarise the state of knowledge.

293 *MM*, 15 Mar 1851, 14 May 1852.

294 *Tipperary Free Press*, 2 Jan 1847 quoting the *Mining Journal*; *The Globe*, 19 Jan 1847. Denman 2000, 19 is ignorant of this engine.

295 Ahrons 1927, 160. This is counting the Chapman bogie geared engines in the north as 0-4-4-0s rather than 0-8-0s.

296 *Welshman*, 5 Nov 1847.

297 *CMG*, 29 Jan 1848.

298 *MM*, 4 Apl 1851.

299 *MM*, 6 Jan 1849.

300 *BM*, 2 Sep 1848. This item does not seem to have appeared in any Monmouthshire paper.

301 *MM*, 4 Apl 1851.

302 *MM*, 13, 20 Jan 1849.

303 *MM*, 4 Apl 1851.

304 Rutherford 2008.

305 *MM*, 4 Apl 1851.

306 *CMG*, 20 Apl 1850. Hill and Green 1999, 286 have it sold in Dec 1852. But it was re-advertised in Jan 1853 (*CMG*, 8 Jan 1853).

307 Hill 2007, 89.

308 Clark 1855, vol. 2, diagram pl. 6 part 2, no. 37.

309 WGAS, D/D NAI L/33.

310 *MM*, 4 Apl 1851.

311 *MM*, 7 Apl, 14 Apl 1849.

312 *CMG*, 7 Dec 1850.

313 Ince 1990, 125; Hill and Green 1999, 285-6. In Oct 1856 the MRCC offered to hire a locomotive to Thomas Powell to haul his trains on the Rumney (TNA RAIL 500/11, Oct 1856), but this is too late for a transfer in July.

314 *CMG*, 14 May 1859.

315 *MM*, 21 Jul 1849.

316 *CMG*, 31 Aug 1850; *Silurian*, 14 Dec 1850; *MM*, 5 Oct 1850.

317 *MM*, 18 May 1850.

318 Ahrons 1927, 104.

319 *Bristol Times and Mirror* 27 Oct 1849.

320 *MM*, 16 May 1851; *The Principality*, 2 Nov 1849.

321 Hill and Green 1999; 286, Jack 2001, 105, 108.

322 *CMG*, 22 Nov 1851.

323 Hill and Green 1999, 285-6.

324 *MM*, 14 May 1852.

325 Ahrons 1927, 119.

326 *Mining Journal*, 4 Aug 1849; *Morning Post*, 6 Aug 1849.

327 *MB*, 18 May 1850.

328 *MM*, 28 Dec 1850.

329 *MB*, 15 Nov 1851.

330 *PP*, 1852-3 lv, 87.

331 *MM*, 16 Jan 1852.

332 *MM*, 6 Jan 1849.

333 Byles 1982, 23-4, 39.

334 *MM*, 29 Jun 1850, 4 Apl 1851, and many references in between.

335 Hill and Green 1999, 285 confirm that at least fifteen were so converted.

336 Two 0-6-0STs, Vulcan Foundry nos. 424 and 425.

337 *MM*, 10 Nov 1855.

338 *HT*, 6 Apl 1839.

339 *Globe*, 27 Mar 1839.

340 *MM*, 26 Jun 1847; *BM*, 4 Oct 1851.

341 Meredith 1913, 231, 240.

342 *MPICE*, 98 (1889), 406.

343 Glam A, DRH/15 f.210.

344 GlamA, DRH/15 f.206.

345 GlamA, DRH/14 ff.172, 214, 241, DRH/15 ff. 206, 210.

346 Rattenbury and Lewis 2004, 74-6.

347 Meredith 1913, 239.

348 GlamA, DRH/ 15 ff.242-3.

349 *Locomotive Magazine*, 11 (Mar 1905), 49.

350 Williams 1908, 71.

351 Meredith 1913, 239.

352 *MPICE*, 98 (1889), 406.

353 Rattenbury and Lewis 2004, 63-5.

354 WGAS, D/D NAI L/22/1, 40/1-16, 42/1-3, 62/2. The latter is a general arrangement by Charles Jordan, Neath Abbey's chief draughtsman at the time, which was redrawn as an engraving in *Engineering*, 15 Nov 1867, 456.

355 GlamA, DRH/15 f.221.

356 GlamA, DRH/21 ff. 154, 181, 209.

357 *CMG*, 5 Feb 1848, 9 Sep 1848; *MM*, 27 Mar 1852.

358 GlamA, DRH/15 ff.267, 276, DRH/52 f.278.

359 WGAS, D/D NAI L41/1-6.

360 NMW, 32.186.

361 GlamA, DRH/15 f.323, DRH/53 ff.170, 300.

362 GlamA, DRH/15 ff.334, 343.

363 GlamA, DRH/85 f.97.

364 *MM*, 2 Oct 1847.

365 WGAS, D/D NAI L/20/17.

366 Rattenbury and Lewis 2004, 74.

367 GlamA, DRH/54 f.81.

368 GlamA, DRH/54 f.82.

369 GlamA, DRH/85 ff. 95-7.

370 *The Atlas*, 13 Dec 1835.

371 The first reports of the accident call it *Superb*, but those of the inquest *Surprise* (*Worcestershire Chronicle* 18 and 25 Nov 1840, both widely copied in other papers.) See also *Locomotive Magazine* 48 (1942), 216.

372 Riden and Owen 1995, 25-6.

373 GlamA, DRH/19 ff.16-17, DRH/55 f.176.

374 Jack 2001, 99, 106-7.

375 *MM*, 4 Dec 1847.

376 GlamA, DRH/85 f.97.

377 *MM*, 30 Nov 1850.

378 GlamA, DRH/21 f.116.

379 GlamA, DRH/85 f.97.

380 An engine of Joseph Latch was derailed (*HT*, 8 Aug 1857); and a train of Messrs Powell, hauled by *Antelope*, was also derailed (*CMG*, 5 Nov 1859).

381 Another Bury allegedly sold by the LNWR to Rhymney in 1852 (Jack 2001, 80-1) seems to be a phantom. There is no mention of the sale in the LNWR minutes nor in the Rhymney Iron Co accounts. The statement in Jack and in Hill 2007, 113 that its boiler exploded in 1859 is wrong: that was No. 9 on the RLR (2.E.iii).

382 GlamA, DRH/12 ff.523,527.

383 *MB*, 9 Sep 1854.

384 GlamA, DRH/85 f. 97.

385 *HT*, 16 Sep 1848.

386 *MB*, 6 Feb 1847. Copied in *Gloucestershire Chronicle*, 13 Feb; *Bell's New Weekly Register*, 21 Feb; *HT*, 27 Feb.

387 Craig et al 2002, 251-3. It was a short-lived concern which, like the Llanelly Railway itself, had strong links with the North East (Denman 2000, 19).

388 *Mechanic's Magazine*, 15 Aug 1846, 165.

389 Patent no. 11, 234; *Repertory of Patent Inventions* 9 (1847), 321-5 and pl. XVIII; Sekon 1899, 168.

390 *Cambrian*, 18 Sep 1846.

391 *MM*, 26 Jun 1847.

392 *MB*, 26 Jun 1847.

393 *CMG*, 27 Nov 1847.

394 *CMG*, 10 May 1849, 4 May 1850.

395 NRM, 2002-8548/75.

396 According to *MM*, 13 Oct 1849 Uskside's first locomotive was *Blaenafon* built in that year for Blaenavon's 3ft 3in tramroad, followed by a similar engine in 1849-50 for the 3ft 6in Bailey's Llangattock Tramroad, of which more anon.

397 *MM*, 19 Nov 1859.

398 *HT*, 28 Feb 1857; *MB*, 4 Apl 1857; *CMG*, 15 Sep 1860.

399 *MM*, 28 Jan 1853.

400 *MM*, 29 Dec 1854.

401 *MM*, 10 Nov 1855.

402 *MT*, 1 Nov 1856.

403 GlamA, DRH/13 f.18.

404 *CT*, 15 Feb 1861. Another, sold in 1862 (an 0-6-0ST), was stated to be standard gauge: *CMG*, 26 Apl 1862.

405 Williams 1908, 71, who also mentions *Star*.

406 Jack 2001, 105, 109.

407 *MM*, 16 May 1857.

408 Williams 1908, 71.

409 WGAS, D/D NAI L/49/1-2, 52/1, 2, 9.

410 For full details, especially of their track, see van Laun 2001.

411 Rattenbury 1980, 51.

412 Rattenbury 1980, 55, 94-5, 55-7; van Laun 2001, 110.

413 *MM*, 11 Dec 1830.

414 *MM*, 18 Dec 1830.

415 *MM*, 11 Aug 1832.

416 Elsas 1960, 182.

417 Lewis 1834, under Llangattock.

418 *Cambrian*, 25 Apl 1835.

419 *CMG*, 18 Apl 1835.

420 *MB*, 21 Oct 1843.

421 *HT*, 26 Oct 1839.

422 *Birmingham Journal*, 18 Sep 1841.

423 E.g. *Aris's Birmingham Gazette*, 27 Mar 1837.

424 Shill 1992, 123.

425 *MM*, 4 Apl 1851, 21 Oct 1853.

426 WGAS, D/D NAI L/2/3.

427 Stephenson Locomotive Society library, P1347.

428 Bick 1987, 63.

429 *MT*, 19 Jul 1856.

430 *Western Mail*, 26, 27 Oct 1871; van Laun 2001, 112-13.

431 *MM*, 4 Feb 1853, 30 Apl 1859, 22 Oct 1859, 11 Dec 1859; *Y Tyst a'r Dydd*, 10 Jul 1874.

432 *South Wales Daily News*, 28 Apl 1881, 4 Jun 1889.

433 *MM*, 13 Oct 1849.

434 'Dean Forester' 1963, 58.

435 *MPICE*, 83 (1897-8), 406-8.

436 Bradley 1992, 35, 151.

437 *HT*, 16 Aug 1856.

438 *MT*, 25 May 1861.

439 Bainton 1972, 137.

440 Lewis 2017a

441 Svedenstjerna 1804, 104; translation, 59.

442 Meredith 1913, 220, 227.

443 Rattenbury 1980, 99-127; van Laun 2001, 141-3.

444 NLW, MS 5155 inside cover. Rattenbury 1980, 101 locates Rosser Thomas's tramroad at Bryn Oer Colliery.

445 Oeynhausen and Dechen 1971, 65.

446 This section is based largely on Rattenbury and Lewis 2004, 55-7.

447 Wrongly dated by Warren 1923, 157 to July 1828.

448 NRM, ROB/4/1.

449 NRM, ROB/3/2/8-10, ROB/2/4/1, f.3.

450 NRM, ROB/4/1.

451 Doubts were expressed in Rattenbury and Lewis 2004, 55-7 and Guy et al 2019, App. 2.

452 Van Laun 2001, 162-4.

453 Rattenbury and Lewis 2004, 56-7.

454 Van Laun 2001, 162.

455 GlamA, DRH/14 f.2.

456 *MPICE*, 98 (1889), 405-8.

457 For the Twynau Gwynion tramroads and their improvements, van Laun 2001, 150-68.

458 *Silurian*, 22 Jun 1850.

459 *Silurian*, 7 Dec 1850.

460 GlamA, DRH/ 21 f.154.

461 GlamA, DRH/13 f.427.

462 *CMG*, 3 Sep 1859; *HT*, 3 Sep 1859; *CMG*, 10 Sep 1859; *CT*, 10 Sep 1859.

463 *CMG*, 27 Oct 1860.

464 *CT*, 27 Jul 1867.

465 *CT*, 21 Jun 1873.

466 The works supplied coffins for the victims: GlamA, DRH/13 f.351.

467 *MT*, 20 Aug 1859.

468 *CMG*, 11 Aug, 1860.

469 *CMG*, 15 May 1858; *MT*, 15 May 1858.

470 *CT*, 27 Nov 1858.

471 *HT*, 5 Feb 1859; *CMG*, 5 Feb 1859; *MT*, 5 Feb 1859.

472 *MT*, 12 Jul 1862.

473 WGAS, D/D NAI L/39, L/39a.

474 *Engineering*, 30 Aug, 13 Sep 1867; *Locomotive Magazine* 46 (1940), 215; Sharman 1989, Plan 73; *RM*, Jun 1941, 248-9; commentary Weaver 1983, 96-7.

475 Van Laun 2001, 232. He thinks it was actually in the mid or late 1860s, which seems too early.

476 Jones 1969, 55.

477 *MM*, 11 Jul 1855.

478 Hill and Green 1999, 156.

479 NWM, 1997-247/2. The photographer was Charles Eastment of Ebbw Vale and Tredegar, who in 1901 copied the old photograph of *St David*. Local directories show that his Tredegar branch existed only from c.1895 to 1905.

480 *MM*, 25 Aug 1855.

481 *MT*, 25 May 1861.

482 *MB*, 25 Mar 1865; *MM*, 27 May 1865.

483 *MT*, 13 Jan 1866.

484 *Western Mail*, 16 Jun 1869; *CT*, 19 Jun 1869; *MT*, 12 Jun 1869.

485 Hill and Green 1999, 155-6.

486 *South Wales Daily News*, 17 Sep 1875.

487 Shore 2017, 43.

488 *Western Mail*, 29 Nov 1869.

489 For the Trevil Railroad, Rattenbury 1989 and van Laun 2001, 135-8, 142-9.

490 *Seren Cymru*, 30 Mar 1866.

491 NWM, 2016-62. Once again the photographer was Charles Eastment.

492 For dimensions, Abbott 1989, 57-9.

493 Tasker 1992, 33.

494 Rattenbury and Lewis 2004, 62.

495 Wear and Lees 1978, 66-8.

496 Jones 1965, 44.

497 Photograph NRM, GWR A1003. Van Laun 2001, 148. The statement in Hill and Green 1999, 155 that the tramroad was converted to conventional edge rail in the late nineteenth century is certainly incorrect.

498 *MM*, 9 Mar 1867.

499 *Merthyr Times*, 28 Jun 1872.

500 *County Observer*, 31 Aug 1872.

501 *South Wales Daily News*, 15 Feb, 16 Feb 1887.

502 *Evening Express*, 14 Sep 1909.

PART THREE
The tramroads at work

THE working of the limestone tramroads having already been described, this part deals only with the lines of 4ft 4in gauge.

TRAMS

For many years from the beginning we have only sporadic references to vehicles and their operators. As shown on the Sirhowy Company seal of 1802 (title page) and Fothergill's Tredegar sketch of 1809 (Fig. 3.01, A), the oldest trams for coal and pig iron were small with sloping sides, and they were subject to the sparsest of bye-laws (Fig. 3.02). A description of 1815 reads,

> The weight generally carried in each waggon on the public tram-roads is two tons and a half. Four tolerable horses will draw 20 tons of iron from Sirhowy and Tredegar iron-works to Newport in one day; the distance is 23 miles. Much of this *halling* is done by hire, which gives employment to many of the lower class of farmers, at such times of the year as they can conveniently attend to it. But the uncertainty of this assistance makes it necessary for the Proprietors of iron-works to keep teams of their own; which perform the two-fold duties of conveying their iron and cultivating their lands.[1]

On the Sirhowy, it was recorded in 1831, four horses normally pulled thirteen trams downhill, on the Rumney four pulled eleven or five pulled thirteen.[2] 'The Company's tramroad horses,' says a modern source, unsubstantiated and surely over-sentimental, 'were always the finest of their kind, powerful, well cared for, and soon known by name to every boy along the route. They became the valley's pride, a new horse never failing to arouse as much interest as it did concern for the one it replaced.'[3] Because of the gradients, the horses had to be changed at frequent intervals, and sometimes, as at Risca, there were lineside cottages where a haulier and his family lived on the top floor, with stables beneath.[4] It has also been said that the horses, on coming off shift halfway along the line, had a ride for the rest of the way in a gambo or dandy cart;[5] but of this there is neither confirmation nor likelihood. On the Sirhowy, unlike many tramroads, shafts were obligatory on coal trams.[6]

As time went on, more hauliers came to be employed directly by the freighters and fewer were freelance. But by 1847, a time of depression, there were still at least twenty-four self-employed

A

B

C

Fig. 3.01
Sirhowy Tramroad coal trams, bar-iron bogies, and possible passenger car, 1809.
(*details, all to same scale, from Fig. 1.26*)

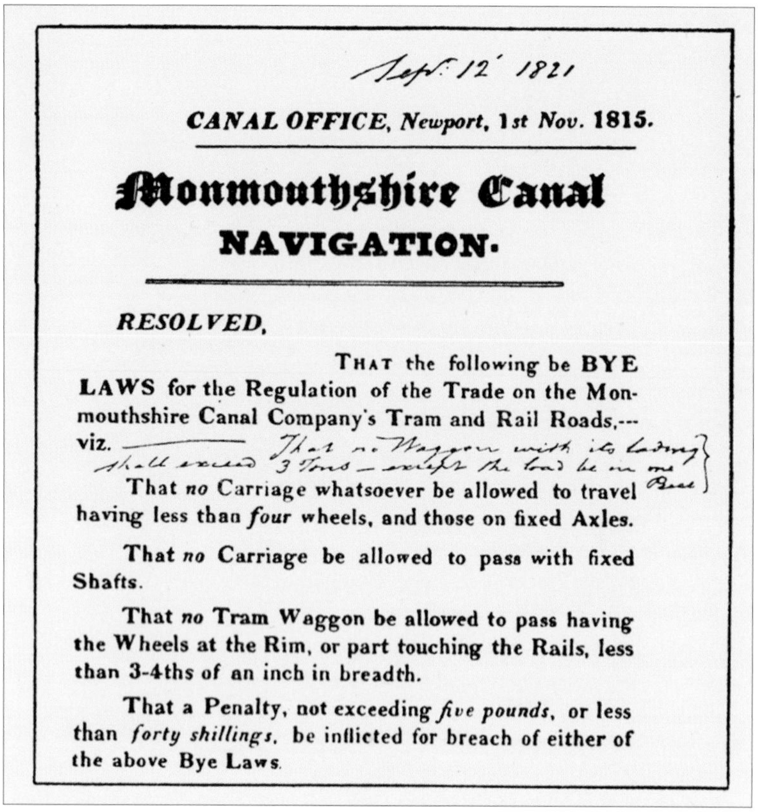

Sep. 12ʳ 1821

CANAL OFFICE, *Newport*, 1st Nov. 1815.

Monmouthshire Canal
NAVIGATION.

RESOLVED,

THAT the following be BYE LAWS for the Regulation of the Trade on the Monmouthshire Canal Company's Tram and Rail Roads,---viz.———— *That no Waggon with its loading shall exceed 3 Tons — except the load be in one piece)*

That *no* Carriage whatsoever be allowed to travel having less than *four* wheels, and those on fixed Axles.

That *no* Carriage be allowed to pass with fixed Shafts.

That *no* Tram Waggon be allowed to pass having the Wheels at the Rim, or part touching the Rails, less than 3-4ths of an inch in breadth.

That a Penalty, not exceeding *five pounds*, or less than *forty shillings*, be inflicted for breach of either of the above Bye Laws.

Fig. 3.02
MCC bye-laws 1815, amended 1821.
(*MacDermot 1931, vol. 2, 105*)

men in the Western Valleys hiring their services to the coalowners and petitioning for a pay rise:

We, the undersigned hauliers on the tramroads to Newport, respectfully beg leave to lay before you the situation we are now placed in. In consequence of the great advance in [the cost of] corn, from the high prices of oats, beans and bran, as well as the enormous advance in horses (in some instances full 50 per cent), we find it will be utterly impossible to continue hauling your coal at the present low prices.[7]

A court case of the same year sheds light on the employment arrangements. Daniel Jones was a haulier who for nine years had been employed by two big coalowners (Sir Thomas Phillips and Thomas Prothero). When he fell into debt and some of his property had to be distrained, the question arose whether his horses were his own or his employers'. Jones had up to twelve or thirteen at a time (all named in the report – Little Captain, Scott, Bowler, Dragon, Violet and suchlike) which he fed and stabled, and in turn employed the drivers. After hearing details from the extremely complex financial accounts, the court decided that the horses were in fact Jones's.[8] The other side of the coin was the large number of company hauliers and company horses. In 1848

the Rhymney Iron Co owned no fewer than 134, individually named in the inventory, although far from all would be working on the tramroads.[9]

On the construction of the trams, an account of the Sirhowy in 1824 runs:

The coal and iron are conveyed upon it in waggons, each carrying about forty-five to fifty hundred weight exclusive of the waggon; and a team of four or five horses will draw about fifteen of these waggons, and take them back, with ease. The waggons are variously constructed according to the fancy of the parties, some are of wood and others wholly of iron; the latter are, however, now more generally approved of. The weight of them is as varied as their construction.[10]

Total numbers at this stage are not on record, but they were considerable. In 1818 Argoed Colliery, beside the line some seven miles below Tredegar, alone had 'one hundred tram waggons, adapted to the Sirhowy Tram-road.'[11] Most were unsophisticated and ill-maintained, but Rumney trams in their early days (Fig. 3.03) boasted 'close ended' wheels, 2ft 6in in diameter and 1in wide on the tread, which involved a closed sleeve attached to the hub and revolving with the wheel (which as usual ran loose on a fixed axle), lubricated with oil fed through a screw-cap (Fig. 3.04).[12] Wheels with 'gothic'-shaped spokes were standard.

By the 1840s the trams had grown in size. We have an actual photograph of them on Hall's Tramroad in 1857, of which more later, and a useful description by a Birmingham waggon builder of one on the MCC lines in 1850 (Fig. 3.05):

The gross weight was 16 cwt, and it carried 3 tons of coals at a rate of three miles an hour, exclusive of the time consumed at the various public houses by the tramway side. The breaking or skidding down the inclines was effected in the most complete manner by means of a slipper or shoe, similar to that on a stage coach, and the stopping of the train by thrusting a bar of wood through the spokes of the wheel, or, as it is locally termed, spragging the wheel. The unloading was effected by means of a gallows and crab, the tram being raised at one end, and the coal discharged by means of the swinging tail board at the other end. It will be observed that no provision is made for buffing, but that the train is articulated by means of the hitching shewn in the drawing. The wheels ran loose upon the axles, and were in most instances dished in the manner of a common road wheel.[13]

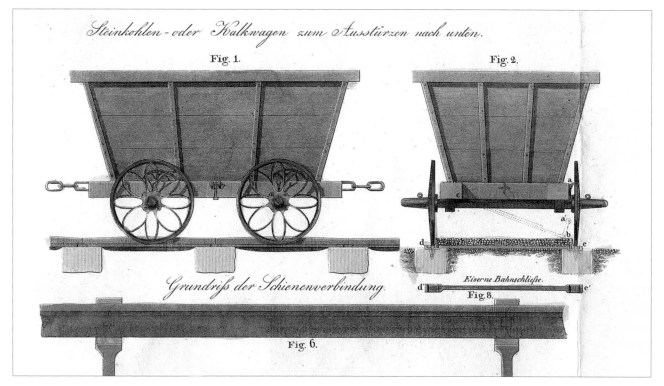

Several points of interest arise from this. In contrast to Shropshire and the North East, where flanged wheels, 3 or 4in wide on the tread, had had friction brakes since time out of mind, plateway trams (and, until quite late in the day, locomotives) had unflanged wheels an inch or less in width, and such brakes were impracticable. Instead, sprags of wood or iron were the norm. Despite the passage quoted above, hardly a mention has been found of shoe or slipper brakes in use in the Western Valleys, even though they

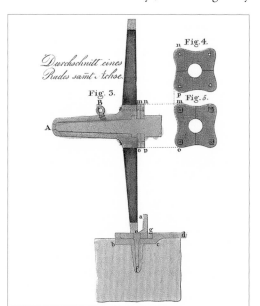

were employed on the Severn & Wye to the east.[14] The sole possible exception came in 1839 at Rhymney: '1 Shoe for Locomotive' costing 7s 2d.[15] Flying sprags caused a number of injuries to those trying to stop trams that were travelling too fast. A full-time spragger, too, was employed at Court y Bella to ensure that every tram stopped exactly on the platform of the weighbridge.[16]

From the beginning, most coal trams were emptied by end-tipping: in 1806 Thomas Edwards of Gellihaf Colliery, already connected to the Sirhowy, was advertising his coal 'in Waggons constructed for the purpose of discharging themselves into vessels.'[17] The gallows at the wharves, typical of South Wales practice (compare those near Swansea in Fig. 3.06), were worked by hand winch until 1849 when Ebbw Vale introduced hydraulic ones.[18] The Rumney trams, by contrast, were emptied through bottom doors (Fig. 3.03).

Fig. 3.03 (Above) Rumney Railway tram and track. The chain couplings are of doubtful authenticity. (Gerstner 1831, Abb. 34)

Fig. 3.04 (Left) Rumney Railway, detail of axle ends. B is the cap for the oil hole. (Gerstner 1831, Abb. 34)

Fig. 3.05 (Below) MCC, old-order tram. (Adams 1850, Plate 17 Fig. 3)

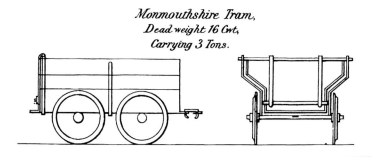

Fig. 3.06

Loading coal with gallows at Landore near Swansea, 1792, by J. C. Ibbetson. The jetties at Pillgwenlly were similar, but probably larger and certainly much more numerous.
(*formerly Wernher Collection*)

The 'dishing' or inclining of the wheels (as in Fig. 2.26) had the purpose, one presumes, of lessening the friction against the rail flange, which could be considerable. To reduce it further, water was sometimes used as lubricant. A haulier in charge of a train of horse trams near Crumlin in 1831 'crossed between the last horse and the tram for the purpose of letting the water out of the box to wet the rail,' and in the dark did not notice a drunk lying across the rails.[19] Another in 1844 was 'riding on the water-box in front of his coal team' when he was knocked off.[20] Oil for lubricating wheels was apparently supplied by the hauliers themselves in the early days, but in 1840 an iron tram carrying 36 gallons of oil was stolen, the property of Crawshay Bailey of Nantyglo, and the theft was traced to 'a man employed to serve out the oil to the men in the works.'[21]

Ellis senior noted the capacity of various trams:

Jany 10th 1844. Weight of coal in Trams for
Pont y gwaith & Tiley's Pit [Tredegar pits]

Small Iron Trams	average 2 Tons
Small Columbus	large Coal 8 Tons
Do Do	Small Do Struck 4 Tons
Large Columbus	Large Coal 9 to 10 Tons
Do Do	Small Coal Struck 6 Tons
New Castle Tram	Small Coal 3 Tons [22]

Of these, the 'Columbus' was a bogie waggon which will concern us later. 'Iron Trams' presumably means trams made of iron rather than for carrying iron. 'Struck' means with the load levelled with the top of the body. While 'New Castle Tram' might mean one made in

Newcastle, as will be mentioned shortly, this date of 1844 seems five years too early.

The only detailed census we have of rolling stock is a Rhymney inventory of 1848:

81	Newport Trams	@ £7
38	Spring Trams	@ £25
22	Common Trams	@ £6
2	Large Iron Trams on Springs	@ £40
14	Iron Trams for Red Ore	@ £22
3	Wooden Trams for Loco Coal	@ £12
30	do do for Red Ore	@ £6
4	Cast Iron Sides for Small Trams	@ £5 10s
8	Wooden Tub Trams	@ £8 6s
201	Hitching Hooks 4 tons 3 cwt	@ £10 per ton [23]

Thus the process of introducing trams with springs was already under way but, compared with the price-tag of £50 that lay in the future, they were still fairly cheap.

In 1849, however, we are given a great deal more detail. From the beginning the freighters – the coal and iron proprietors – had carried their own products not only down the public and private feeder tramroads such as the Sirhowy but also along the MRCC's lines which continued on to Newport. They used their own miscellany of trams, whether horse- or steam-hauled. By the late 1840s the MRCC, backed by parliamentary powers, was intent on dragging its system into the Railway Age by easing the curves, by banning horse haulage, by insisting on traction by its own locomotives, and by imposing on the freighters a standard pattern of waggon, with the ultimate intention of replacing the plate rails with edge.

Over the feeder lines it could of course exert only indirect control. The freighters, frightened for their pockets, protested vigorously with a series of petitions, and in April 1849 the Railway Commissioners sent Captain J. L. A. Simmons R.E. (later a Field Marshal) to arbitrate in the dispute. His report is a fascinating document,[24] although the full details of the complex saga cannot detain us here.

It obligingly provides a table of the numbers of vehicles owned by the freighters. Four-wheeled coal waggons were by then in the great majority. The MRCC described them as of

a variety of shapes, sizes and frames … so rudely constructed, being without either springs or buffers, and having frames of irregular heights, and wheels so out of perpendicular that they cannot be drawn in a train without great danger and hazard … They cost from £8 to £10 new; they are without springs, have bent axles, with small cast iron wheels, with no brakes, and a system of spragging having been adopted, the wheels have as many sides as there are holes in the wheel, instead of being round. The present wheels are very narrow at the edge, and are most destructive to the Company's plates, by cutting a groove therein. The coal on these waggons is piled up above the side boards to a height nearly equal to the depth of the waggon, and if hauled by locomotive power, at a speed of 10 miles per hour, the coal would be shaken off, and the remainder so crushed as to be much injured for shipment.

Although plenty of these waggons were already locomotive-hauled, it was at less than 4 mph. Simmons confirmed that the existing four-wheeled waggons had an average tare weight of 17 cwt, and carried when piled nearly 3 tons. They were 'connected by stiff drawbars' or hitching hooks rather than by coupling chains, and were drawn in trains of 20 to 24, the number being limited by the ability of the horses to pull the empties back up. They cost £8 or £10 apiece. In contrast, the proposed standard waggon with combined wheels cost £60. The nub of the freighters' complaint was that on 14 Nov 1848 the company had instructed them to replace something like 3,500 old trams with the new version by 1 August 1849. Apart from some technical reservations, they were objecting to so huge a capital outlay at such short notice. The table shows that by April 1849 only Ebbw Vale had even started on the process of replacement.

TABLE of the ROLLING STOCK in use upon the TRAMWAYS in the WESTERN VALLEYS belonging to the MONMOUTHSHIRE RAILWAY and CANAL COMPANY.

NAME.	Coal-Waggons on Four Wheels.			Coal-Waggons on Eight Wheels.			Waggons for Iron.			Locomotives.			Miscellaneous.		
	No.	Value.		No.	Value.		No.	Value.		No.	Value.		No.	Value.	
		£.	£.		£.	£.		£.	£.		£.	£.		£.	£.
Mr. Prothers	530	8 to 10	4,930												
Messrs. Larch & Co.	420	8	3,360												
Mr. Powell	560	8	4,480												
Mr. Henry Marsh	160	8 to 10	1,440												
Sir T. Phillips	136	8 to 10	1,404												
S. Homfray & Co.	70	8 to 10	630	97	75 to 80	7,469	70	35 to 40	2,625	9	800	7,200	5	..	450
Romney Iron Company	..	..	..	..	..	..	208	..	2,176	6	..	6,600			
Mr. Morrison	240	8 to 9	2,040												
Mr. Roger Lewin	123	8	1,000												
Mr. Cartwright	210	8 to 10	1,890												
Mr. Crawshaw Baillie	200	8 to 10	1,800												
Ebbw Vale Iron Company	50	8	4,000	..	..	..	15	50	750	6	800	4,800	5	..	450
	18	60	1,080	..	..	..	25	45	1,125	..	..	..	5	..	100
							30	30	900						
							34	..	1,020						
							20	..	160						
							20	..	560						
Cwm Calyn and Blaina Iron-works.	20	10	200	..	..	..	30	..	450	2	..	1,600	4	..	306
							20	..	720						
							9	..	180						
							7	..	280						
							4	..	120						
Abercarn Collieries	185	8 to 10	1,665												
Mr. Russell	370	8 to 10	3,330												
Mr. John Jones	73	8 to 10	657												
Mr. Joseph Jones	70	8 to 10	630												
Various parties for the haulage of goods and passengers on the tramways.	..	..	..	..	..	..	..	..	..	..	..	..	76	10	760
Total	3,477	..	34,556	97	..	7,469	492	..	11,006	23	..	20,200	95	..	2,066

Alongside these 3,477 four-wheeled coal waggons were 97 eight-wheeled ones which, according to the table, belonged solely to Tredegar, although a year later Ebbw Vale also had them.[25] Their value, £75 to £80 each, presumably represents their cost new, and gives some idea of their size and complexity compared with the crude four-wheelers. As the most expensive waggons listed, they must correspond to the 'coal-waggons which … are propelled by locomotive steam-engines … and which are on springs' mentioned in a petition to which Homfray was a party. They also correspond to those mentioned by the MRCC itself: 'there are waggons now owned by some of the freighters which have eight wheels, are 16 feet in length, weigh from 3 to 5 tons, and carry a load of about 10 tons.' With only 70 four-wheelers as opposed to 97 eight-wheelers, Homfray clearly had a predilection for the latter. They will come in for closer scrutiny later.

Of the 'waggons for iron' in Simmons's table, the report regrettably tells us no more. The cheaper ones which cost between £8 and £15 were evidently as small and simple as coal trams, and may have carried pig iron. If they are ignored, the average value of the remainder was £33, running as high as £40 at Blaina and Tredegar, or £50 at Ebbw Vale. This implies a larger size and a much more complex design than the four-wheelers for coal, though not as complex as Homfray's large coal waggons; and it seems likely that some at least had more than four wheels. A vehicle for carrying rolled iron bars needs length, but it also needs forked bolsters rather than the solid sides that a coal tram does. Nor (if we disregard the effect on the track) is it so strong a candidate for springs as a large waggon full of fragile lump coal. Probably, then, the more expensive waggons for iron in 1849 were unsprung but multiple-wheeled. This ties in with an advertisement for the sale of Blaina in 1844 that included '48 pairs of bar iron carriages, 4 covered carriages each weighing 24 cwt.'[26] The latter no doubt correspond to Blaina's four miscellaneous vehicles in 1849.

Simmons's recommendations were a compromise. He approved the exclusive use of company locomotives. But the freighters, he said, should be allowed two years to replace their trams, and until the Western Valleys lines could be converted, within a time limit of five years, he would sanction the continued use of the 4ft 4in-gauge plate-railed track.

In parallel with improvements to the track which we will shortly explore, waggon capacity on the MCC lines grew larger. For four-wheelers the maximum permitted gross weight was increased from 56 cwt in 1806 to 60 cwt in 1821, 61 cwt in 1828, and 70 cwt in 1830.[27] Whether or not the limit of about 75 cwt obtaining in 1849 was authorised or tacitly overlooked, the permitted gross weight had grown since 1821 by at least half a ton, and the axle loading of four-wheelers was now of the order of 1¾ tons. But by 1849 Homfray's eight-wheelers had a gross weight of 13 to 15 tons,[28] or an axle loading of 3¼ to 3¾ tons. This can only have been with the company's approval, quite likely because they were now sprung and therefore easier on the track. Tredegar's first locomotive weighed nearly 9 tons or 3 tons per axle, and its successors built by Thomas Ellis weighed about 13 tons or 4⅓ tons per axle. All these engines had springs, which was no doubt what exempted them, like the eight-wheeled waggons, from the standard weight limit.

To return to the new and supposedly superior four-wheeled trams. In the trials of 1849 there were 'two model trams' belonging to freighters rather than to the MRCC,

the one built under the entire superintendence of Messrs. Nicholas Wood, of Newcastle-upon-Tyne, and Thomas Bouch, resident engineer and manager of the Edinburgh and Northern railway, and formerly of the Stockton and Darlington railway [and later of Tay Bridge infamy]; and the other waggon designed and built by Messrs. Fox, Henderson, and Co., Birmingham. These waggons are each of the same cubical contents as that of the Canal Company, and adequate to carry five tons of coal each. The wheels are not on the principal [sic] set up by the company set up [sic] under their waggon, known as the 'combination wheel,' but are made expressly for the use of a tram road. One horse drew these waggons.[29]

A Shildon Works drawing dated 26 February 1849 survives of a 'Coal Wagon to Carry 5 tons of Coals on the Monmouthshire Tram Way.'[30] Sprung but with simple plateway wheels, it borrows far more from current standard-gauge than from tramroad practice, and is presumably the Wood and Bouch version (Fig. 3.07).

There were also in 1849 five new model trams as specified by the MRCC and built by Smith & Willey of Liverpool. These were large and supposedly sturdy, 10ft long, 2 tons 19 cwt in weight and 5 tons-odd in capacity, and had springs and combined edge/plate wheels of the sort to be described shortly. A train of ten of them carrying

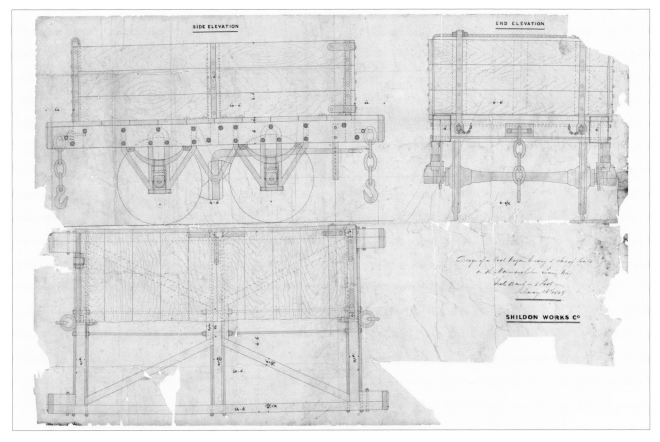

SIDE ELEVATION

END ELEVATION

SHILDON WORKS Cº

Fig. 3.07

MRCC 'Model' tram built by Shildon Works, 1849. (*NRM, 1998/11 11 37/1*)

55 tons 13 cwt of coal, hauled by five horses from Abercarn to Newport, was reported to run far more smoothly than the old versions, and with much less breakage of coal.[31] But some users had harsher words. Under the old regime, it was said,

six horses brought down 60 tons of coals and 16 tons of trams. The same power was required to take up the empty trams. Dead weight in the trams was consequently of vital importance. This tramway is now being worked with Locomotive power and permanent waggons, the Tramroad Company finding power, and the freighters waggons. The same care, which influenced the private haulier and caused him to equalize his upward to his downward load, does not now influence the freighter, and has been lost sight of by the Company. In the eye of the freighter the waggon which is strongest and heaviest is the best, and the consequence is, that waggons weighing 3 tons are conveying but 5 tons of load … In place of a perfect horse tram-road heavy engines are being hammered, and are hammering to pieces a bad road with bad gradients and extremely bad curves.[32]

Nor was James Brown of Ebbw Vale served well by the new rolling stock. A persistent thorn in the flesh of the MCC and later of the MRCC,

in 1853 he took the company to law for damaging his trams. The courtroom, surprisingly for so mundane a piece of litigation, was packed, and the press recorded the proceedings in minute detail. An MRCC locomotive, it transpired, had brought down from Nine Mile Point a train of eight columbuses, each carrying 11 tons of coal, with thirteen of Brown's new-style trams hitched on at the back. These, unlike the columbuses which by now sported proper buffers and chain couplings, had 'a mere continuation of the wooden framework of the carriage, with a soft and yielding substance attached to the surface, so as to avoid the effects of a collision.' At Court y Bella the locomotive ran round the train and, at full regulator, pushed it towards the weighing machine. Brown's trams were now between it and the heavy columbuses.

'Well,' said counsel, 'they placed the engine behind, whether to try the strength of poor Mr Brown's carriages, or to get that experience of which it is said railway companies stand so much in need, I don't know; but there was the engine, puffing and thumping away at their back – until, upon the principle that the weakest must go to the wall, poor Mr Brown's carriages went to the ground. (Loud laughter).'

Two of the new trams, proving less sturdy than was thought, succumbed to the pressure, rather as in the episode of 1843 recounted above when a train was squashed between two locomotives. After many expert witnesses declared that a train of that sort, weighing 206 tons, was perfectly safe to pull but hopelessly dangerous to push, Brown won his case, and damages.[33] The company, however, had the last laugh. It 'determined to give Mr Brown notice to provide trucks in accordance with the requirements of the company's bye laws, and to discontinue the use of about fifty of those at present carrying his coal.'[34]

The Rhymney Iron Co likewise had improved trams, sold in 1854 as the Rumney was being converted, which held four to five tons of coal or, with heightened side-boards, three tons of coke.

Their axles ran in grease boxes and brasses.[35]

Trains could be long and heavy, even prodigiously so. That of 12 April 1849, listed below, was an astonishing 350 yards long. Some recorded examples are shown in the table below.

The timber mentioned in 1849 – largely, no doubt, pit props – reminds us that back carriage was considerable. From the early 1830s more and more iron ore was imported, and from the start 'market trams' or 'luggage trains' brought in almost everything that the mushrooming population required. 'The opening of the tramroad,' says Tredegar's historian, 'was the means of supplying the town with a regular and constant supply of provisions; farmers brought their produce to the market weekly, which made Tredegar the market town of the surrounding neighbourhoods.'[36]

			No. of trams	tons net	tons gross		
18 Dec 1821	horse		18		79½	coal, two trains	John Thomas painting
27 Apl 1822	horse		74		empty?		*Cambrian* 4 May 1822
17 Dec 1829	*Britannia*			53	c.80	iron	*MM* 26 Dec 1829
20 Jul 1830	*Speedwell*		20	50½	70+	coal	*Cambrian* 31 Jul 1830
7 Jun 1834	*Britannia*		27	103½	146	mostly iron	NLW 5160 f.23r
Apl 1839?	*Fanny*				174	iron	NLW 5159
10 Apl 1848	*St David*			201½	237	iron	*MM* 21 Apl 1849
18 Apl 1848	*St David*				180	iron	NLW 5159 f.69
22 Apl 1848	*St David*				210		NLW 5159 f.69
10 Apl 1849	*St David*			129	179	mostly coal	*MM* 21 Apl 1849
12 Apl 1849	*Abbey/EV*		124		115	up, timber	*MM* 14 Apl 1849
May 1850	MRCC loco		130				*MB* 18 May 1850
14 Jun 1853	MRCC loco		21		206	coal	*MM* 12 Aug 1853

Fig. 3.08

Penydarren rolling mills with wooden bar-iron bogies in foreground and centre right, Thomas Hornor *c.*1817.

(*Sir Arthur Elton Collection, Ironbridge Gorge Museum*)

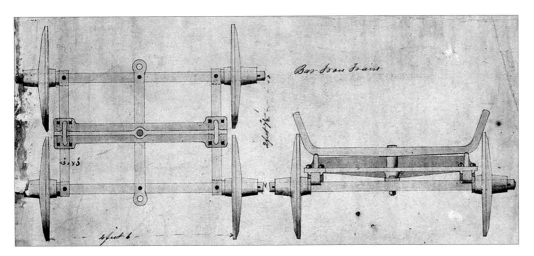

Fig. 3.09
Dowlais iron bar-iron bogie,
27 Jun 1843.
(*GlamA, DG/P/1/127*)

Fig. 3.10
Plymouth (Merthyr
Tramroad) bar-iron bogies.
(*Engineer, 11 Jul 1924, 38*)

BOGIE WAGGONS

The concept of bogie waggons, mentioned a number of times already, seems to have been born in South Wales.[37] Special vehicles to carry long bars of wrought iron were almost a corollary of the rolling mills that produced them. We do not know which ironworks led the way. At Penydarren in 1803 'two waggons coupled together and loaded with five tons of bar iron are comfortably hauled by one horse,'[38] which might very well be bogies. But the earliest firm evidence is Richard Fothergill junior's sketch of Tredegar in 1809 (Fig. 3.01, B), whose rolling mill had been opened in 1807.[39] These vehicles were doubtless two separate trucks joined only by a drawbar rather than a solid frame. Such was the case in later years with the wooden bolsters at Penydarren (Fig. 3.08) and the iron versions used on the Merthyr Tramroad by Dowlais and Plymouth

(Figs. 3.09-10).[40] As we have seen, included in the sale of Blaina Ironworks in 1844 were '48 pairs of bar iron carriages.'[41] The same arrangement, provided for in its bye-laws of 1811, was adopted on the Severn & Wye Railway for carrying large blocks of stone,[42] very likely in imitation of the ironworks bogies; and also on the Bodmin & Wadebridge, for which Neath Abbey drew a plan of a 'double carriage' in 1833.[43] The principle was carried through into the Railway Age, as for instance in the bogies for timber up to 50ft long found on the Liverpool & Manchester in 1842.[44] It is possible too that the Hay Railway, whose main purpose was to carry coal inland from the B&A at Brecon, imitated the Sirhowy. In 1822 it ordered a weighing machine long enough to take 'double tram waggons' with a capacity of up to 3 tons, twice the normal load. These could also be bogie vehicles.[45]

Fig. 3.11
Tredegar 8-wheel bogie coal waggons, capacity 5 tons, 1821 (*detail from Fig. 1.28*)

It was seemingly Homfray in 1821 who first applied the bogie principle to waggons for coal, which necessarily had a continuous frame (Fig. 3.11). Most of the vehicles in John Thomas's picture have sides and, according to figures painted on them, hold five tons. But the leading three are flat trucks carrying vast blocks of coal that weigh up to 4½ tons apiece. Carriage of such monstrous lumps was surely not standard practice but a one-off publicity stunt, and maybe after the event these trucks were converted to waggons by adding sides. But two of them have twelve wheels at equal intervals (Fig. 3.12), and it is open to argument how they worked: two sets of six or three sets of four? At this early date, in the absence of springs to help keep six wheels in contact with the rails, the latter seems more likely, with the central set not pivoted but capable of sliding sideways in a manner not unlike the much later Cleminson patent.[46]

The period immediately following December 1828, when Thomas Ellis junior travelled to Newcastle and met Robert Stephenson, saw the adoption of the bogie on American railways. In that very month, or perhaps the following one, it is specifically stated that Stephenson recommended the bogie to a visiting party of American engineers.[47] They included Ross Winans of the Baltimore & Ohio, who unlike his colleagues stayed on in Britain until at least October 1829, and who took out a British patent for a hand-powered railway carriage with reduced friction which was tried on the Liverpool & Manchester.[48]

Outside South Wales, the pioneer of the bogie was undoubtedly William Chapman on Tyneside, who as we saw incorporated it in his locomotive patent of 1812,[49] and next year suggested, for a proposed railway at Sheffield, long passenger carriages 'placed on two separate sets of wheels, 8 in all.'[50] It seems likely that his was an independent invention rather than imitated from pre-existing South Wales practice., and it took no immediate root in the North East whereas the Welsh version became commonplace. On American locomotives it was put into effect in 1832 on the Delaware & Hudson with Horatio Allen's articulated engine and John B. Jervis's 4-2-0 *Experiment*, the prototype for subsequent American design.[51] For American waggons and carriages its first use is commonly ascribed to Ross Winans on his eight-wheeled passenger car *Columbus* of 1831 for the Baltimore & Ohio, which he patented.[52] But his claim to originality was (and remains) dubious, and gave rise to years of litigation. Much the same thing had been patented in Massachusetts in 1827, bogie waggons were in use on the Quincy Granite Railroad in 1829, and in 1830 the Baltimore & Ohio had bogies for timber.[53] One suspects a degree of independent invention as well as of cross-fertilisation, some of which could well have come from the Sirhowy.

The dates make it perfectly possible that knowledge of the Sirhowy bogies reached Winans either indirectly through Stephenson or, if their visits coincided, directly from Ellis himself.[54]

Fig. 3.12
Tredegar 12-wheel bogie truck, 1821. (*detail from Fig. 1.28*)

Even more pertinent is the name 'columbus,' found from 1840 and unique to Tredegar and later to Ebbw Vale, which was applied only to bogie coal waggons in particular and to some degree to bogies for iron. In default of any other plausible explanation, was not the name borrowed by Tredegar from Winans's passenger car called *Columbus*? Might it confirm that Ellis and Winans met at Newcastle in 1828 and perhaps corresponded thereafter? If so, it was a case of the name crossing back over the Atlantic in return for the initial inspiration or influence. [55]

In local parlance the word 'columbus' became corrupted:

Large 'clumbers' were constructed, capable of conveying about 5 tons each of coal with ease; three of these clumbers were deemed a suitable train for one locomotive. Small low carriages were also constructed for the purpose of conveying rails, &c.; two or three of these carriages were placed under a length of rails, and connected together with iron hooks. These low carriages were the cause of a great loss of life and limb; being low, incautious people would attempt to jump upon them for the sake of having a 'ride with the engine' while the train was in motion; a large number fell victims to these rash acts. [56]

Three bogies under a load of iron bars would make a twelve-wheeler, which adds credibility to the suggestion above that Homfray's twelve-wheelers for coal also had three sets of wheels.

If the original bogie trams of 1821 held five tons of coal, by 1844 they held ten and by 1853 eleven. This increase was probably due not only to improvements in the track and the use of springs, but also to the coming of steam, and it seems that thereafter they were always hauled by locomotive, never by horse. The technical snag was that, until the introduction of hydraulic winches, they were too large to be tipped at the wharves, and therefore had to be unloaded by hand. [57] They are last mentioned in 1854, and were probably withdrawn when modernisation of the MRCC was complete. Yet one may claim that they were the Western Valleys' most important if unsung contribution to railway technology. For fifty years after their inauguration, however, their wider influence was limited, by way of the initial borrowing of 1828, to America. Joseph Wright's British patent of 1844 for vehicles on four-, six- and even eight-wheeled bogies was doubtless quite independent, and sank without

trace. [58] Only in the 1870s, as is well known, did the bogie passenger carriage reach Britain, in imitation of American practice. But the concept had originated in South Wales, and few who travel by train today know whom to thank, at root, for the smoothness of their ride.

TRACK

There is still current an odd folk tale, first recorded by Evan Powell in 1884, featuring Richard Fothergill (1758-1821) and Waun y Pound Chapel in Ebbw Vale, which opened its doors in 1793.

A curious incident occurred at this old place of worship during service on a Sunday morning. 'Old' Mr Fothergill was very punctual and attentive at Waunypond Church, but at the time of constructing tramroads at Sirhowy Works the old gentleman's inventive faculties had been strained and taxed to extremes. Partings and crossings were not invented, which was an insurmountable difficulty when roads were required to be constructed in various directions. The old gentleman pondered and planned, planned and pondered; crossings and partings were preying upon his mind in the works, in the house, and in the church. But on the said Sunday morning the floor of the church was adorned with a thick coat of strewn sawdust. While the Rev 'Price Bach' was proceeding with the morning service Mr Fothergill was seen drawing a plan with the point of his staff in the sawdust, and at last ejaculated 'That is it by —,' whereupon the officiating clergyman paused; the old gentleman lifted up his head, and with a smile said, 'Go on Mr Price, it is all right now;' and the plan of the crossing had been completed. [59]

This must be a tale misremembered and garbled. The date can hardly be before 1794, when Fothergill bought himself into the Sirhowy partnership. Maybe he was working out some specific points-related problem rather than inventing the principle which, whether for edge or plate rails, was already well known. [60] The Dadford brothers as professional engineers would hardly need help from novice ironmasters. Another version of the tale involving Samuel Homfray and St George's church at Tredegar (which was built only in 1836) is even less credible. [61]

For the first few decades the MCC's track followed a typical pattern of improvement. It has been said that in 1808 the original 67lb rails were replaced with 76 lb ones.[62] These weights, inordinately large for the period, must mean per yard run, i.e. that each plate weighed 33½ and 38 lbs respectively. But this is highly dubious. According to the advertisement of 1802 requesting tenders, the original rails were considerably heavier at 45 lbs,[63] and were soon 51 lbs.[64] In 1830, immediately after the arrival of Tredegar's first locomotive, relaying began with 55 lb plates, still 3 ft long but with a bellied rib underneath and held in chairs or cast-iron sills on stone blocks.[65] In 1837 the MCC ordered 100 tons of 6 ft plates weighing 180 lb, but apparently found them too long, for in 1841 it ordered 800 tons of 4 ft 6 in plates weighing 148 lb.[66] The Sirhowy seems to have followed a very similar pattern (Figs. 3.13-14); and the Rumney began life in 1828 with 4 ft plates weighing 65 lb, with male and female ends and a bellied rib below, and held in cast-iron sills through which, rather unusually, they were also spiked to the blocks (Fig. 3.03).[67] In 1842 the MCC (and perhaps the Sirhowy too) began to lay wrought-iron plate rail in 16 ft lengths held sometimes in quite low chairs, sometimes in chairs of extraordinary height (also visible in Fig. 2.14), and mounted at 2 ft 8 in intervals on transverse wooden sleepers. By 1849 only two miles of old cast-iron plates remained. The new wrought rail greatly reduced both the breakages and, with so many fewer joints, the rolling resistance. In 1850 much of it was replaced with a heavier version weighing 75 lb/yard in 19 ft lengths.[68] At least latterly, there was superelevation on curves.[69]

The decade from 1850 to 1860 was dominated by the conversion of the MRCC and its connections into an up-to-date standard-gauge railway system, and it is as confusing to us in retrospect as it surely was at the time. It invites comparison with the much better known conversion of the last 177 track miles of the Great Western's broad gauge in 1892, which was carried out with military precision over a single weekend by slewing one line of rail inwards to the new gauge and installing new, mainly prefabricated, pointwork. That was a massive operation indeed, but straightforward in that the Great Western owned all the track and most of the rolling stock. The MRCC's task, by contrast, was far more complex. It had to convert its Western Valleys tramroads and its locomotives to standard-gauge edge rail, while at the same time to persuade or compel its customers – the multiple owners of the feeder tramroads – to change all their track and all their wheels too. This could not possibly be done in one fell swoop. In fact it took ten years.

There were two ways of approaching the problem. One was to lay 'combined rails' on which both flanged and unflanged wheels could run. The other was to fit rolling stock with 'combined wheels' which could run on either plate or edge. The advice given to the MRCC by its engineer conflicted with that from one of its most influential committee members; and confusingly (and in retrospect misguidedly, because it involved unnecessary cost) it adopted both. Let us start with combined rails.

The principle had first been applied in 1838-9 on the Ticknall Tramroad in Leicestershire, another line built by Outram, in order to carry standard-gauge waggons from the adjoining Coleorton Railway (Fig. 3.15A).[70] Then in 1843 the same idea was patented – no doubt in sublime ignorance of this precedent – by Crawshay Bailey (1789-1872), ironmaster of Nantyglo and dominant partner in the Rumney Railway, which was confronting just the same need to modernise as was the MRCC.[71] His version, held

Fig. 3.13
Centre, underside of original Outram plate rail; STRC = Sirhowy Tram Road Company. (*Oxford House Industrial History Society, Risca*)

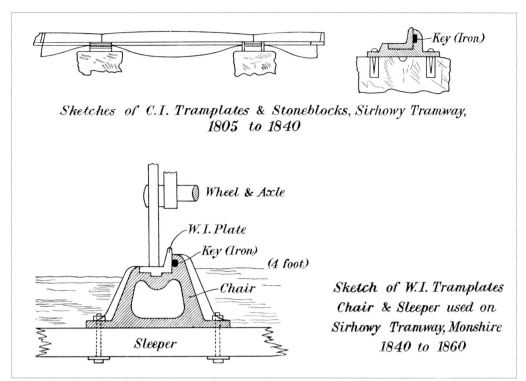

Sketches of C.I. Tramplates & Stoneblocks, Sirhowy Tramway, 1805 to 1840

Wheel & Axle

W.I. Plate

Key (Iron)

(4 foot)

Chair

Sleeper

Sketch of W.I. Tramplates Chair & Sleeper used on Sirhowy Tramway, Monshire 1840 to 1860

Key (Iron)

Fig. 3.14
Sirhowy Tramroad track. The earliest rails were in fact not held in chairs but spiked directly to stone blocks.
(*Barrie and Lee 1940*)

in heavy chairs, resembled a GWR bridge rail with one wide flange for the tram wheels to run on, and was called a 'union rail' (Fig. 3.15B).[72] As on the Ticknall, the edge rail part also served as the flange to guide the tram wheels, but was necessarily on the outside of the track, not the inside as was the norm for plate rails. By a stroke of luck the plate rail gauge of 4ft 4in fitted nicely with the standard gauge of 4ft 8½in, or rather of 4ft 8in over the wheel flanges. At some point an inside flange was added to the Rumney rails (Fig. 3.15C).[73] This was imitated, under the name of the 'Sir John Guest rail,' by Dowlais and Plymouth Ironworks at Merthyr, with an inside flange but without the strengthening rib underneath (Fig. 3.15D).[74] Designing, fabricating

and maintaining pointwork for such track must have been a nightmare.

In 1847 Crawshay Bailey said that he would very likely convert the Rumney to combined rails, and in March 1850 the change began there.[75] The MRCC followed suit, the first suggestion that it should do so being made by James Brown in 1847.[76] Nothing however was done until April 1850 when Crawshay Bailey, who was a member of the MRCC committee, persuaded it to lay an experimental mile of combined rail, supplied by himself, northwards from Pillgwenlly.[77] It seems to have closely resembled his patent design, and supposedly weighed as much as 120lb/yd.[78] There was at the time no intention of using it beyond Nine Mile Point and Abercarn, where

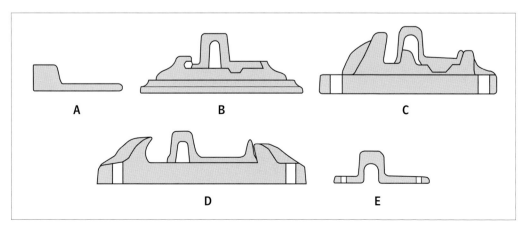

A   B   C

D   E

Fig. 3.15
Combined rails.
A, Ticknall (NRM, 1977-850);
B, Bailey's patent, 1843;
C, Rumney (after *RM*, 24 (Apl 1909), 272);
D, Plymouth Ironworks (Lewis Collection, Ironbridge Gorge Museum); Tredegar.
(*after NRM, GWR A1002*)

the Sirhowy and Penllwyn and Hall's Tramroads joined.[79] But in the event it was installed in 1853 up to Aberbeeg, north of which the track was converted directly to edge rail.[80] However, the MRCC's combined rail, of which no illustration is known, was only a temporary measure. By the end of 1855 every yard of it had been replaced with straightforward edge rail,[81] and the Company, having for the time being done all that it could do by itself, had achieved the first half of its strategy. The next step was to bring the freighters into line. They were already simmering with fury at the Company's edicts. In 1851 the ban on old ramshackle trams had finally been enforced, which caused the temporary closure of fourteen collieries that possessed no other rolling stock.[82] In 1853 tram wheels were banned which were not vertical, because the commonly-used wheels that inclined outwards, while reducing friction against ordinary inside flanges, markedly increased it against outside flanges such as combined rails had.[83]

All this was part of the MRCC's second line of strategy, to force its customers to adopt the combined wheel which could run on either kind of rail. The freighters had no option but to comply, because from 1855, while the feeder lines were still tramroads, the main lines were now railways. We first meet the concept of the combined wheel in 1832 – unusually forward-looking for so early a date – when it was proposed by Neath Abbey for the Sirhowy yard engine and the Ebbw Vale-Sirhowy tunnel engine (Figs. 2.34, 36). At the same date it was found at Dowlais too, on *Yn Barod Etto*, another four-wheeled yard engine by Neath Abbey; and its *John Watt* of 1838 and several of its locomotive tenders of the period likewise had edge/plate wheels.[84] The idea was later fostered by Somers Harford of Ebbw Vale, who in 1840 was advocating it for the MCC lines,[85] but only from 1848 was it recommended by Edward Scott Barber the chief engineer, and in 1849 applied to the Company's model trams. There was a set-back when Captain Simmons expressed disapproval both of combined wheels and of combined rails. He suggested instead a dedicated standard-gauge track laid eccentrically to the tramroad, which the Company refused to contemplate because of the cost. But it found a way round the dilemma. When the line to Blaina was inspected by Captain R. M. Laffan in 1850 prior to its opening for passenger traffic, he gave it his blessing even though the locomotives were fitted with combined wheels.[86] This the Company

took as the go-ahead, and over the next few years urged their adoption, helped by the engineering firm of James Murphy of Newport who supplied combined wheels of the approved pattern with replaceable wrought-iron tram tyres, and even complete waggons on combined wheels and rubber springs.[87]

We have a fascinating photograph taken in 1857 (Fig. 3.16) when the great Crumlin viaduct was almost completed. It shows two trams, one full of coal, one derailed and empty (apart from a bunch of navvies from the viaduct construction gang), on the Kendon (Cefn Coch) arm of Hall's Tramroad. One intriguing feature is that the rails are a mixture of cast and wrought, apparently still on stone blocks, and the trams are of the traditional plateway-only type: there is no sign of combined rails or combined wheels. This suggests that these trams no longer ran on the MRCC proper, and that when the old sort was banned in 1851 the owner, rather than re-equip his whole branch, had installed tipplers to empty the coal into new model trams.

The Rumney was on the same course, but now lagging a little behind because it was short of materials and was waiting to see the results of conversion on the MRCC. It announced in March 1854 that it was going to complete its relaying by 1 January 1855, with combined rail on the lower part and solely edge rail on the top 11 miles, by which time all freighters must have adopted combined wheels.[88] Whether it achieved its aim is not wholly clear. While by the deadline there was still work to be done on cuttings and walls, 'the old tramway, which was one of the most useful as it was also one of the most dangerous tramways in existence, has just been converted into a railway ... The whole of the conversion, extending over about 24 miles, has only been six months in hand.'[89] Yet in August 1857 it could be said that 'The old Rhymney tramroad ... is still in part a tramway.'[90]

What with plateway and combined wheels running on simple plate rails, on simple edge rails and on combined rails, there were many permutations possible, more than one of which might be found in the same train. Combined wheels gave endless trouble when they moved from edge to plate or vice versa, and especially at points. An interesting case in May 1855 involved a Rhymney locomotive which derailed and overturned at a set of points at Bedwas. The driver, sacked for speeding, complained bitterly about the lack of maintenance which led to

Fig. 3.16
Hall's Tramroad at Crumlin, 1857. Taff Vale Extension viaduct in background. The two counterweights on the left probably belong to a coal chute or tippler down to the MRCC main line below. Note the pile of tram wheels. (*Stephen Rowson collection*)

regular derailments. He had narrowly escaped 'an accident from a rail being completely out of the chairs and lying in a ditch at the roadside,' and had asked the railway company staff why they had not noticed it. 'They had plenty to do,' they replied, 'to replace the rails after the passage of every team.'[91] He took the Rhymney Iron Co to court for wrongful dismissal, maintaining he was going no faster than 8 mph. A witness said it was more like 30 mph. At points, it was said, it was not unknown for the engine to take one line and its train the other. In this case the real culprit was a wooden 'guard rail,' that is, a check

clout-nails … [This guide was] quite loose – so loose I could move it with my foot. The rails were very much out of gauge at the spot. Next morning, I took our engine through the crossing three or four times, very slowly, and the engine jumped on the box, showing that the guard-plate did not do its work.

Interestingly, the Rhymney engine in question had ordinary standard-gauge flanges, whereas, as we saw, one of Marshall & Knowles' locomotives with combined wheels and therefore deep flanges took the points in its stride.[92]

So things continued, on the MRCC, for four years after the end of combined rails. But combined wheels were only another temporary stage, because, while they were compatible with standard gauge track as laid by the MRCC, they were not compatible with standard gauge track elsewhere. The wheel flange had to be deep enough to raise the tread, when a combined wheel was running in plateway mode, high enough to clear the flanges of the plates and the check rails at crossings (Fig. 3.17-18). It was therefore 3in deep, nearly three times the norm, and, in the interests of strength, thicker than a normal flange. Thus on ordinary chaired edge rails it would foul the chairs, and was too deep and wide for ordinary flangeways alongside check rails and at crossings. To complete the conversion, therefore, wheel flanges had to be made of normal size, and the flangeways in the track made of normal width and depth.

Thus in November 1859 the edict went forth:

As the combined wheels which are in use will not run on any railway of ordinary construction, and have been found, from four years' experience, to add greatly to the amount of wear and tear of the rails, and to lessen the effective power of the locomotive engines … wheels with tyres and flanges of the shape objected to will not be admitted on the Western Valleys Railway after the 1st of January, 1860.[93]

This final edict drove the freighters to their final revolt. At a stormy meeting of the MRCC, Richard Powell Davies for Tredegar and Samuel Homfray for the Sirhowy Tramroad insisted that there was no hope of anyone, especially owners of small feeder tramroads, converting all their wheels in time. They pointed out that the MRCC Act of 1853 gave the Penllwyn and Hall's Tramroads specific permission to use combined

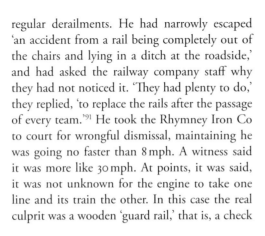

Fig. 3.17
Combined wheels on edge and plate rail. Note the double flanges of check rail on right.

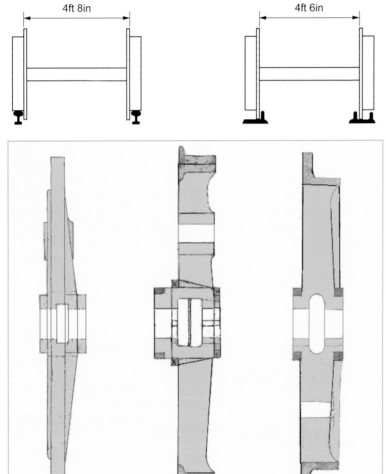

Fig. 3.18
Neath Abbey locomotive wheel profiles, 1831-39. Left to right, plateway, ordinary edge rail, combined wheel. (*after drawings in WGAS*)

rail. The Rumney Railway Co claimed that 'in the transition state of the road, the wooden guards were sufficient, and as good as iron, if in due order.' To which the Iron Company's traffic manager retorted,

These guides were generally made with half a sleeper, and lined with sheet iron, nailed on with

wheels.[94] This, they argued, meant that other feeders did not have permission, which could only be supplied by new parliamentary authority. The MRCC therefore agreed to suspend the notice to allow time for further thought.[95] Thought was taken, tempers cooled, and the revolt petered out. Six months later it was announced that the Penllwyn and Hall's would be converted to edge rail by 30 September 1860, and that Tredegar would change its combined wheels for ordinary railway ones as soon as possible. It was resolved

That immediately after the 30th of September 1860, the points and crossings on the Western Valleys lines whenever the changing of any of them may from wear and tear become necessary, shall be replaced with points and crossings similar in their opening spaces [i.e. flangeways] to those upon the Eastern Valley lines and all other lines of narrow [i.e. standard] gauge railways; and that notice of this intended alteration to be given to the owners of wagons fitted with combined wheels, so that they may take steps to adapt those wheels to the alteration in the railway by the above-named day.[96]

Thereafter no plateway vehicles could run on even the furthest tentacles of the main-line system, and September 1860 may be taken as marking the end of the MRCC as a tramroad. Its conversion into a railway, said a local paper when the process was almost complete, 'has not been effected without much individual and social injustice.'[97] How very true.

The Sirhowy itself embarked on a similar course, but a later and more ingenious one. In the absence of Tramroad Company papers the details are obscure. But by February 1858 – probably in 1857 – edge rails of Vignoles or flat-bottomed section[98] had been laid on the portion from Nine Mile Point to Tredegar Junction (at Pontllanfraith, where it was crossed by the new Taff Vale Extension). The portion from there to Sirhowy was already under conversion,[99] which was certainly completed by November 1859.[100] For the transition, these rails were laid on their side in very heavy special chairs (Fig. 3.19), the tram wheels running on the web and the edge-rail wheels on the side of the head.[101] When the time came to complete the conversion into the Sirhowy Railway, the rails were simply turned upright, whether spiked direct to the sleepers or in chairs.[102] It seems, however, that inside Tredegar works a simple combined rail without chairs was employed for relatively light track (Fig. 3.15E).[103]

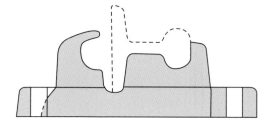

Fig. 3.19
Sirhowy Tramroad chair for flat-bottom rail on edge. (*after NRM, GWR A1005*)

LIFE AND DEATH

In their mingling of steam- and horse-drawn traffic, the Sirhowy Tramroad, the Rumney Railway and the Western Valleys lines had much in common with the fledgling Stockton & Darlington, where everyone from manager and engineer to fireman and platelayer was feeling his uncertain way through the pitfalls of a new form of transport, ever prone to organisational and operational mistakes.[104] But if standard-gauge lines of the early Railway Age had little to boast of in terms of safety, Welsh tramroads had even less. In one poignant incident in 1845 a haulier on the Rumney fell between two of the trams in his train and was crushed to death. It transpired that both his father and his brother had died in the same way.[105] With the growth of traffic and the coming of steam power, accidents proliferated, to the point where newspapers sometimes printed callously off-hand lists of the nastiest. An example from 1853: 'There was quite a chapter of accidents here [Newport] last week;—A poor fellow was knocked down on the Western Valleys Railway, on Saturday, by an engine, and cut to pieces.— On Monday, a driver fell off an Engine and had his head cut off,' and so forth.[106] By this date the malign effects of tramroad locomotives seem, after twenty-four years of incessant tragedies, to have lost the power to shock.

At inquests, a verdict of accidental death was almost a foregone conclusion. On only the rarest of occasions did jury or coroner criticise employers, and more often it was left to the press to voice unhappiness about working practices.

At the lowest end of the scale, derailments were so frequent that the press normally mentions them only if they led to something serious. But the episode at *Britannia*'s debut in 1829 when its wheels 'got out of the tram-plates' raises the question of how derailments were righted. The Rhymney Ironworks inventory of 1848 lists (under the heading of Trams) '2 Bars for Prizing' at 4s each, '1 Iron Jack' at a mere 3s, and '1 Double Action Rack Jack' at £1 10s.[107] But in 1855 John Raymond, a Rhymney engine driver whose death in 1859 by boiler explosion we have already recorded, was charged with hauling a derailed tram a quarter of a mile up the line, bumping over the sleepers with great damage to the chairs. By the rules, he should have used jacks to rerail it. But it was common practice, he said, to pull trams along the ballast until the next turnout, where rerailing was easier. 'Our company ought to give us jacks,' he added, implying that the jacks normally lived in the store rather than on the engines.[108] Indeed the accounts record a number of small payments of a pound or two for 'Getting Engine on Road.'

Another device is recorded in 1815 (Fig. 3.20).

> In all tram-roads it is very useful to have, at the distance of every two or three hundred yards, a tram-plate with two turn-up edges, the outer one being a segment of a circle. This plate assists the waggon to regain its proper station on the tram-plates, whenever (as will sometimes happen) it is thrown off the track by the interruption of loose stones lying on the plates; by imperfections in the wheels or axles; or by the carelessness of the driver, in not keeping the horses in the regular line of drawing.[109]

These special rails may be the 'horn plates' mentioned in Fig. 3.21 On the matter of accumulated dirt, one practice found on a few South Wales tramroads was to clean it off the running surfaces by scraping them with a hoe-like implement,[110] and there are a few references to cleaning the road in the Rhymney accounts.

There were other mechanical mishaps, as when

> An accident occurred to the 9.0 a.m. down mineral train from nine mile point. Several of the Tredegar Iron Company's columbusses containing coal, and six or seven cars loaded with iron, were proceeding towards Newport, and when passing through Tredegar Park, the wheel of one of the columbusses came off, and threw the carriages across the line, blocking up the spot for nearly six hours.[111]

More serious accidents, involving death or injury, were almost beyond count. For their victims there was seldom any personal compensation whatever. Property, in those days, was valued more highly than people. The iron companies regularly shouldered responsibility for damage they caused, whether to trams or horses or fixtures, but in almost all cases the injured parties were not employees of the iron company and might have sued for damages. We have seen, for example, how Homfray paid the owners of demolished property at Blackwood. The Rhymney accounts are full of compensation payments for setting woodland, hedges, fences, straw and even barns on fire: the spark arresters on the engines were clearly not infallible. The works paid up for killing horses, cows, donkeys and sheep, and regularly bought coffins (15s 0d apiece) for its servants killed on active service and once 'a wooden leg for Wm Pugh' (£1). The only instance when we hear of a company accepting the smallest liability for personal injury or death

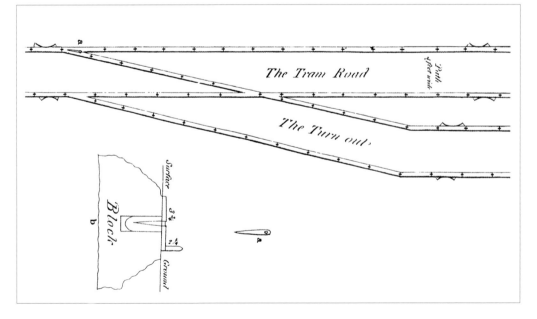

Fig. 3.20
Points and re-railing plates.
Bottom centre, a, latch.
(*Hassall 1812, pl. 2*)

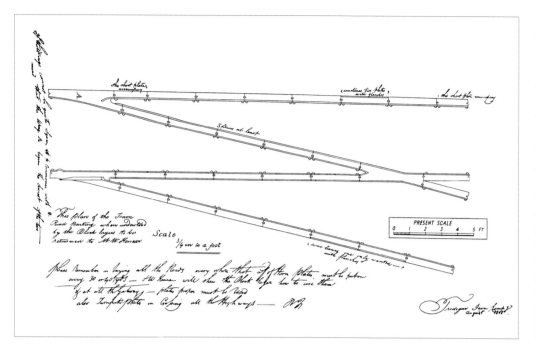

Fig. 3.21.
Tredegar points. The captions read: 'This plan of the Tram Road parting when understood by the Block Layers to be returned to Mr W. Kenear. Tredegar Iron Compy August 1808,' 'Please remember in laying all the Roads every where that a Pr (?) of Horn Plates must be put on every 30 or 40 yds — W Kenear will shew the Block Layer how to use them and at all the Gateways — plates proper must be used also Turnpike Plates in crossing all the Highways. RF [Richard Fothergill],' (sideways) 'If the Wings cannot be quite square to commence with mind that the Wing A begins the soonest of the two;' (beside rails) 'this short plate unnecessary,' 'sometimes two Plates with flanches,' '5 Pairs at least,' 'sometimes only one wanted with flanches'. (TNA, RAIL 1014/4/26)

concerned William Roberts, one of the Tredegar engine drivers, who had lost a leg in an accident about 1836. He was given the post of watchman at Tyley's Pit, a Tredegar colliery; and when, twenty-eight years later, his cottage was burnt down, the company rebuilt it for him.[112] How far the iron companies were insured is not clear. The only record is of Rhymney paying £4 5s 6d to insure its locomotives in July 1848;[113] given that it then had eight engines valued at £5,894, this seems a very modest premium.

Medical aid for those injured on the tramroads was, needless to say, rough and ready, and the surgeons employed by the ironworks were rarely of much competence. A good (or bad) example is recorded in 1831.

Whilst Thomas Phillips was spragging the wheel of a tram of coal at Ebbw Vale Iron-works his clothes became entangled in the wheel, and he was dragged in that state upwards of sixty yards, the wheel passing across the palm of his hand, which fractured two of his fingers, and divided the integuments of both sides of his hand. He applied to the surgeons of the Works, who put him upon the *antiphlogistic system*, with an outward application of bread and water, for eight days; the poor sufferer, finding himself getting worse, went to Crickhowell, and obtained admission into the dispensary, under the care of Mr Wakeman, surgeon, who extracted from his hand ten pieces of coal and a splinter of wood. He is now in a fair way of recovery, and will again be able to use his hand. This is the fourth case from the Iron-works that has been relieved at that charitable institution within the last three months.[114]

Amputation of leg or arm was commonplace, but at least, in mid-century, chloroform became available. In a single week in December 1847, within a month of its first clinical demonstration at Edinburgh, a surgeon at Newport Dispensary (which was established as late as 1839) used it in three operations on men injured by trams.[115]

The fundamental reason behind this toll of life and limb was identified in 1841.

The number of fatal and distressing accidents continually occurring on the tram roads is indeed appalling: scarce a week passes away without one or two dreadful accidents, causing either instant death or leaving the unfortunate sufferer a cripple for the remainder of his days … A great majority of the accidents are caused by the carelessness of the men.[116]

It was likewise said, a few years later, 'since the introduction of locomotive engines on your roads, the number of accidents from the bursting of the boilers, the breaking of engine and carriage axles, and other misadventures, outstrip those of all the railways in the kingdom.'[117] Whether or not that was true, the number of deaths and injuries seems appalling. But it must be viewed in context. Early railways were indisputably dangerous. Locomotive boilers had been bursting ever since Blenkinsop's at Leeds in 1814, and a glance through the newspapers of 1830 reveals, both before and after its opening, a whole catalogue of accidents on the Liverpool & Manchester, which was a concern vastly better regulated than any in South Wales. On the Sirhowy, the MCC and the Rumney, carelessness does indeed seem to have been the watchword. This happy-go-lucky approach might do little harm on a horse-operated line that saw relatively little use, but growth of traffic and the coming of locomotives altered the whole picture.

Two categories of accident mentioned in the newspaper accounts were of a distressingly common kind, and deserve explanation. The first concerns the fireman. Early locomotives were narrow, with little projecting sideways outside the wheels. Footplates were therefore narrow too, and if the fireman's foot, in clambering up or down as the engine was moving, slipped off the step, it landed on the rail and in the path of the wheels. As locomotives and footplates grew wider, such a slip would land the fireman's foot on the ground outside the rails.

The second concerns the latchman (later sometimes called the breaksman or watchman), the third member of the standard engine crew. His job was to shoo away trespassing livestock and, above all, to set the latches or points. This was a simple matter of moving by hand the short wrought-iron switch visible on Fig. 3.20 and on a fine Tredegar drawing of 1808 which was sent

by Richard Fothergill senior to the MCC for the guidance of their blocklayers (Fig. 3.21). There was no way of locking the latch. The latchman's normal post was the locomotive's fore-plate, as seen on the Neath Abbey *Camel* on the Bodmin & Wadebridge (Fig. 3.22), from where it was easy to jump off the moving engine for the purpose, and if necessary to drop sand 'from a plentiful store placed on a platform in front of the engine.'[118] His job carried its own particular perils. Typically, in 1852 on the Rumney,

William Thomas, the breaksman, fell from his seat in front of the engine [the *Bute*], and suffered amputation on the rail, of a leg, a hand, and the thumb of the other hand, by the wheels passing over him … The practice of allowing the breaksman to ride up a narrow shelf of iron fixed to the front of the engine, from which he might be shaken off by a slight jolt, or on jumping from which, he might easily stumble, and be killed on the spot, is at once most dangerous and reprehensible, and requiring an immediate alteration.[119]

In the absence of turntables, locomotives ran chimney-first uphill. On the downhill journey the latchman changed ends, although on the tender there was no such obvious perch as the fore-plate. Many cases are recorded of him falling off, or of stumbling as he jumped off, and being run over. Likewise in 1846 a man lost a hand 'while

Fig. 3.22

Bodmin & Wadebridge Railway *Camel* with latchman on fore-plate, 1834.

(*Sir Arthur Elton Collection, Ironbridge Gorge Museum*)

shutting the "latch" on the tramroad, in order to turn off the trams … [and] not withdrawing his hand sufficiently quick.'[120]

Danger too attended the latchman when coupling trams which, as was general in South Wales, were connected not by chains but by rigid bars called hitchings. Of varying length, these were bent over at the ends like overgrown staples and dropped into holes in the drawbars (Fig. 3.23, and see Fig. 3.05).[121] The account of another accident underlines the hazards they posed and the fact that the buffers – mere extensions of the wooden frames, if they existed at all – rarely matched those on the neighbouring tram.

It appears that the Ebbw Vale engine[122] was returning to Newport with a number of loaded coal waggons attached, and that the pin of the 4th waggon fell out, causing the shaft of that carriage [presumably the coupling bar] to stick in the ground, and throwing the carriages behind it in all directions, breaking and scattering the coals all over the road. The engine proceeded onward with the three large columbusses a little distance before they could stop, as they were going at a rapid pace.[123] A haulier … had a narrow escape of his life. He was standing on the buffer of one of the carriages, and the buffer belonging to the next carriage happening to skim along the side of the one on which he was stationed, threw him several yards on the road, and rendered him insensible at the time. Luckily the circumstance happened as it did; for if the buffer had come on his carriage instead of the side it would have smashed him to pieces. The damage done to the different carriages is very serious. No fault can be attached to the engine driver, as it was caused by the hitchings of the trams belonging to the Ebbw Vale Company.[124]

It is clear that, had the trams been loose-coupled, misaligned buffers would have locked or overridden and led to constant derailments; hence the rigid bar hitchings. The downside was that the starting load of such a train was immense: it could not be gradually taken up by means of the slack in the loose chain couplings that were the norm elsewhere. The upshot, once again, was that drivers increased the pressure by tampering with the safety valve.

Here as elsewhere, the convergence of roads and railways was always a problem. Sparks from engines alighted on passers-by – a girl in Newport, for instance, was badly burned when

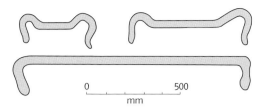

Fig. 3.23
Tram coupling bars from Penydarren and Dowlais. (*after Young 2016, fig. 9*)

her dress was set alight – and equally they set hedges and woodlands on fire.[125] Horses took fright at the 'Vesuvius-like belchings' of locomotives and went out of control.[126] Road vehicles skidded or shed their drivers or overturned when crossing the rails diagonally. Plates for level crossings were normally made as double-flanged troughs in order to keep them as clear as possible of dirt from the road metalling, and the flanges were scalloped on top to give road wheels a grip.[127] 'Pieces of wood should be laid on each side of each rail, in the same manner as on the level crossings of [main-line] railways, for the protection of vehicles passing over.'[128] But when the Tredegar mail coach came to grief near Risca and injured several passengers it was found that the rail flange here was single and the timber ramp between the metalling and the rail was defective. 'The wood affixed to the flange to make the approach gradual being worn away,' the shock of the wheel hitting the flange threw the driver off and overturned the coach.[129]

Such problems with highways were generic; but in South Wales they were made worse by a peculiarly local phenomenon. Whereas tramroads elsewhere tended to pick their way through an existing infrastructure of roads and streets, in these remote and undeveloped landscapes it was often the tramroads that came first. It was remarked in 1843, for example, admittedly by the advocate of a rival railway, that apart from the indifferent and extremely roundabout road via Abergavenny, the MCC tramroad was still the only route between Nantyglo and Newport for vehicles of any kind. But it was

formed, in many parts, on the edge of a precipice, without any fence or other protection, and of so steep a gradient, that trams, let loose, will run down of themselves, to the great danger of any living being, with which they may come in contact.[130]

Nor was there any pre-existing road between Ebbw Vale and Aberbeeg and, hard as the MCC tried to prevent them, travellers naturally

Fig. 3.24

The Welshman who couldn't speak English. (*MM, 4 Apl 1846*)

followed the route on foot or horse or cart, and sometimes they paid the physical price. In 1841, we hear, 'it appeared that Richard Lowe was driving a tram through Risca, and that from some carelessness on his part, he drove it on the wrong road.' He knocked down a pauper woman who had already walked 21 miles from Glamorgan that day, and broke her leg.[131] In the 1840s we hear of children in Ebbw Vale having to cross multiple tramroads on their way to school and 'dodging the trams like street Arabs dodging the traffic.'[132]

What also ensued, when new settlements were created and old ones burgeoned, was ribbon development beside the line. As Captain Simmons put it in his report of 1849,

The various tramways have in many instances been used as high roads, and villages have been erected upon them having no other roads of communication, even from house to house; and in the town of Newport good houses have been built with no means of access to any public road except across the tramroad.

Here the rails passed, in places, within 5ft 8in of the front of houses.[133] Thus trams and road vehicles and pedestrians shared the same right of way, with no fencing or demarcation whatever, and with inevitable outcomes. We have seen one result when the Sirhowy inconsiderately altered the road at Blackwood. It had already been complained

that the tramroads of the Canal Company … cross the public roads and highways, and in many places are carried along the streets, and the houses on each side are in no way protected therefrom … That numerous accidents have occurred under the present system of hauling along the tramroads by horse power, which casualties, it is feared, will much increase when steam power is used upon them.[134]

Newport itself being thick with ungated level crossings, numbers of inhabitants came to a sticky end there, whether through their own lack of caution or the failure of engine drivers to sound their whistles.[135] Another factor, especially in Newport although line-side pubs engendered similar behaviour, was that hauliers often left their trams standing on the main line without bothering to park them in sidings. Many were the summonses they earned for obstructing the highway, not to mention obstructing the tramroad. A classic case was when the driver of an unnamed Tredegar locomotive was charged with 'leaving his steam engine upon the tramroad, while he went to see a fight some distance off.'[136] Another such case in the police court involved a none-too-bright miscreant (Fig. 3.24).[137]

A level crossing could even supply the opportunity of cocking a snook at the local gentry. One Thomas Newell was driving his trams along the Crumlin line when Sir Benjamin Hall called to him to stop to allow his carriage to cross. The haulier replied that

'he cared no more for a Baronet than for any other man,' and proceeded until he reached the crossing, when he pulled up, and deliberately detaching the horses from his train, he led them away to a considerable distance to water, thereby preventing the passage of Sir Benjamin along the turnpike road. After the lapse of nearly an hour, defendant returned, and having hooked on his horses, proceeded on his way.[138]

Public access to the track contributed to a further problem. Stealing coal was endemic, and not merely, despite the presence of night watchmen, from trams parked on the sidings at the wharves. In 1848, for example, a man was gaoled for a month having been caught red-handed.

Isaac Stephens is an engine driver to the Tredegar Iron Company. On the 9th of March he was at the machine; there was a tram weighing there, and he with a lot of trams was waiting till the machine could be engaged for his trams. He saw three persons on the road who had no business there. He got under a tram, and one of those persons, the prisoner at the bar, passed him; and he afterwards heard coal falling from the tram, and running out, caught the prisoner with coal on his shoulder.[139]

Nor was trespassing necessary. It was easy to reach into trams as they passed at walking pace along the streets – a case was reported of one man taking three hundredweight of coal at a time [140] – and it was easier still to scavenge lumps that had fallen out. In the infamous Blue Books of 1847 the parliamentary commissioners enquiring into education in Wales, who had not a word of Welsh between them, took much of their evidence from Anglican clergymen of mind-blowing insensitivity and arrogance, who never bothered their heads with the causes of the poverty that drove their flocks to theft. One of them deposed,

> In my opinion, a *tramroad* for the conveyance of coal from the hills to the sea-port for exportation, tends to demoralize the district through which it passes to an inconceivable degree. The results are theft, drunkenness, and prostitution. Women and children of all ages, sent out expressly by their parents, are seen at all hours following the tram-waggons, to obtain by any means, save by a pecuniary purchase, coals for the use of their respective families. The *haltiers* [sic] of the trams, from a knowledge and intimate acquaintance with the parties, oftentimes aiding and assisting in the plunder of their employers. [141]

This witness was Rev Augustus Morgan, rector of Machen on the Rumney Railway and son of none other than Sir Charles Morgan of Tredegar who had amassed a huge fortune from tolls on the Golden Mile that crossed Tredegar Park.

In similar vein, Martin Morrison the freighter deplored

> the crime which prevailed on the tramroad… They were all aware what depredations were committed. It was most lamentable to see so many children brought up thieves. On one occasion he counted upwards of eighty persons following the trams for the sake of plunder. [142]

For this reason if for no other, the new, large and sprung coal waggons of 1849, despite their cost, pleased the coalowners.

> Another most important advantage derived by their use, is that whatever weight of coal is loaded at the collieries will be delivered in Newport. The average loss from breakages and pilfering in transit now amounts to nearly five per cent upon the total quantity. In the new waggons breakage is precluded by their great strength; and, as in the columbuses

used by Mr Homfray at Tredegar, the swarms of marauders who infest the roads, are completely non-plussed by being unable to reach the top of the waggon. [143]

But even scavenging came at a price. As an entirely typical example,

> One of those shocking accidents, which occur so frequently to persons employed on and about our tramroads, befell a poor boy, eleven years of age. His means of subsistence depended on his picking up the bits of coal, which fall from the coal trucks. Tempted by a large lump, which fell close to the wheels of the tram, he eagerly ran to gather it up, when the wheels of the next truck passed over his hand. [144]

Nor was coal the only target. Tram wheels, or even whole trams, might be stolen and sold on, [145] or 'borrowed' without permission, even though those of independent hauliers were marked with their initials. In 1841 a wheel marked HP was borrowed by someone who thought, he said, it belonged to Harry Price, whereas it was actually the property of Hopkin Perkins. [146] In 1849 a very small urchin, son of a tinker, was caught red-handed and in broad daylight trying to unscrew a brass band on a locomotive boiler, having already succeeded in removing the whistle. [147] Rails were quite often stolen for their scrap value, including latches (point switches) and guard plates (check rails). So too, from the trams, were beans, oats, turnips, straw and hay, and even wine (stolen by a lad 'aged 16 but an old offender'). [148] On one occasion two Risca men, having purloined from a tram a puncheon of rum destined for a Tredegar pub, sat down beside the track to drink themselves into a stupor. One fell across the rails, where his head was cut off by a passing train. The other's life was only saved by a stomach pump. [149]

Even more dangerously, in 1851,

> Thomas Vaughan, one of the engine drivers of the Tredegar Iron Works Company, was charged with being drunk, while in charge of one of the company's engines, on the Western Valleys railway. This was an extraordinary case. The defendant, last Thursday evening, got drunk, and was seen driving his engine and tender up and down the line, without carriages attached, as if for amusement. Other engines were expected down, and had a collision taken place, the drunken fellow, who was occasioning such danger, and now and then lying down in his tender, would no doubt have been completely smashed. The piece

of line selected for this dangerous folly, was between Tydee and Rumney Junction [i.e. Pye Corner]. At the latter place, the station officer jumped on the engine, stopped her, examined the fire and boiler, and found that the latter was nearly empty. He therefore pulled out the fire; but the drunken fellow wished to increase the fires, and a pretty explosion might have been expected, if the defendant had not been stopped.

From 1850, when the MRCC finally took over haulage, Tredegar engines should have been restricted to the Sirhowy Tramroad, transferring their trains at Nine Mile Point. Yet it seems that, at least on this occasion, Tredegar locomotives still ran on MRCC metals. Vaughan was given the option of a £5 fine or two months' imprisonment.[150]

Alcohol, indeed, featured large in the hauliers' lives.

In the Forties the Western Valley Railway was not regulated (or at least it seemed so), for the locomotives stopped at nearly all the public houses from Ebbw Vale to Newport like the proverbial 'miller's horse', and many publicans reaped a substantial harvest from that custom. It was the origin of more than one big fortune.[151]

It was also the origin of countless delays to traffic. On the Rumney, even after it had ceased to be a plateway, old habits died hard, for the philosophy remained lackadaisical and the engines gimcrack. We have an account from 1856 by someone who, through knowing the right people, had obtained a footplate pass.

Mounted one of these steam snorters at the Victoria Inn, Brithdir, steam strongly to Pontaberbargoed where a train of lime drawn by a horse and a tram of dung pushed by a man obstructed progress 8 minutes. The old engine snorted angrily and snail-like crept around Fiddlers Elbow Turn; at Pontaberpengam I got off to seek a friend, wetted the whistles of the directors of the engine with a pot of XXX and started again: at Place Level stopped engine to shake hands with my friend; thence merrily to Twynyrudw – platelayers reparing road 15 minutes delay; steam full up, pelted away making a terrible noise and clatter to a feeding place where engine got dry; a little trial of patience, then on again to the Bedwas Turn when bang over the plates went the greater part of the train, which I then left and padded the hoof to my destination ... Thundered along [said the same writer of a later

trip] until near Ystrad Mynach when lo! a soung [sound?] whist-s-st and clouds of steam. I leaped off the tender, thought the 'biler busted,' but it turned out to be only one of the tubes which evidently they could not soon 'fettle.'[152]

The opposite danger to tardiness, especially recurrent after the MRCC began to turn itself into a 'proper' railway with modern locomotives, was drivers exceeding the speed limit. An up goods train was approaching Abercarn when

the train suddenly came into collision with the tender [meaning what?], through some unknown cause, when the engine ran off the line. The impetus which was still on it drove the engine over the bank, the edge of which is there very close to the rails, and in a moment the engine went down the precipice at a frightful speed. The driver fortunately had presence of mind sufficient to induce him to leap off before the engine reached the bottom.

The wreckage took two days to clear.[153] This incident prompted a letter to the press complaining about recklessly fast driving. It named several drivers, whether as paragons or as public dangers, and claimed that down passenger trains often reached Risca six minutes early.[154]

A few months later a light engine was returning tender-first from Abertillery to Aberbeeg in the charge of James Austin.

Austin – who was described as a careful driver and named by his colleagues "The Swift," in derision, he being prudent and slow – appears to have lost all awareness of duty and self-preservation.

He put on steam immediately on leaving Abertillery and accelerated at 25-30 mph down a gradient of 1 in 54, where the speed limit was 7 mph, while 'the stoker was struggling like a madman at the break.' At a set of points on a curve, the wheels climbed the flange of the rails (which were still plates), and the engine ran for a further 90 yards on the ballast, smashing a string of eleven trams that were standing on a siding. The driver, it was said, was not drunk; but he was killed instantly.[155]

There was, of course, until almost the end, no signalling system whatever. The basic rule, as elsewhere, was that empty trams gave way to loaded ones, whether hauled by horse or steam, and that the trams nearest to a junction took priority. In 1841, for example, the complainant, Isaac Williams, was driving down along the Rumney tram-road towards Pie Corner, a team of trams loaded with coal, the property of Mr Prothero; and the defendant, Thomas Jones, was driving down a team of trams, loaded with iron, along the Tredegar tram-road, towards the same place. The two roads in question join at Pie Corner, and there terminate in one line of road. It was clearly proved by Williams and another person, that Jones must have been well aware, when he was between 200 and 300 yards from the junction of the roads, that Williams was much nearer the junction than he was, and that it was impossible for him (Jones) to take the lead; that notwithstanding this, Jones was riding on one of the iron trams, which were going at a terrific rate, and left in the charge of a boy about ten years of age. The consequence was, that the iron trams became unmanageable, forced the horses across the tram-road, into the turnpike road, and came in collision with the last of the coal trams, upset it, and broke two of the wheels, but fortunately the horses received no injury.

Jones, upbraided by the court for 'leaving a mere child in the care of the team,' was fined 15s for damages plus 17s costs.[156]

The truth is that for decades there was no concept of timetabling or even of interval running. Hauliers, whether by horse or steam, started their journey when they saw fit and proceeded at the rate they saw fit. It was only in 1849 that the company, armed with its new parliamentary powers, began slowly to turn chaos into order. It created a rudimentary operating department, and from the Newport police force it recruited its first policeman, Superintendent John Huxtable, to try to enforce the bye-laws.[157] He was a Bristol man, a competent and respected officer, whose wife ran a refuge for down-and-outs. Next year sixteen 'Semaphore, Station, Distance and Branch Signals' were installed on the MRCC, along with twenty sets of level crossing gates.[158] But even in 1851, even after the Blaina line had been approved by the Railway Inspectorate and had begun to carry passengers, an engine coming down from Blaina ran into a stationary one that was taking on water, luckily with no lives lost. As the press very reasonably remarked,

> We should have thought that a signal of some description ought to have been given when engines stop on the road in the above manner to take in water, there being a curve in the line before coming to Aberbeeg, so that the engineer and fireman are

prevented from seeing what is going on a few yards before them.[159]

And even when safety regulations were in place, there was no guarantee they would be observed. In 1853 a man and boy, despite being refused permission by the station master at Pye Corner, pushed a tram up the line by hand. The driver of a following train, warned by a red light, proceeded cautiously and was able to stop in time.[160] Next year three gangers were loading old rails onto a trolley on a single track section, without, as they should have done, planting a red flag 400 yards away in each direction. When a train bore down on them at 20 mph, they only just got the trolley into a siding before the train scraped past. They were fined.[161] All these cases were on the relatively go-ahead MRCC; the Sirhowy and Rumney lagged far behind in terms of regulation, which allowed inexcusable head-on and tail-end collisions as late as 1858.

Another problem was overtaking. Horse-drawn trams inevitably travelled more slowly than locomotives, and in 1849 the freighters complained of the Company engineer 'taking up the intermediate partings of their roads, thereby preventing engines from passing horse teams.'[162] Yet barely a year later Richard Jackson, driver of the MRCC's No. 3, was taken to court by Huxtable charged with 'taking an engine on the wrong line of road ... in order to pass a tram drawn by horses which was dodging along before him at a slow pace, much slower than the railway speed the defendant wished to proceed at.' Unfortunately

> the crossing where he intended to resume his proper course, was in an unfinished state, and the engine and train there met with a check, which threw about seven large waggons [i.e. columbuses], loaded with coals, off the road, by which they were much damaged; and about two days elapsed before the line could be freed from this obstruction.

Jackson's excuse was that not only did the drivers regularly drive on the wrong line, but

> that the head engineer had done so himself, and that Superintendent Huxtable had directed an engine driver to go on the wrong line in order to pass an obstruction of this sort, and bring him to Newport by a certain time; and, further, that the engine drivers had duly reported in writing when they went on the wrong line; but no notice had been taken by the company of those reports.

The magistrates, while they reprimanded senior Company officials for considering themselves above the law and thus condoning 'this very dangerous practice,' made an example of Jackson by fining him £2.[163]

These tales only underline the impression that locomotive crews considered themselves superior to humble horse hauliers, as a report from the Rumney suggest.

> William Davies and William Hawkey, who work an engine on the Rhymney tramroad, were charged with having assaulted, beaten, and kicked William Wells, a haulier on the same road. It appears that Wells, who was only a 'common haulier', offended the dignity of the engine-men by not moving his 'trap' out of their way; whereupon they jumped down, and played a game something like shuttlecock with the head of poor Wells, which they hit from one to the other until the unfortunate man fell down, and then they made a football of him, and kicked him unmercifully. They were fined 10s and 7s costs each, or one month's imprisonment.[164]

Possibly Rumney enginemen were particularly belligerent members of the species.

When a passenger service to Blaina began at the end of 1850, it necessarily had to follow, or try to follow, a timetable. So too, increasingly, did freight trains. We first hear of this in 1853, when Rumney trains were supposed to leave Pillgwenlly at 11.00 a.m and 5.00 p.m., but by no means always did so.[165]

One commodity carried on the tramroads has not yet been mentioned. Explosives, in constant demand for mining and quarrying, carried their own dangers. In 1850 a spectacular collision, which might so easily have been a major disaster, took place on the MRCC between Ebbw Vale and Aberbeeg.

> On Friday afternoon last, between four and five o'clock, a man named Charles, in the employ of the Ebbw Vale Company, was in charge of two of the large iron carriages of that establishment [i.e. columbuses], containing about twenty tons of iron. He wished to remove these carriages from a particular spot, at the Victoria works, and desired one of the Ebbw Vale engineers to move them forward a little with his locomotive, in order to place them upon the line for the upper works. This was done, but the break which Charles placed in the wheel to stay the motion thus given, being suddenly snapped off, the two heavily laden carriages started off, and were speedily careering at such a velocity as to be beyond all human controul. Thus left, the velocity attained by such an immense weight on the incline, became most frightful . . .
>
> At this time a man named Williams, of Tydee, owner of a small one-horse covered tram, in which his wife usually rode with him on his journeys, was quietly jogging along with sixty barrels of gunpowder piled beneath his coverlid. He had reached Llanhilleth, when suddenly in the distance, he perceived the two iron-laden carriages wildly thundering down. In a second, apprehending the fearful state of the case, and thanking Providence that the constant partner of his journeys was not with him, he instantly slipped out the pin that fastened the shafts to his tram, and dashed down the declivity with his frightened horse, just in time to avoid the destructive clash; for quick as lightning the twenty tons of rail iron ran into his car, and among his powder barrels, which, of course, were smashed; whilst the crazy tram was smashed and comminuted beyond all carpentry skill. The collision caused some sparks of fire, and the matting around the shattered powder casks speedily took fire; and then an explosion, awfully grand, something perhaps like the magazine display at Moultan,[166] ensued; fifty-one barrels having been blown high into the air, shaking the neighbouring houses, and frightening their tenants, as if an earthquake had taken place; while the narrowly-escaped Williams, who wished himself safely back once more with his good wife at Tydee, stood with his old horse looking on in terrible amazement, until his hat being blown off his head by a shock, or knocked off by a piece of his tram wheels, he considered it high time to decamp. Very fortunately, indeed, no life was lost, nor greater damage done, than the destruction of the powder and the haulier's tram. We understand that the Monmouthshire Railway and Canal Company have just received from the manufacturers, an air-tight powder carriage, which comes opportunely to replace the old vehicle of Williams, which had hitherto been used for the purpose. We have heard that for the loss which poor Williams has suffered, he will be fully compensated by the Ebbw Vale Company.[167]

Another instance of compensation. Finally, in early February 1859, during the Sirhowy's twilight zone between tramroad and railway, there was a further spectacular runaway.

> Two accidents, which might have resulted in serious loss to life and limb, occurred on the Sirhowy tramroad … and we regret to state that

each was occasioned, there is too much reason to believe, through the malice of some evil-disposed persons. In consequence of the large amount of traffic on the Sirhowy tramroad, trains of coal and merchandise have for some time been despatched by night as well as by day, and on Wednesday night last one of these, on arriving near the Argoed siding, instead of pursuing its course along the main line, turned into the siding and came into collision with some trucks standing there. The force of the shock detached the tender from the engine, and the tender and trucks – some of which were laden with coal and ore, the leading truck with stones, and the others were empty – passed over the siding on to the main line, down which they proceeded until they arrived at Nine Mile Point. Here a stop-block upon the line was forced from its position by the front truck, loaded with stones, and the truck was thrown off the line and emptied of its contents, the truck itself going down the embankment, a depth of about thirty feet. The remainder of the trucks continued their course, in their progress carrying away and completely destroying the gates placed across the Western Valleys Railway at Tynycwm and Pontymister. The tender remained upon the line near the Black Vein Pit at the Risca Works, two of the empty trucks stopped at Tynycwm, and three others at Pontymister, but the progress of the four trucks loaded with coal was not arrested until after they had passed through Tredegar Park and arrived at the Gaer Pool, where they were found by one of the company's policemen on the down line of rails. Two of the coal trucks belonged to the Tredegar Iron Company, and two to Mr Cartwright, to whom also belonged the whole of the empty trucks. Upon an investigation being made into the cause of the accident it was found that the points at the Argoed siding had been opened, and were kept in that position by being firmly wedged up.[168]

The first of these two accidents, when *Tredegar* was derailed down the embankment, had also been caused by sabotage to points, and has already been recounted. In this second case, because it happened to the last train of the day and because at this late hour in midwinter the line was otherwise deserted, there were mercifully no injuries. By this date the Sirhowy had just been relaid with edge rails, and the trams were on combined edge/plate wheels. The last surviving waggons of the ill-fated train ran a good sixteen miles by gravity alone, which they assuredly would not have done on plate rails.

PASSENGERS

Passenger carriage on the Sirhowy began very early; conceivably even earlier than 25 March 1807, when the famous service on the Oystermouth Railway was inaugurated which is the first verified instance of formal passenger carrying.[169] No doubt from the start people hitched informal lifts on the trams, with or without payment to the driver and with or without his connivance; and, to judge by the reports of accidents, they did so in considerable numbers. An interesting example from 1843 concerns a navvy in search of work who paid the engine driver 1s 6d for a lift for himself and his probably considerable baggage from Newport to Ebbw Vale, on an Ebbw Vale train. His companion tried to walk alongside but, his smock catching on the tram, was pulled off his feet and run over. The inquest jury expressed 'in the strongest terms their disapprobation of the conduct of the Ebbw Vale Company in so allowing their servants to permit travellers to be conveyed by their carriages after the frequent loss of life that has arisen therefrom.'[170] A more typical case was when a miner, 'a little worse for drink,' cadged a lift to Tredegar and 'notwithstanding the remonstrances of the engineer, he would persist in riding in the tender, on which he lay down at full length,' only to roll off to his death.[171]

The same had happened, usually with less dire results, on horse-drawn trains. But tram horses plodded at no more than walking pace. It is usually said that faster and more formal passenger services from Newport to Sirhowy were started only in 1822 by John Kingson, a Newport innkeeper, who next year built a covered 'Caravan' at a cost of £70, for which the MCC charged him a toll of sixpence (later a shilling) for every twice-weekly trip.[172] But his was not the first such vehicle. The magnificent aquatint of Risca viaduct (Fig. 1.20), published on 1 June 1810 and based on a drawing of no earlier than 1807, includes an open-topped carriage

Fig. 3.25
Sirhowy Tramroad passenger tram, 1810. *(detail from Fig. 1.20)*

conveying at least eight passengers. This, with its long wheelbase, is clearly not converted from an ordinary tram (Fig. 3.25). Any suspicion that it might be artistic licence or wishful thinking is dispelled by the Scottish engineer Robertson Buchanan. In a report of 23 September 1811 he mentioned the Sirhowy on which

passengers are often carried upward, on *a rise of one foot in two hundred*, at the rate of *six or seven miles an hour*, by one horse; and with a motion more easy and pleasant, than can be well conceived by those who have not experienced it.[173]

Given the sledge-hammer jarring of unsprung wheels on plates with a joint every yard, the claim of comfort should be taken with a goodly grain of salt. But there is no reason to doubt the service existed.

Earlier still, Richard Fothergill junior's drawing of Tredegar on 7 August 1809 (Fig. 3.01, c) includes a single vehicle carrying three unidentifiable objects. With its large body and very large wheels, it is no ordinary tram. Can it be a car carrying three passengers? If so, the sketch predates by three weeks our first picture of the Oystermouth carriage. The question therefore arises: did the passenger service go back even further than 1809 or 1810? Until 1800, as we saw, Sirhowy was a small and remote community. Then, with the new works at Tredegar, the population almost exploded. But the only road communication to the south comprised wretched tracks meandering along the ridges, and the tramroad's Act of 1802 therefore stipulated that a cart road, on which tolls were charged, should also be built alongside the line. It was not until well after 1810, however, that the Sirhowy completed its section of the road,[174] so that until then the only sensible route to Newport, for people as for iron, was the tramroad. Even so, ordinary trams took seven hours to make the journey,[175] whereas a single light car could do it in half the time. Given these circumstances, was a regular passenger service provided from the completion of the Sirhowy Tramroad in 1805, two years ahead of the Oystermouth? We do not know.

In the mid-1820s, according to Powell, 'Passengers to and from Tredegar, Argoed, Blackwood, Newport, &c., were conveyed in wooden trams, by a large number of contractors, who also furnished the town with a constant supply of provisions, &c.'[176] Directories list such carriers as Samuel Robins and John Price plying from Newport to Tredegar 'by railway' every Monday and Friday in 1835, and Henry Morgan likewise 'occasionally per tram' in 1849.[177] Such trams no doubt carried passengers too. Small-scale carriage of goods – other, that is, than the principal traffic of iron and coal – was always toll-free on the Sirhowy if not on the MCC.[178] In 1839, among expenses for repairing damage after an accident at Pye Corner, we have the bald entry 'Passenger to Tredegar, 5[s] 9[d]:' presumably the full distance and probably return.[179] There were even private trams: included in a sale of domestic effects at Blackwood in 1834 was a 'Pleasure Tram.'[180] In 1843 an unnamed merchant, possibly at Nantyglo, had urgent business to transact in Newport, and the only conveyance available on 'that abominable road' was 'a small spring tram.' His journey was twice delayed by permanent way works at Crumlin and Risca, where despite his pleas to let him pass, the workmen's 'exertions seemed to relax into the most perfect slothfulness.'[181]

Even road vehicles could serve their turn on rails. In 1844 'a capital four wheeled Phaeton' was advertised for sale, 'made to fit the Tram-road.'[182] One Rees Morgan of Ebbw Vale stated that 'before 1845, I used to go from Ebbw Vale in Mr Brown's gig, that fitted the flanges of the tramroad. I travelled that way nearly twenty years.'[183] The other way round, one Charles Bishop was summonsed in 1848 for injuring the road surface near Newbridge 'by placing a coach upon tram wheels and running the same on the highway.'[184]

These passenger services were small-scale and horse-drawn, but when added together they were not insubstantial. It was said of the MCC that

the existence of the tram-road brought vast numbers of people from the Hills every Saturday to the Newport market. On that day no engines were allowed to be used, for fear some accident might happen to those who came down in the train drawn by horses. At this time the line was single, with partings in various places; consequently, very great delay was frequently caused in passing.[185]

Accidents, needless to say, still happened. In 1846 John Williams was driving his single horse-drawn tram, carrying goods and several passengers, up the double track from Newport to Risca when, for reasons not explained, he changed from one line to the other. In the process his tram was hit by a down train – also horse-drawn – and the occupants were spilled out. The only injury was a woman's broken leg.[186]

None of these passenger services were advertised in the press, no doubt because everyone interested already knew of them and because far from all could read. But they were clearly well used. Captain Simmons's table of 1849 includes, over and above the 3,996 trams and columbuses for coal and iron, 76 vehicles 'for the haulage of goods and passengers on the tramways.' Indeed his steam-hauled inspection train was twice held up on the Aberbeeg, for four or five minutes each time, by passenger trams coming down within minutes of each other, as if the second was carrying the overflow from the first.[187] Next year James Brown, as usual deploring the management of the MRCC, recorded of the Western Valleys that

> trams, laden with passengers by thousands every month, were wont to run to and from Newport, at charges of about one halfpenny per head per mile. Wretched as was this system, still for want of a better, it answered the purpose tolerably well in fine weather.[188]

Thus, as we have seen, 'canvas-covered omnibi plod primitively to town with their market-going coteries.'[189] Until the onset of the confusion that attended the transformation of the system, 'on one of these lines public horse-coaches and the mails travelled daily,' and 'the public had been accommodated with mail vans, cars, trams, &c &c, to the number of twenty or thirty.'[190] Another source speaks of the public 'in gigs and carriages, the wheels of which were adapted to the flanges of the tramroad,'[191] yet another of 'a sort of ramble-tumble coach.'[192]

Then from 1 August 1849, under the Act of 1848, the public was restrained from using MRCC tramroads as highways. Where alternative roads simply did not exist, as on the Beaufort and Crumlin, this caused much hardship and anger.[193] The company also withdrew permission for all private-enterprise passenger services. The use of steam haulage for passengers was restricted to special occasions and even then to the elite, as when the new rolling mills at Tredegar were ceremonially opened in 1849 and 'two Locomotive Carriages will be in readiness in the Morning at Pillgwenlly, to bring Visitors from the Neighbourhood of Newport.'[194] Otherwise all that the MRCC provided was a single steam-hauled third-class carriage, 'but as this did not stop save when and where it pleased the engine driver himself, it afforded little or no real accommodation.'[195] A 'kivered carriage' (the meaning is doubtful: a kiver was a bowl or trough) sometimes sprung, sometimes not, left Ebbw Vale for Newport at the crack of dawn and returned last thing at night. It was perhaps from this 'passenger tram' between Ebbw Vale and Newbridge that two men leapt in 1850 when a collision threatened, and were lucky to escape with their lives.[196] One of them was 77-year-old Richard Brown, father of Thomas and James, who had helped construct the boiler of Trevithick's Penydarren locomotive. The tram ran over his legs, and he died a year later, possibly as a delayed result.

There were also (or were they the same?) conveyances 'of the most execrable description, distinctively y'clept "mail vans."' In one of them, James Brown revealed, so mighty a man as the chairman of the MRCC himself, 'in consequence of the failure of the "Doctor," was necessitated to ensconce himself.' In order to explain to readers, he adds, 'the rate and style of travelling with these venerable vehicles, it will suffice to mention, that the post office authorities are unable to get the mail conveyed from Newbridge to Nantyglo (a distance of only 11 miles) in less than 2 hours 20 minutes.'[197]

With the growth of the ironworks and commercial premises in the iron towns, a well-used tramroad would seem to be an obvious and reliable route for the carriage of mail, but there was little of it. The nearest post towns were Newport and Abergavenny, and a private post, by road, between Tredegar and Newport was early established and jealously fostered by Samuel Homfray senior. By 1816 it was extended to serve (on payment) Sirhowy, Beaufort, Ebbw Vale and Nantyglo as well. Local tradespeople had attempted in 1832 to employ ordinary hauliers to carry letters on the Sirhowy, the legality of which was queried. But with the coming of the Penny Post in 1840, private mails became pointless, and the Post Office took over everything. It still sent most of the mail by road, and its mail service by tram from Newbridge to Brynmawr and Nantyglo was the only one in the Western Valleys, the bags being transferred to it at Newbridge from the Tredegar-Newport road coach. This is said to have been given up in favour of road carriage by 1844,[198] but in fact it continued until the embargo of 1 August 1849, 'in consequence of which the two mail-vans then running were stopped.'[199] That having been said, however, on 10 September 1849 'the mail train' was derailed and overturned a mile and a half out of Newport. This was hardly the Newbridge-Brynmawr service.[200] Perhaps it was a brand-new and longer-distance one.

Passenger services, however crude and intermittent, were thus in existence in the 1840s. True, one girl who grew up in Ebbw Vale in that decade had forgotten them when she wrote her reminiscences.

> I can only remember one mode of going from Ebbw Vale, and that was on foot. There was one exception, a conveyance called the Pleasant Tram, for the use of officials of the works, and to us schoolchildren it was a wonderful thing (so grand as we thought). Poor thing, its grandeur consisted in having red velvet cushions! I fancy it would seat about six, and as we always used to know when it was going to be used, for it was brought out to be cleaned about the time we went to school, and we went a little out of our way in order just to step into it, to have an idea of what a ride on it would be. It took the officials to Newport along the Western Valley Railway, which was used then, but not for passengers. If I remember rightly, it was opened for passengers in the year 1850.[201]

The long-awaited formal services, steam-hauled, in 'proper' carriages, and duly approved by the inspectors of railways, were finally inaugurated from Newport to Blaina on 23 December 1850 and to Ebbw Vale on 19 April 1852, still running on plateway wheels.[202] At Newport, the passenger station was at first at Court y Bella, and from 1852 at Dock Street a mile further east. Not that everyone was happy about the services:

> Very few of the second and third class passengers know that the seats in the carriages belonging to the Monmouthshire Railway and Canal Co are settled by the Railway Commissioners to carry or accommodate *four* passengers only... and servants of the Company very often insist on five or more being accommodated... The ride we get is a very rough one – the speed slow, and the charge high, and I, for one, intend to insist upon availing myself of all the comfort that the law allows me.[203]

If the Western Valleys lines were thus slowly creeping out of the Dark Ages, the Sirhowy

Tramroad was not. We have seen that in 1847 the enigmatic *Brithdir* was supposedly proposed (but doubtless never used) for passenger work to Tredegar. And in 1850, when the MRCC promised to start passenger trains on its branch to Nine Mile Point, the Sirhowy eagerly decided to follow suit by buying six carriages built by Joseph Wright of Saltley (precursor of the Metropolitan Carriage & Wagon Co). Three were third-class only – 'equal to the Great Western second-class' – and three were composite third, second and first – the latter compartments 'fitted up in a style suitable to the tastes and requirements of those who at home recline on Grecian couches.'

> The first-class compartment bears upon the panel of the door the Sirhowy Company's arms – a pick, mallet, and spade, crosswise – with the words "Sirhowy Company, 1802," surrounding the emblems. The whole are now on the Tredegar Wharf, at Pillgwenlly, in this port. The carriages are supposed by some parties to be too lightly constructed for the road; but it is a question whether a light carriage is not preferable on a road which is much inferior to the railroads of the age.[204]

But, beguiling though the image may be of luxurious Grecian couches on board a plateway vehicle, alas once more for fond hopes. In the event the MRCC did not give Nine Mile Point its passenger service, it still forbade private-enterprise vehicles, and the branch was not converted to edge rail until 1855 nor given a passenger service until 1865. The spanking new Sirhowy carriages were sold off to the MRCC in 1852 for £1,350,[205] and a Tredegar omnibus that was proposed to meet the (non-existent) MRCC trains at Nine Mile Point never materialised.[206]

Thus for fifteen years from 1850 the Sirhowy Tramroad languished without formal passenger trains. Whether the old-fangled informal ones survived on it, we do not know. The landlady of the Argoed Arms who died when *Bedwellty* was derailed in 1858 was probably only hitching a lift on an ordinary tram.[207] But occasional specials were run. In 1855 R. P. Davies, the Tredegar manager, laid on a picnic excursion to Nine Mile Point when 240 of the town's inhabitants piled into twenty-six 'carriages;'[208] and in 1861 visitors to the Machen Flower Show were 'conveyed over the Sirhowy tramroad free of charge, and the company allowed the use of their carriages for the purpose.'[209] In both cases the 'carriages' were no doubt ordinary waggons dolled up for the occasion. Also in 1861 it was reported that unauthorised passengers were carried in the brake van of goods trains on paying a contribution towards the driver's beer.[210] But for all this time, as far as most people were concerned, Tredegar was effectively cut off. 'Travellers from Tredegar to Newport,' it was lamented as late as 1864, 'have at present to go to Ebbw Vale, and to get there they must either walk two miles over a mountain, or be jolted three or four miles along a circuitous road in a tilted cart called "the bathing machine."'[211] This was presumably the omnibus already mentioned. Proper passenger trains only reached Tredegar – and, for that matter, Nine Mile Point – when the modernised Sirhowy Railway was opened in 1865.[212]

The Rumney was equally dilatory, and with better excuse in that its catchment was not so heavily populated. Less provision was made for passengers than in the other valleys and, as usual, riding on the trams was clearly commonplace. Thus in 1855 near Bedwas,

> the engines of two trains on the Rhymney [sic] railway came suddenly close to each other, at ordinary speed, on a curve near this place. The drivers and stokers seeing that a collision was inevitable, the distance between the two trains being very small, leaped off their engines, and many persons who were riding on the trains, followed their example. The collision took place with great violence, and one of the engines was much injured. A female who was riding on a tram, was considerably hurt, but all the other persons escaped.[213]

We hear of nothing in the least formal until 1850 when

> Mr Williams, the omnibus proprietor who runs between Newport and Caerphilly, has undertaken to run a 'bus' on the Rhymney tram road having obtained the consent of the company for that purpose. This will be a very great convenience for the inhabitants of Rhymney and neighbourhood to visit our markets[214]

Whether it materialised we do not know. But in 1859 James Brown was ranting about 'the wretched conveyances, outside the King William the Fourth [a Newport pub], which pass between Machen and Newport,' and were presumably road omnibuses, the only public transport available.[215]

THE END

Conversion of the Western Valleys lines was set in motion by two Acts of 1845 and 1848 (the latter changing the name from MCC to MRCC),[216] and it was complete, in the limited sense that standard-gauge stock could use them all, by November 1855, and wholly complete by September 1860.[217] The transition of the MRCC from tramroad to railway was therefore prolonged, as curves and gradients were eased and signalling, fences, stations and gated level crossings installed. Conflicts too still arose between considerations of safety (on the part of the Company) and the desire (on the part of the freighters) to expedite the flow of traffic.

Over to the west, the Rumney tried to keep pace with the MRCC. There was some limited work in the early 1850s to improve curves, and some years before 1859, like the MRCC, it forbade horse traction.[218] The building of the Rhymney Railway, sponsored by Bute interests, was authorised on 24 July 1854 from the ironworks to Hengoed where it met the Taff Vale Extension of the Newport Abergavenny & Hereford, and from thence to Cardiff.[219] It was opened throughout on 25 February 1858 and, as intended and expected, drained much Rhymney traffic away from Newport to Cardiff. It paralleled the top half of the Rumney, but followed the opposite (west) side of the river before veering westwards. The Old Rumney, making the best of a bad job, had itself reincorporated as a railway company on 1 August 1861, with powers to upgrade the line for high speed passenger working, which meant in places building a new road alongside to remove pedestrian and horse traffic from the line.[220] But the old order was still reluctant to be improved.

In 1860 it had offered itself for £110,000 to the MRCC, which would bid no higher than £65,000.[221] It was again reported in 1862 that the board had agreed to sell the Old Rumney to the MRCC;[222] but once more it fell through. Next year the old complaint was voiced again, 'the district has for years been crying out against the lethargy and want of activity evinced by the proprietors.'[223] And at last help was found from an unexpected quarter. On 28 July 1863, for about £90,000, the Old Rumney was bought by the Brecon & Merthyr Railway,[224] whose real stamping ground lay well to the north. Although ambitious, it was not a wealthy company, and it took time to relay the track and ease the many curves. After two failed inspections, passenger traffic began from Newport to Pengam on 14 June

1865 and thence to Rhymney on 16 April 1866.[225]

Just as relations were often strained between the MCC and its freighters, so they were between the MRCC and the Sirhowy, with fault no doubt on either side. Samuel Homfray, although he had retired from the Tredegar Iron Co in 1853, remained chairman of the Tramroad Company. But as he aged he lost his former zest. In the nature of things the Sirhowy Tramroad Company, while in theory independent, was in practical terms always in the Tredegar Iron Company's pocket, and its driving force, until his death in 1860, was now Richard Powell Davies, Homfray's new-broom successor as manager of Tredegar. He seems to have been something of a tyrant and precious little of a diplomat; hence, one might guess, the Blackwood debacle outlined above.

If it is difficult to define a single point at which the MRCC ceased to be a tramroad and became a railway, so it is with the Sirhowy. In both cases 1860, with the end of combined wheels, is perhaps the closest we can get. As we saw, the Bill to transform the Tramroad Company into the Sirhowy Railway Company was thrown out by Parliament in 1859. The Company tried again, and in 1860 it succeeded, with powers for a number of diversions.[226] Even so, the line took five more years to modernise fully. After hopes were several times raised and dashed because negotiations were under way to sell the line to a larger concern,[227] it was finally opened as a fully-fledged passenger-carrying railway on 19 June 1865.

By this time the writing had been on the wall, in effect, for thirty-five years. In England, it is true, a few plateways of some significance survived into the twentieth century: the Derby, Ticknall and Peak Forest Canal tramroads are the prime examples: none of which, be it noted, had graduated to steam traction. But on major Welsh lines like the Sirhowy and the MRCC, the old order simply could not be allowed to continue. Just as with Brunel's broad gauge a generation later, modernisation was inevitable. To quote for the last time the sardonic James Brown of Ebbw Vale,

> The company's system of management was defective. As long as horse teams were continued … so long would they be acting under a wrong and antiquated system. The common practice now carried on upon the road – locomotives coming down and mixing with horse teams – led to constant and serious inconvenience to the trade. Matters could never be improved until the company became the general carriers for the freighters. How were they now often situated? A horse team was coming down before a locomotive which was followed by another horse team. After proceeding a certain distance, the horse team would be stopped, and the man who had the charge of it would leisurely throw down hay before the horses. In the meanwhile the locomotive was detained – could not get on; and oftentimes the driver had to give men who had the care of horse teams the sum of five shillings in order to get them to move out of the way, otherwise an explosion could not be avoided; and was that system to be tolerated?[228]

Yet, after this comment was aired in 1847, thirteen further years went by before these anachronisms were finally and fully ironed out. The surprise is that it took so long. But we may be glad that the process was slow, for it has bequeathed us a most instructive chapter of railway history in which an antiquated tramroad system could, in terms of length and traffic, still rival and even outdo many a normal standard-gauge railway.

Meanwhile the economic map was being changed as the traditional pattern of north-south tramroads was augmented by new railways running east-west across the grain of the country, which favoured Cardiff rather than Newport. The broad-gauge South Wales Railway (1852) hardly matters, because it followed the coastal plain. The standard-gauge Taff Vale Extension of the Newport Abergavenny & Hereford (1857, which included the great Crumlin viaduct, at 208ft the highest in Britain) had links to each of the old lines it crossed. The Merthyr Tredegar & Abergavenny (1862-71) demanded equally heavy engineering but falls effectively outside our period. After seeing off proposals for rival north-south lines in the Western Valleys, in the Eastern Valley the MRCC finally opened its own Newport & Pontypool Railway in 1852. In 1875 the Sirhowy Railway was leased to the London & North Western, while in 1880 the MRCC was amalgamated with the Great Western. The Rumney had already, in 1863, been bought by the Brecon & Merthyr Railway.[229] Later still, towards the end of the nineteenth century and the beginning of the twentieth, most of the ironworks closed. But although the 4ft 4in gauge was effectively dead by 1860, the narrow-gauge limestone tramroads lingered on for decades more. The Tredegar-Trefil remained at work until 1915, not only the last survivor of a tradition already well over a hundred years old in the Western Valleys, but the last South Wales plateway of any significance.

Notes to Part Three

1   Hassall 1815, 111.

2   Gerstner 1831, Bd. 1, 638-9.

3   Jones 1969, 43.

4   Barrie 1980, 30-1.

5   Byles 1982, 13.9

6   *MB*, 31 Aug 1844.

7   *MM*, 23 Jan 1847.

8   *MM*, 10 Apl 1847.

9   GlamA, DRH/85 ff.114-118.

10   Cumming 1824, 29-30.

11   *Cambrian*, 22 Aug 1818.

12   Gerstner 1831, Bd. 1, 621).

13   Adams 1850, 29-30, Plate 17 Fig 3.

14   *MB*, 18 May 1839.

15   GlamA, DRH/15 f.353.

16   *MM*, 18 Sep 1848.

17   *GJ*, 12 May 1806.

18   *MM*, 9 Feb 1849.

19   *MM*, 18 Nov 1843.

20   *MM*, 24 Aug 1844. Palmer 1823, 18 had recommended that water be carried on the front tram to use as lubricant.

21   *MB*, 27 Jun 1840.

22   NLW, MS 5155.

23   GlamA, DRH/85 f. 97.

24   Report of the Commissioners for Railways for 1849, Appendix 74, 157-178 = *PP* 1850, vol. xxxi, 179-200, from which many details are drawn. Discussed in Lewis 1996.

25   *MB*, 10 Aug 1850.

26   *MM*, 2 Mar 1844.

27   Hadfield 1967, 148.

28   By 1853 the gross weight of some Ebbw Vale ones, with buffers and chain couplings, was 17 tons (*MM*, 12 Aug 1853).

29   *MM*, 14 Apl 1849.

30   NRM, 1998/11 11 37/1.

31   *MM*, 28 Apl 1849.

32   Adams 1850, 30.

33   *MM*, 12 Aug 1853.

34   *MB*, 27 Aug 1853.

35   *MM*, 10 Mar 1854.

36   Powell 1902, 32.

37   The word 'bogie' in its modern sense was not then in use, but emerged in the early 1840s. For its antecedents see Lewis 1997.

38   Svedenstjerna 1804, 96; translation, 55, wrongly giving ten tons.

39   Powell 1902, 23; Jones 1969, 44.

40   A set of Plymouth bogies found its way to the Baltimore & Ohio Transportation Museum, and replicas are in NWM.

41   *MM*, 2 Mar 1844.

42   Paar 1963, 39; Paar and Pope 1997.

43   WGAS, D/D NAI L/6/2a.

44   Whishaw 1842, 205.

45   Rattenbury and Cook 1996, 53, 75.

46   Paar and Pope 1997; Pope 1997.

47   Colburn 1871, 96.

48   Patent no. 5796; Thomas 1980, 69, 183.

49   Dendy Marshall 1953, 62.

50   Lewis 2014, 210.

51   For the dispute between Allen and Jervis over priority, see Fitzsimons 1971, 90-101.

52   Dendy Marshall 1953, 250.

53   White 1978, 8-9, 18.

54   Lewis 1996; Gwyn 2004. On the American visits, Heydinger 1954.

55   Paul Reynolds suggests the name may be borrowed from the ship *Columbus*, launched in 1824, claimed to be the largest in the world, and the talk of the day. Did some wag in Tredegar compare this outsize ship with Homfray's outsize waggons?

56   Powell 1902, 55-6. 'Clumber' is also found in *RM*, 9 (Nov 1901), 422.

57   *CMG*, 18 Mar 1848; cf. *MM*, 17 Feb 1849.

58   Patent 10,173 of 7 May 1844.

59   Powell 1902, 46.

60   Lewis 2019a.

61   Tasker 1992, 23.

62   Baxter 1966, 50.

63   *GJ*, 8 Nov 1802.

64   *Cambrian*, 14 Feb 1808.

65   *Cambrian*, 17 Apl, 5 Jun 1830.

66   *MM*, 29 Apl 1837, 30 Jan 1841.

67   Gerstner 1831, Bd. 1, 620.

68   *MM*, 18 May 1850; MacDermot 1931, vol. 2, 112.

69   *MM*, 12 Aug 1853.

70   Clinker and Hadfield 1958, 69. Specimen in NRM, 1977-850. Called a 'rim and tram rail,' it was devised by a local blacksmith named Hallam (*RM*, 6 (Mar 1900), 211).

71   Patent 9582 of 11 Jan 1843, 'Construction of rails for tramways and railways;' *London Journal of Arts*, 23 (1843), 254 and pl. xii; *The Principality*, 3 May 1850.

72   *MM*, 27 Apl 1850; *PP* 1851, vol. xxx, 457.

73   *RM*, 24 (Apl 1909), 272.

74   Specimen in Lewis Collection, Ironbridge Gorge Museum; Dendy Marshall 1938, pl. 73; Mercer 1948, 101-2; 'Dean Forester' 1963, 60; van Laun 2001, 26-7

75   *CMG*, 22 May 1847; *MM*, 10 Nov 1855.

76   *MM*, 15 Apl 1847.

77   *MM*, 27 Apl 1850.

78   Byles 1982, 31.

79   *MM*, 27 Apl, 18 May 1850; *CMG*, 23 Nov 1850; *MM*, 4 Apl 1851.

80   *Silurian*, 19 Jun 1852; *MB*, 20 Nov 1852; *CMG*, 21 May 1853.

81   *MM*, 18 May 1855; *MB*, 24 Nov 1855.

82 *MM*, 21 Nov 1851.

83 *C&MG*, 21 May 1853.

84 Rattenbury and Lewis 2004, 69-77.

85 NLW, Tredegar Estate III 57/136.

86 *MM*, 14 May 1849; *MB*, 29 Mar 1851; *MM*, 4 Apl 1851; *MB*, 10 May 1851.

87 *MB*, 8 Oct 1853; *MM*, 11 Aug 1854. Illustrations in MacDermot 1931, vol. 2, 112 and Byles 1982, 25 both purportedly show a combined wheel, but are in fact of an ordinary tram wheel.

88 *MM*, 3 Mar, 16 Jun, 23 Jun 1854.

89 *HT*, 13 Dec 1855.

90 *CMG*, 15 Aug 1857.

91 *MM*, 18 May 1855.

92 *MM*, 10 Nov 1855.

93 *MB*, 12 Nov 1859.

94 16-17 Vic. c. 195.

95 *C&MG*, 19 Nov 1859.

96 *C&MG*, 19 May 1860.

97 *C&MG*, 15 May 1858.

98 Meredith 1913, 229-30, Moore 2017, 61.

99 *MB*, 27 Feb 1858.

100 *MB*, 19 Nov 1859.

101 A close counterpart was Plymouth Ironworks' bullhead rail laid flat in special chairs in Morlais quarries (van Laun 2001, 179). Double-headed rails laid flat were used on some Rhymney tramroads by at least 1857; but these were wasters – that is, of too low a quality to sell (*Engineer*, 6 Feb 1857, 109).

102 Meredith 1913 229-30.

103 Inadequately reproduced in MacDermot 1931, vol. 2, 114.

104 See the chapter 'The First Railwaymen' in Rolt 1960, 128-45, and the chapters 'Operating the railway' and 'Accidents' in Thomas 1980, 186-215.

105 *MM*, 31 May 1845.

106 *Silurian*, 15 Oct 1853.

107 GlamA, DRH/85 f. 97.

108 *MB*, 11 Aug 1855.

109 Hassall 1815, 121.

110 Guy and Rowson 2011.

111 *MB*, 21 May 1853.

112 *MT*, 17 Dec 1864.

113 GlamA, DRH/55 f.178.

114 *MM*, 23 Apl 1831.

115 *MM*, 18 Dec 1847.

116 *GMBG*, 24 Jul 1841.

117 *MM*, 17 Apl 1847.

118 *MM*, 29 Apl 1843.

119 *MM*, 27 Mar 1853.

120 *MM*, 18 Apl 1846.

121 Specimens from Penydarren and Dowlais trams found at Ffos y Fran: Young 2016, Fig. 9. Similar rigid coupling bars saw some use on the Stockton & Darlington in 1828, as well as the chains which Hackworth preferred (Allen 1953, 131).

122 At this date 'the Ebbw Vale locomotive' probably means that it was the MRCC engine No. 2, named *Ebbw Vale*.

123 In 1845 the speed limit for locomotives on the MCC lines had been raised from the previous 5 to 10 mph (Hadfield 1967, 151).

124 *MB*, 10 Aug 1850.

125 *MM*, 31 May 1845, 8 Apl 1854, 27 May 1858.

126 *MM*, 4 Oct 1845.

127 Lewis 2010.

128 *HT*, 24 Nov 1855 (at Penderyn).

129 *Silurian*, 17 Aug 1850; *HT*, 16 Aug 1851.

130 *MM*, 14 Jan 1843.

131 *MM*, 13 Mar 1841.

132 'Hen Gymraes' 1998, 42.

133 *HT*, 11 Aug 1855.

134 *MM*, 28 Mar 1846.

135 For a typical report, *MM* 24 Feb 1854.

136 *MM*, 25 Apl 1846.

137 *MM*, 4 Apl 1846.

138 *MM*, 8 Dec 1838.

139 *MB*, 1 Apl 1848.

140 *MM*, 6 Jul 1839.

141 Report of the Commission of Inquiry into the State of Education in Wales, *PP* 1847, vol. xxvii part 2, 302.

142 *GMBG*, 14 Jan 1843.

143 *MM*, 28 Apl 1849.

144 *MM*, 18 Nov 1848.

145 *MM*, 17 Nov 1849.

146 *MM*, 1 Jan 1842.

147 *MM*, 15 Sep 1849.

148 *MM*, 19 Jan 1855; *MB*, 3 Apl 1841; *MM*, 22 Dec 1849; *CMG*, 26 Jan 1850.

149 *MM*, 3 Oct 1835.

150 *MM*, 20 Feb 1852.

151 'Hen Gymraes' 1998, 46.

152 Meyrick 1973-4, 41.

153 *Silurian*, 19 Mar 1853.

154 *MM*, 1 Apl 1863.

155 *MM*, 7 Oct 1853. The driver's name was really Anstice, not Austin.

156 *MM*, 2 Oct 1841.

157 *MM*, 29 Sep 1849.

158 *MM*, 18 May 1850.

159 *CMG*, 22 Nov 1851.

160 *MM*, 20 May 1853.

161 *MM*, 28 Jul 1854.

162 *MM*, 20 Jan 1849.

163 *CMG*, 9 Mar 1850; *MM*, 16 Mar 1850.

164 *MM*, 3 Mar 1854.

165 *MM*, 29 Jul 1853.

166 The magazine in the citadel at Moultan in India, supposedly containing a million

pounds of powder, exploded shortly before its capture by British forces in 1848.

167 *MM*, 26 Jan 1850; *CMG*, 26 Jan 1850.

168 *Western Daily Press*, 7 Feb 1859.

169 The whole question is discussed by Lewis 2014, 203-7.

170 *MM*, 1 Apl 1843.

171 *HT*, 1 Jan 1848.

172 TNA, RAIL 500/6, 6 Jun 1823. In 1824 the service ran every other day, not twice weekly (Gray-Jones 1970, 78). Kidner 1994, 314 wrongly says that the Sirhowy Act authorised passengers.

173 Buchanan 1811, 16. Peter Cross-Rudkin, in his article on Buchanan in Skempton et al 2002, 94, also mentions this reference to the Sirhowy and adds 'where passengers had been carried for four years'; but he cannot track down his source.

174 It was still not in place in 1823 (TNA, RAIL 500/6, Nov 1823); but some informal sort of precursor is shown on the Ordnance Survey drafts of 1813.

175 Jones 1969, 44.

176 Powell 1902, 41.

177 Pigot 1835, 262; Hunt 1849, 142.

178 *MM*, 30 Jul 1859.

179 NLW, MS 5155.

180 *MM*, 15 Mar 1834.

181 *MM*, 21 Jan 1843.

182 *MM*, 8 Jun 1844.

183 *MM*, 24 Oct 1851.

184 *MM*, 30 Dec 1848.

185 *MM*, 13 Apl 1867.

186 *MM*, 20 Jun 1846.

187 *MM*, 14 Apl 1849.

188 *MM*, 16 Mar 1850.

189 *MM*, 26 Jun 1847.

190 *MM*, 16 Mar 1850.

191 *MM*, 24 Oct 1851.

192 *MM*, 4 Oct 1862.

193 *Silurian*, 5 Oct 1850.

194 *CMG*, 17 Mar 1849.

195 *MM*, 16 Mar 1850.

196 *MM*, 30 Mar 1850.

197 *MM*, 13 Jan 1849.

198 See Reynolds 2010, 181-223 for an overall history of mail carriage in the Western Valleys, and especially 194, 192 and 207-8.

199 *Silurian*, 5 Oct 1850, a complaint by inhabitants of Brynmawr.

200 *HT*, 15 Sep 1849.

201 'Hen Gymraes' 1998, 43.

202 *MM*, 23 Apl 1852.

203 *MM*, 22 Oct 1852.

204 *MM*, 24 Aug 1850.

205 TNA, RAIL 500/8, Jul 1852.

206 *CMG*, 31 Aug 1850

207 Moore 2017.

208 *MT*, 8 Sep 1855.

209 *MM*, 20 Jul 1861.

210 *MT*, 2 Feb 1861.

211 *MT*, 17 Dec 1864.

212 *CMG* 23 Jun 1865.

213 *MM*, 18 Aug 1855.

214 *MB*, 2 Nov 1850.

215 *CT*, 19 Mar 1859.

216 8-9 Vic. cap.169, 31 Jul 1845 and 11-12 Vic. cap. 120, 14 Aug 1848.

217 For this period see Barrie and Lee 1940, 20-3 and Byles 1982, 30.

218 *MM*, 23 Jun 1853; *MB*, 16 Apl 1859.

219 17-18 Vic cap. cxciii.

220 23-24 Vic cap. ccxxvii.

221 TNA, RAIL 500/12, Oct 1860.

222 *CMG*, 11 Aug 1862.

223 *CT*, 1 May 1863.

224 26-27 Vic cap. ccii.

225 Barrie 1980, 91.

226 23-24 Vic cap. lxxi, 25 May 1860.

227 *Western Daily Press*, 2 Oct 1863, 16 Mar 1864. See Barrie and Lee 1940, 22-3.

228 *CMG*, 27 Nov 1847.

229 See in general Barrie 1980.

Abbreviations

B&A	Brecknock & Abergavenny Canal
BL	British Library
BM	*Bristol Mercury*
CMG	*Cardiff & Merthyr Guardian*
CT	*Cardiff Times*
ER	*Early Railways*: 1, ed. Andy Guy and Jim Rees (London 2001)
	2, ed. M. J. T. Lewis (London 2003)
	5, ed. David Gwyn (Clare 2014)
	6, ed. Anthony Coulls (Milton Keynes 2019)
GA	Gwent Archives, Ebbw Vale
GJ	*Gloucester Journal*
GlamA	Glamorgan Archives, Cardiff
GMBG	*Glamorgan Monmouth & Brecon Gazette*
HJ	*Hereford Journal*
HT	*Hereford Times*
IRR	*Industrial Railway Record*
JRCHS	*Journal of Railway & Canal Historical Society*
MB	*Monmouthshire Beacon*
MCC	Monmouthshire Canal Company
MM	*Monmouthshire Merlin*
MPICE	*Minutes of Proceedings of Institution of Civil Engineers*
MRCC	Monmouthshire Railway & Canal Company
MT	*Merthyr Telegraph*
NEIMME	North of England Institute of Mining and Mechanical Engineers, Newcastle
NLW	National Library of Wales, Aberystwyth
NMW	National Museums of Wales
NRM	National Railway Museum, York
NWM	National Waterfront Museum, Swansea
PIME	*Proceedings of Institution of Mechanical Engineers*
PP	*Parliamentary Papers*
RCHS TGOP	*Railway & Canal Historical Society, Tramroad Group Occasional Papers*
continued as	
RCHS ERGOP	*Railway & Canal Historical Society, Early Railway Group Occasional Papers*
RLR	Rhymney Limestone Railway
RM	*Railway Magazine*
TNA	The National Archives, Kew
TNS	*Transactions of Newcomen Society*
WGAS	West Glamorgan Archive Service, Swansea

Bibliography

Abbott, Rowland A. S., *Vertical Boiler Locomotives* (Headington 1989)

Aberconway, Lord, *The Basic Industries of Great Britain* (London 1927)

Adams, W. A., 'On railway carrying stock,' *PIME* 1850, paginated within paper

Allen, Horatio, 'Diary of Horatio Allen 1828 (England),' *Railway & Locomotive Historical Society Bulletin* 89 (1953), 97-138

Ahrons, E. L., *The British Steam Railway Locomotive* (London 1927)

Andrieux, –, 'Description d'un chariot à vapeur (steam carriage) imaginé par M. Blenkinsop,' *Bulletin de la société d'encouragement pour l'industrie nationale* 14 (1815), 80-6

Anon, *Observations on the proposed Rail-way or Tram-road, from Stockton to the Collieries, by way of Darlington* (Durham 1818). Copy in Durham County Record Office, D/PS/3/48

Baber, Colin, 'The construction and operation of the Monmouthshire Canal and its tramroads,' *JRCHS* 19 (1973), 9-16

Bainton, John C., 'Reminiscences of Bryn-Mawr,' *Brycheiniog*, 16 (1972), 125-38

Barrie, D. S., *The Brecon & Merthyr Railway* (Lingfield 1957)

Barrie, D. S., *South Wales*, Regional History of Railways, Newton Abbot 1980)

Barrie, D. S., and Charles Lee, *The Sirhowy Valley and its Railways* (London 1940)

Bassett, A., 'The port of Newport and its coal field,' *Transactions of South Wales Institute of Engineers* 5 (1866), 134-64

Baxter, Bertram, *Stone Blocks and Iron Rails* (Newton Abbot 1966)

Bick, David, *The Gloucester and Cheltenham Tramroad* (Headington 1987)

Bradley, V. J., *Industrial Locomotives of North Wales* (London 1992)

Buchanan, Robertson, *Report relative to the Proposed Rail-way from Dumfries to Sanquhar* (Dumfries 1811)

Burland, Len, Foster Frowen and Lionel Milsom, 'Abercarn Blast Furnace,' *Gwent Local History* 82 (1997), 16-43

Bye, Sheila, 'John Blenkinsop and the Patent Steam Carriage,' in *ER2* (2003), 134-48

Byles, Aubrey, *History of the Monmouthshire Railway and Canal Company* (Cwmbran 1982)

Clark, Daniel Kinnear, *Railway Machinery* (Glasgow 1855)

Clements, Paul, *Marc Isambard Brunel* (London 1970)

Clinker, C. R., and Charles Hadfield, 'The Ashby-de-la-Zouch Canal and its railways,' *Transactions of Leicestershire Archaeological and Historical Society* 69 (1958), 53-76

Colburn, Zerah, *Locomotive Engineering and the Mechanism of Railways* (London 1871)

Combes, Charles, *Traité d'exploitation des mines* (Paris 1845)

Coxe, William, *An Historical Tour in Monmouthshire* (London 1801)

Craig, R. S., R. Protheroe Jones and M. V. Symons *The Industrial and Maritime History of Llanelli and Burry Port 1750 to 2000* (Llanelli 2002)

Cumming, T. G., *Illustrations of the Origins and Progress of Rail and Tram Roads* (Denbigh 1824)

'Dean Forester,' 'Mr Keeling buys a locomotive,' *IRR* 3/4 (1963), 58-61.

De Havilland, John, *Industrial Locomotives of Dyfed & Powys* (London 1994)

De Pambour, F. M. G., *A Practical Treatise on Locomotive Engines upon Railways* (London 1836)

Dendy Marshall, C. F., 'Links in the history of the locomotive,' *Engineer*, 29 Jan 1937, 130-1

Dendy Marshall, C. F., *A History of British Railways down to the year 1830* (Oxford 1938)

Dendy Marshall, C. F., *A History of Railway Locomotives down to the end of the year 1831* (London 1953)

Denman, Michael, *Railways around Llanelli: a history of the railways of East Carmarthenshire* (Huntingdon 2000)

Dickinson, H. W., and Arthur Titley, *Richard Trevithick, the Engineer and the Man* (Cambridge 1934)

Dowden, M. J., 'Land and industry: Sir Charles Morgan, Samuel Homfray and the Tredegar lease of 1800,' *National Library of Wales Journal* 28 part 1 (1993), 22-37

Elsas, Madeleine (ed.), *Iron in the Making: Dowlais Iron Company Letters 1782-1860* (Cardiff 1960)

Eyles, Joan M., 'William Smith, Richard Trevithick and Samuel Homfray: their correspondence on steam engines, 1804-1806,' *TNS* 43 (1970-1), 137-61

Fitzsimons, Neal, *The Reminiscences of John B. Jervis* (Syracuse NY 1971)

Forward, E. A., 'Notes on Trevithick's locomotives, from the Journals and Memoranda of Simon Goodrich,' *Engineer* 26 Aug 1921, 211-12

Forward, E. A., 'Links in the history of the locomotive,' *Engineer*, 24 Jan 1930, 94-5 and 31 Jan 1930, 128-9

Forward, E. A., 'Chapman's locomotives, 1812-1815,' *TNS* 28 (1951-3), 1-13

Forward, E. A., 'Links in the history of the locomotive,' *Engineer*, 22 Feb 1952, 266-8

Frowen, Foster, 'Hall's Tramroad: Abercarn,' Part 1, *Archive* 54 (2007a), 27-38; Part 2, *Archive* 56 (2007b), 30-54; Part 5, *Archive* 66 (2010), 2-33

Gerstner, Franz Joseph von, *Handbuch der Mechanik* (Prague 1831)

Gibbon, Richard, 'Rings, springs, strings and things: the National Collection pre 1840,' in *ER1* (2001), 208-16

Gooch, Daniel, *Diaries of Sir Daniel Gooch, Baronet* (London 1892)

Gray-Jones, Arthur, *A History of Ebbw Vale* (Risca 1970)

Guy, Andy, 'North eastern locomotive pioneers 1805 to 1827: a reassessment,' in *ER1* (2001), 117-44

Guy, Andy, et al, 'Penydarren re-examined,' in *ER6* (2019), 147-92

Guy, Andy, and Paul Reynolds, 'Joseph Tregelles Price on tramroad practice in south Wales: a letter of 1818,' *RCHS TGOP* 138 (1999)

Gwyn, David, 'Artists, Chartists, railways and riots,' in *ER2* (2003), 37-51

Gwyn, David, 'Tredegar, Newcastle, Baltimore: the swivel truck as a paradigm of technology transfer,' *Technology & Culture* 45 (2004), 778-94

Hadfield, Charles, *The Canals of South Wales and the Border* (Newton Abbot and Cardiff 1967)

Hassall, Charles, *General View of the Agriculture of the County of Monmouth* (London 1815)

'Hen Gymraes', 'Ebbw Vale in the 1840s,' *Gwent Local History* 84 (1998), 35-49

Heydinger, Earl J., 'The English influence on American Railroads,' *Railway and Locomotive Historical Society Bulletin* 91 (1954), 7-45

Hill, Geoffrey, *Industrial Locomotives of Mid & South Glamorgan* (Melton Mowbray 2007)

Hill, Geoffrey, and Gordon Green, *Industrial Locomotives of Gwent* (London 1999)

Hilling, John B., 'Britain's first industrial town? The development of Tredegar, 1800-1820,' *Gwent Local History* 94 (2003), 55-76

Hodge, John, *South Wales Valleys: railways and industry in the Western Valley, Newport to Aberbeeg* (Barnsley 2016)

Hughes, Stephen, *The Brecon Forest Tramroads* (Aberystwyth 1990)

Hunt & Co's Directory and Topography for Gloucester and Bristol etc (London 1849)

Ince, Laurence, 'The locomotives of the Neath Abbey Iron Co,' *IRR* 121 (1990), 120-31

Ince, Laurence, *Neath Abbey and the Industrial Revolution* (Stroud 2001)

Jack, Harry, *Locomotives of the LNWR Southern Division: London and Birmingham Railway, London and North Western Railway and Wolverton Locomotive Works* (Sawtry 2001)

Jones, Oliver, 'The Sirhowy Tram Road and its locomotives,' *Presenting Monmouthshire* 20 (1965), 34-44

Jones, Oliver, *The Early Days of Sirhowy and Tredegar* (Risca 1969)

Jones, Oliver, 'The Sirhowy-Ebbw Vale Tunnel,' *Presenting Monmouthshire* 31 (1971), 21-6

Kidner, R. W., 'Passenger carriages on tramroads', *JRCHS* 31 (1994), 313-16

King, P. W. 'Pont Gwaith yr Haearn,' *Gwent Local History* 75 (1994), 13-16

Kirby, Maurice W., *The Origins of Railway Enterprise: the Stockton and Darlington Railway 1821-1863* (Cambridge 1993)

Lewis, M. J. T., *Early Wooden Railways* (London 1970)

Lewis, M. J. T., 'Bogie waggons on Welsh Tramroads,' *RCHS TGOP* 110 (1996)

Lewis, M. J. T., 'Origins of the Bogie,' *RCHS TGOP* 117 (1997)

Lewis, Michael, 'Tramroad locomotives in South Wales: addenda and corrigenda,' *RCHS TGOP* 159 (2001)

Lewis, Michael, 'How did the plateway cross the road?' *RCHS ERGOP* 211 (2010)

Lewis, Michael, 'Early passenger carriage by rail,' in *ER5* (2014), 199-220

Lewis, Michael, 'Crawshay Bailey's Engine yet again,' *RCHS ERGOP* 233 (2017) (a)

Lewis, Michael, 'An early Welsh incline,' *RCHS ERGOP* 236 (2017) (b)

Lewis, Michael, 'Pointwork to 1830,' in *ER6* (2019) (a)

Lewis, Michael, 'A new locomotive drawing from the 1820s, *JRCHS* 39 (2019), 476-86 (b)

Lewis, Michael, and John van Laun, 'A proposed railway at Merthyr Tydfil, 1766-67,' *RCHS TGOP* 171 (2001)

Lewis, Samuel, *Topographical Dictionary of England*, 3rd ed (London 1835)

Liffen, John, 'F. P. Smith's journal of his search for Trevithick engines in Cornwall and South Wales in June 1862,' *RCHS ERGOP* 239 (2018)

Lloyd, John, *The Early History of the Old South Wales Iron Works* (London 1906)

Longridge, Michael, *Remarks on the Comparative Merits of Cast Metal and Malleable Iron Railways* (Newcastle 1832)

Lovering, G. W., 'Thomas Powell of the Gaer, Newport,' *Gwent Local History* 84 (1998), 4-14.

MacDermot, E. T., *History of the Great Western Railway* (London 1931)

Madison, Nathan Vernon, *Tredegar Iron Works, Richmond's foundry on the James* (Charleston SC 2015), unpaginated

Manby, G. W., *An historic and picturesque guide from Clifton through the Counties of Monmouth, Glamorgan and Brecon* (Bristol 1802)

Mercer, Stanley, 'Trevithick and the Merthyr Tramroad,' *TNS* 26 (1948), 89-104

Meredith, W. L., 'The Sirhowy Valley, South Wales,' *Journal of Permanent Way Institution* 24 (1906), 252-6, reproduced in *RCHS TGOP* 47 (1988)

Meredith, W. L., 'A century of railway developments in South Wales and Monmouthshire,' *Journal of Permanent Way Institution* Dec 1913, 216-65

Messenger, Michael, *The Bodmin & Wadebridge Railway* (Truro 2012)

Meyrick, Howard G., 'Taken for a ride,' *Gelligaer* 10 (1973-4), 41-2

Moore, Graeme, 'William Lewis Meredith (1843-1924),' *Journal of Permanent Way Institution* 135 part 3 (2017), 60-1

Morgan, Bryan, 'The location of Edward Jones's 1799 tramroad: an assessment based on contemporary correspondence,' *JRCHS* 228 (2017) 45-52

Morris, David (Eiddil Gwent), *Hanes Tredegar* (Tredegar 1868)

Morris, J. H. and L. J. Williams, *The South Wales Coal Industry 1841-1875* (Cardiff 1958)

Mulholland, Peter, 'The first locomotive in Whitehaven,' *IRR* 75 (1978), 177-19

Myrone, Felicity, 'Peter van Lerberghe, artist, printmaker and "capital" collector,' *British Art Journal* 15 part 3 (2015), 71-81

Napier, James, *Life of Robert Napier of West Shandon* (Edinburgh 1904)

Oeynhausen, C. von, and H. von Dechen, *Railways in England 1826 and 1827* (Cambridge 1971)

Overton, George, *A Description of the Faults and Dykes of the Mineral Basin of South Wales* (London 1825)

Paar, H. W., *The Severn & Wye Railway* (Dawlish 1963)

Paar, H. W., *The Great Western Railway in Dean* (Dawlish 1965)

Paar, Harry, and Alec Pope, 'Bogie waggons on Welsh Tramroads,' *RCHS TGOP* 116 (1997)

Pigot & Co's National Commercial Directory, Derby … North & South Wales (London 1835)

Palmer, Henry R., *Description of a Railway on a new Principle* (London 1823)

Pope, Alec K., 'Twelve-wheel tramroad waggons: some thoughts,' *RCHS TGOP* 119 (1997)

Potts, Martin and G. W. Green, *Industrial Locomotives of West Glamorgan* (Oakham 1996)

Powell, Evan, *The History of Tredegar* (Newport 1902, but written in 1884)

Prujean, John, *Map of the Iron-works and Collieries and their means of Communications by Railroad Tramroad & Canal with the Ports of Newport and Cardiff* (London 1843)

Rattenbury, Gordon, *Tramroads of the Brecknock & Abergavenny Canal* (Oakham, 1980)

Rattenbury, Gordon, 'Penllwyn Tramroad,' *JRCHS* 27 (1983), 189-97 (a)

Rattenbury, Gordon, 'Jones' Tramroad, Risca,' *JRCHS* 27 (1983), 288-90 (b)

Rattenbury, Gordon, *The Sirhowy Tramroad* (unpublished 1987)

Rattenbury, Gordon, 'Hall's Tramroad,' *JRCHS* 29 (1988), 170-83

Rattenbury, Gordon, 'The Trevil Rail Road Company,' *JRCHS* 29 (1989), 454-69

Rattenbury, Gordon, and Ray Cook, *The Hay & Kington Railways* (Mold 1996)

Rattenbury, Gordon, and M. J. T. Lewis, *Merthyr Tydfil Tramroads and their Locomotives* (Oxford 2004)

Rees, Jim, 'The strange story of the Steam Elephant,' in *ER1* (2001), 145-70

Reynolds, P. R., 'A "high state of perfection:" Cox's Hendreforgan Colliery, 1814-1833,'

Morgannwg, 30 (1986), 42-64

Reynolds, P. R., 'Tramroad Locomotives in South Wales,' *RCHS TGOP* 156 (2000)

Reynolds, Paul, 'George Stephenson's 1819 Llansamlet locomotive,' in *ER2* (2003), 165-76

Reynolds, Paul, *The Ironmasters' Bags: the postal service in the South Wales valleys c.1760 to c.1860* ([London] 2010)

Reynolds, Paul, 'Was there ever a Blenkinsop locomotive in Wales?,' *Bulletin South West Wales Industrial Archaeology Society* 128 (Feb 2017), 9-12

Reynolds, Paul, 'William Stewart of Newport, Drogheda and Bordeaux,' *RCHS ERGOP* 247 (2019)

Riden, Philip and John G. Owen, *British Blast Furnace Statistics* (Cardiff 1995)

Rolt, L. T. C., *George and Robert Stephenson: the Railway Revolution* (London 1960)

Rowson, Stephen, 'Early Photography in Cardiff,' *National Library of Wales Journal* 29.3 (1996), 305-28

Rowson, Stephen, 'Benjamin Hall's Tramroad and the promotion of Chapman's locomotive patent,' *RCHS ERGOP* 251 (2019)

Rutherford, Michael, 'Some notes on the Monmouthshire Railway & Canal Company. Part 2,' *Backtrack* 22 (Jun 2008), 368-78

Schofield, R. B., *Benjamin Outram 1764-1805* (Cardiff 2000)

Scrivenor, Harry, *History of the Iron Trade* (London 1854)

Sekon, G. A., *The Evolution of the Steam Locomotive* (London 1899)

Sharman, M., *Boultons Sidings including Contractors Locomotives* (Oxford 1989)

Shill, R. A., *Industrial Locomotives of West Midlands* (London 1992)

Shore, Leslie M., *The Tredegar Company: one of the South Wales coalfield's 'Big Three'*, (Lydney 2017)

Skempton, A. W., et al (eds), *A Biographical Dictionary of Civil Engineers in Great Britain and Ireland*, vol. 1 (London 2002)

Steggles, Don, 'The Monmouthshire Canal Company tramroad trials, 1849,' *RCHS ERGOP* 201 (2009)

Svedenstjerna, Eric Th., *Resa igenom en del af England och Skottland, åren 1802 och 1803* (Stockholm 1804); trans. E. L. Dellow, *Svedenstierna's Tour of Great Britain 1802-3* (Newton Abbot 1973)

Tasker, W. W., *Railways in the Sirhowy Valley* (Headington 1992)

Thomas, Brinley, 'A cauldron of rebirth: population and the Welsh language,' in Geraint H. Jenkins (ed.), *The Welsh Language and its social domains 1801-1911* (Cardiff 2000), 81-99

Thomas, R. H. G., *The Liverpool & Manchester Railway* (London 1980)

Tomlinson, W. W., *The North Eastern Railway* (Newcastle 1914)

Trevithick, Francis, *Life of Richard Trevithick* (London 1872)

Van Laun, John, *Early Limestone Railways* (London 2001)

Warren, J. G. H., *A Century of Locomotive Building by Robert Stephenson & Co* (Newcastle 1923)

Wear, Russell, and Eric Lees, *Stephen Lewin and the Poole Foundry* (London 1978)

Weaver, Rodney, 'Ancient Britons,' *IRR* 96 (1983), 89-96

Whishaw, Francis, *The Railways of Great Britain and Ireland* (London 1842)

White, John H., *The American Railroad Passenger Car* (Baltimore 1978)

Wilberforce, Robert Isaac and Samuel, *Life of William Wilberforce* (London 1838)

Wilkins, Charles, *History of Merthyr Tydfil* (Merthyr 1867)

Wilkins, Charles, *The South Wales Coal Trade* (Cardiff 1888)

Wilkins, Charles, *History of the Iron, Steel, Tinplate and other Trades of Wales* (Merthyr 1903)

Williams, John, 'West Midland goods engines,' *Locomotive Magazine* 14 (1908), 71

Winstanley, Derek, 'The Evolution of Early Railways in Winstanley, Orrell and Pemberton,' in *ER5* (2014), 112-31

Wood, Nicholas, *A Practical Treatise on Rail-roads* (London 1825)

Young, Robert, *Timothy Hackworth and the Locomotive* (London 1923)

Young, T. P., *Metalwork from Ffos y Fran* (GeoArch Report 2016/01, Caerphilly 2016): http://www.geoarch.co.uk reports/2016-01%2 Ffos-y-fran%20metalwork_%20 revised.pdf

Index

INDEX